Illuminating History

Illuminating History

A RETROSPECTIVE OF SEVEN DECADES

BERNARD BAILYN

W. W. NORTON & COMPANY
Independent Publishers Since 1923

Frontispiece: The author, with friend, 2018.

For information about permission to reproduce selections from this book, write to
Permissions, W. W. Norton & Company, Inc., 500 Fifth Avenue, New York, NY 10110

For information about special discounts for bulk purchases, please contact
W. W. Norton Special Sales at specialsales@wwnorton.com or 800-233-4830

Manufacturing by Lake Book Manufacturing
Book design by Chris Welch Design
Production Manager: Julia Druskin

Library of Congress Cataloging-in-Publication Data

Names: Bailyn, Bernard, author.
Title: Illuminating history : a retrospective of seven decades / Bernard Bailyn.
Description: First edition. | New York, N.Y. : W. W. Norton & Company, [2020] |
    Includes bibliographical references and index.
Identifiers: LCCN 2019050520 | ISBN 9781324005834 (hardcover) | ISBN
    9781324005841 (epub)
Subjects: LCSH: United States—History—Colonial period, ca. 1600–1775—Biography.
    | United States—Civilization—To 1783. | Bailyn, Bernard. | Historians—United
    States—Biography.
Classification: LCC E187.5 .B34 2020 | DDC 973.2—dc23
LC record available at https://lccn.loc.gov/2019050520

W. W. Norton & Company, Inc., 500 Fifth Avenue, New York, N.Y. 10110
www.wwnorton.com

W. W. Norton & Company Ltd., 15 Carlisle Street, London W1D 3BS

1 2 3 4 5 6 7 8 9 0

To Lotte

Beloved companion

Who has been with me through all of this

And so much more

It's her book

Contents

List of Illustrations

Illuminating History

Introduction

ENTERING THE PAST

I saiah Berlin was wrong in his entertaining game of classifying writers and thinkers into hedgehogs, who focus on one great theme, and foxes, who study and write about many themes and see the world though many lenses—wrong at least as far as historians are concerned. Many, like me, are both. Repeatedly I have been involved deeply and at length in a single absorbing subject, then have moved on to another, but touching, as I go along, smaller interests that come and go. Diverse as my interests have been, however, they reflect my intention in studying history that I had decided on in the chaotic months that followed my discharge from the army in June 1946. I had had much time in the army to think about what I might do—three and a half years, as I went through various army assignments, a year longer than the time I had had as an undergraduate.

But the story really begins further back than that. In retrospect it seems to me that my education began in an addiction I had somehow acquired to reading. By the time I entered high school I had been reading everything I could get hold of. Much of what I read I knew was over

Witkower's Bookstore, 1940. The window displays copies of William B. Goodwin's The Story of the New World *and weapons related to the Spanish conquest.*

my head, but I read on anyway. I remember going through a series of illustrated classic adventure books by James Fenimore Cooper, Jules Verne, Walter Scott, and Robert Louis Stevenson, then drifted on to Dickens, though only *Barnaby Rudge*, a novel of the Gordon riots of 1780 and mob violence against Catholics, I can still clearly remember. My parents were complicit in this addiction, and they had an expert to advise them. Hartford's biggest and best bookstore, which once had sold books to Mark Twain, was then owned by a friend of theirs, Israel Witkower, an émigré from Vienna.

He knew about books of all kinds, in several languages, and visiting his store, with its deep central corridor crowded with books, its alcoves, and its jumbled bargain basement, was an adventure.[1] Occasionally through him or his son, I would receive things to read. The main gift that I can recall was given by my parents on my thirteenth birthday. It was a six-volume set of Kipling's writings. I read it all, but with much confusion, since I had no idea of the Raj or of Kipling's world views or of many of the specific references to places and events, especially in the short stories. I still have that set of books, each volume dated by me: October 1935. Somewhat later, for some reason I can't recall, I got into Eugene O'Neill's plays, one of which affected me profoundly.

History was of no special interest, but I recall two books, besides *Barnaby Rudge,* that I read before high school and that I later realized were historical in essence. I read and reread them, and I never forgot them. One was a big coffee-table book with a deeply embossed purple cover, published, I think by the *Collier's* magazine company, largely consisting of close-up photos of the great men and events of the early twentieth century. The pages were printed in the brownish, "rotogravure" process, but to me they were vivid, and the commentary was readable. The faces of the presidents and other celebrities were intriguing. But it was the battle scenes of World War I that mainly gripped my imagination, and of them, the scenes of the gas attacks at Passchendaele were the most gripping. I can still recall the ominous fog surrounding the men hiding in trenches and the trails of blinded men marching in a row. Some stared at the reader through hideous, wide-eyed gas masks that made them look like wildly glaring sea monsters. The comments were innocuous, but the scenes were fearful and unforgettable.

The other book of those pre-high-school years that was so memorable and implicitly historical contained a series of comparisons on facing pages of towns in England and in New England that bore the same names. Thus there were photos with comment on the towns of Biddeford, Devon, and Biddeford, Maine; of Bath, Somerset, and Bath, Maine; of Portsmouth, Hampshire, and Portsmouth, New Hampshire; of Newhaven, Sussex, and New Haven, Connecticut; and of Hertford, Hertfordshire, and my own town, Hartford, Connecticut. It was only later that I would understand that these were mainly towns of England's West Country and south coast, and why their names would have carried over to New England. But it was enough for me, then, to search for the similarities and differences of these towns on either side of the Atlantic, and to puzzle about how that could have come about.

By the time I reached Hall High School in West Hartford, I was a compulsive reader, and of that affliction I have never been cured. In the high-school years I tried everything at least once, from acting in the school plays (at which I was at least not completely embarrassing) to sports of all kinds (at which I was totally embarrassing). The school's curriculum was traditional, but the teachers I knew best were excellent. In math, unfortunately, only algebra vaguely interested me, but in French I galloped ahead, to disaster. For some reason I had convinced myself that my pronunciation of the French language was good if not excellent, and so I entered the Connecticut High School French Pronunciation contest (a state program I now cannot believe could ever have existed) and to the rage of the head of my school's French department, I came in last. Years later I recalled his outrage when in a Paris café I got into a debate with a fierce young Maoist (I was told he later became a banker). The café's patrons were much amused, not about the debate but about my French, which was perhaps more or less fluent, but to listeners it sounded like some lost dialect of Appalachia.

But I flourished in two of the school's major programs. The two or three years of Latin I took, I enjoyed—whether because the rule-bound declensions and conjugations seemed so neatly logical, even when irregular, or whether in what I could actually read in Latin, I sensed in some small way the drama of the lives of those who had spoken the language. For whatever reason, I liked the Latin I studied and profited by it. But it was in English that I found my footing, largely the result of having two extraordinary teachers. One was Alfred A. Wright, then an elderly man soon to retire, who for years had refined his teaching of English grammar and in 1935 had published the fruit of his life's work, *Words in Action: A Study of the Sentence*. A disciplinarian, he led us through the book chapter by chapter and tested us again and again with questions of increasing complexity. I recently went over Harvard's copy of the book and was impressed with how elementary the beginning was and how complex the

My high-school English teachers: Alfred A. Wright (left) and Samuel B. Gould.

concluding chapters. It was a schoolbook, not a reference work, designed for teachers and students, but rigorous and clear throughout.

The other English teacher could not have been more different from Wright. Samuel B. Gould, born in the obscure Connecticut town of Shelton, was in his twenties when he taught at Hall High School (1932–38), but that must have been the time that his innovative ideas on teaching were developing, and we, unknowingly, were the first beneficiaries of them. We read short stories, parts of books, some poetry, with Gould explaining, inspiring, and sharing his own enthusiasm. I don't think at that point he had any theory of how he was teaching; he seemed to like to teach, and had a keen sense of literary values that he conveyed to us so that we gained a sense of style as well as knowledge of selected works. But his gifts as a teacher and educator could not be confined to high-school instruction. When he left the high school he studied briefly at Oxford, took a doctorate at Harvard, and went into educational administration, where he flourished. I am now amazed but not surprised to discover that he became president of Antioch College, then chancellor of the University of California at Santa Barbara, and in 1964 was appointed president of the State University of New York, which under his guidance had its greatest physical and academic expansion that featured new technologies in teaching and nontraditional study opportunities. In retirement he worked on educational problems in Venezuela and accompanied his friend, Vice President Nelson Rockefeller, on a tour of Latin America. In the end he returned to Connecticut to serve as interim chancellor for higher education.

I was well prepared for college, and after a discouraging look at Princeton I decided on Williams College, where I had friends and where I felt comfortable even before I matriculated.

My experience there, short as it was, in various ways shaped much of what followed. A small, all-male institution in the Berkshire hills, the college was traditional in its arts and sciences curriculum, and traditional too in its fraternity tribalism, antisemitism, and male chauvinism. But among its faculty there were men (there were no women) who were devoted to their fields of study and sensitively and generously responsive to students who showed interest. To one, John William Miller, it is true, a charismatic Hegelian philosopher and Emersonian aphorist who himself was intriguing and whose lectures were brilliant, I developed a strong antipathy. Looking over the three short volumes of his essays published just before and after his death, I can still see why. I became aware that his kind of aphoristic, metaphysical talk, brilliant as it was, was beyond criticism and beyond validation; it seemed to me that you could say anything that came into your head. And that was especially true of some of Miller's students, whose philosophical chatter struck me as simply pretentious. That resistance led me to a tough-minded medievalist and historian of the Crusades, Richard Newhall, a wounded veteran of World War I whose tragic experiences on the battlefield, in which his left shoulder and arm were shattered, I have only recently discovered.

An empiricist with a doctorate from Harvard, wry and reserved, he was the opposite of Miller. While I did not take his courses, I knew what they were, and I found his devotion to the facts and his skepti-

Richard A. Newhall, a medievalist, who chose to teach in a small liberal arts college. "If I have contributed to the intelligent, social and political awareness of the young men who go out into business and government service I have done better, I contend, than if I had persuaded them to follow in my own footsteps."

cism entirely congenial. More recently I have found in his published correspondence the extent of his devotion to teaching in a small liberal arts college—a career he deliberately chose over the life of scholarship that he might well have had.*

But my main studies continued in literature, for which I had several

---

* James Carl Nelson, *Five Lieutenants: The Heartbreaking Story of Five Harvard Men Who Led America to Victory in World War I* (New York, 2012), 252–70. See also Russell H. Bostert, *Newhall and Williams College: Selected Papers of a History Teacher at a New England College, 1917–1973* (New York, 1989), and Alvin Kernan, *In Plato's Cave* (New Haven, 1999), chap. 2.

excellent instructors. One was Nelson Bushnell, who taught courses on creative writing as well as on English literature. He helped me greatly in prose composition and self-criticism in writing.

Hallett Smith, a Shakespearean scholar then teaching a broad course on poetry, introduced me to Gerard Manley Hopkins, whose strange verse and stranger theories of poetry had a special fascination for me, and I read everything I could of his publications and biography.

But, as I recalled in my sixtieth-year class report, in those two and a half years at Williams, living apart from the dominant fraternity world and left to follow my own instinct, I mainly

> wrote—and wrote and wrote, first under the instruction of Bush-nell, and then in other courses and noncourses. I wrote long letters, course papers, short stories, a long play (based on various translations of the Antigone story: I still have it—it's pretty awful, but not as bad as it might have been), and pieces for the student magazine. My teachers were encouraging and indulgent, but my contemporaries were neither, and the combination, as I think back on it, was perfect. One senior I respected looked over a short story I had written and said it was hopeless since I had nothing really to say beyond what I felt. He was right. Ever since I've been writing history, where you have lots of real things to write about and where you're not supposed to make things up.

I had already moved into history almost without realizing it. I had chosen to write a thesis on Laurence Sterne, but I discovered that what really interested me was not *Tristram Shandy* and the rest of Sterne's writing so much as the provincialism of Sterne's Ireland and Yorkshire and the sophisticated social and cultural world he found in metropolitan England, and how the two related.* "How all that got done in two and a

---

* Twenty years later Laurence Sterne and his scatterbrained, garrulous, comic hero Tristram Shandy reentered my life in a strange way. A brief note of mine to the sociologist Robert Merton on the historical origins of the expression "on the shoulders of giants"

half short years," I concluded in my sixtieth-year report, "I'll never know. The intensity must have been fierce, the openness to new experiences infinite, and the intellectual atmosphere supportive in the best way. . . . God knows how I could have survived the full four years at that pace."

My months as an undergraduate, with army service looming, passed quickly, and none of my plans were completed when I left Williams. But despite my deficiencies in course credits, I was awarded the BA degree in 1945 while in uniform and awarded, too, a fellowship for two years of study at Oxford. That touched off a peculiar problem—a problem that had something to do with Robin McCoy.

I had met McCoy, a private school teacher ten years my senior, during the war, at a testing and relocation center at the Citadel in South Carolina. He was on a break reading Dante the afternoon I met him, and we began a series of conversations that continued after the war. A midwesterner, he had graduated from Harvard in 1935 with a concentration in math, then had gone to the University of Cambridge where he earned another BA and also an MA in history, and had returned to Harvard for an MA in classics. We talked again and again on all sorts of subjects, mainly academic, and especially of Cambridge, where he had studied history most intensely. Cambridge, the university and its style of life, had deeply affected him. Soon after the war, in 1946, he would establish—together with the philanthropist Charles E. Merrill, Jr. (son of the founder of Merrill Lynch Co.), and Graham Spring—the Thomas Jefferson School, a largely boarding school patterned after the Cambridge colleges, with emphasis on history, languages (including required Greek), and math. He would serve the school as headmaster for thirty-four years.[2]

Much of what he talked about at the Citadel and elsewhere during the war was his experience at Cambridge, which I remembered clearly when

---

inspired, he said, his writing a book-length, mock-scholarly "Shandean Postscript" on the supposed derivation of that famous metaphor. My note, he wrote, was "the occasion of it all," and he began the book, to my surprise, by reprinting my note to him as a preface to the book. He was justifiably proud of that immensely learned, witty Shandean spoof, which he referred to fondly by the acronym OTSOG.

Robin McCoy. Devoted to the curriculum and style of England's schools and colleges, he created his own version in the Jefferson School in Missouri, over which he presided for three decades.

thinking about the Oxford fellowship. The result was that I wrote the sponsors of the fellowship and told them that I preferred the University of Cambridge and asked if they could transfer the fellowship. They asked why, and I recall writing a finely argued answer, which probably carried more conviction than I really had. The reply was swift in coming. They said they understood my preference, and thought I should indeed go to Cambridge, but their fellowship was for Oxford, and they wished me luck. So with no idea how I might negotiate entrance to Cambridge on my own, I applied to the Harvard graduate school and was accepted.*

I brought with me to the graduate school from my time in the army something important, for which I was, and have been ever after, deeply grateful. I had been assigned to the Signal Corps, eventually to the Army Security Agency, and had various duties ranging from Japanese radio traffic analysis to courier service in the distribution of codes in Europe. But before I was actively engaged in any of those activities I was caught up in the preparations that were being made for the eventual occupation of Germany. For that, knowledgeable German-speaking officers and NCOs were needed, and since not enough were available, the army set about training them (as they did for Italian, Russian, Chinese, and other language speakers) by creating the Army Specialized Training Programs established on selected college campuses. For me, it meant a concentrated, intense education, at Clark University in Worcester, Massachusetts, in all things German: language, literature, economy, geography, history, and politics.

Of course, it was perverse, since I had qualified in French, but they put me into the German program—a typical army kind of thing. For weeks on end we studied German language and culture in the most intense way, all of which was a blessing, as I think about it now. I became extremely interested in German history and ended up with a fairly basic control of the German language. I also came under the influence of some excellent scholars in the field. Henry Donaldson Jordan, a professor of English history, was there teaching European and diplomatic history; he impressed me with his command of information and his clear, succinct lectures. The Dutch geographer Samuel Van Valkenburg, a leader in his field, a flamboyant man, got me interested in cultural geography. A Swiss professor, Henry Bosshard, taught us some aspects of German literature and, miraculously, got

---

* Twenty-five years later I had the privilege of delivering the Trevelyan Lectures at the University of Cambridge and in 1986–87 served as Pitt Professor there and became an honorary fellow of Christ's College.

us acquainted with both Gothic lettering and German *Schrift,* the cursive handwriting that was then still being used. And for conversational German we had a wonderful instructor, a young refugee, Hilda Weiss, whose official, and accurate, academic title was Drill Master in German. She certainly did drill us, and often exploded into colorful, colloquial expressions that sent us scrambling to the dictionaries and to native German speakers to figure out what she was talking about. Thus, European history focused on Germany was an important part of my experience in the army.

At the start in graduate school I had little use for German; in fact, it may have contributed to the confusion of those first weeks in the fall of 1946. The graduate school was a scene of chaos. Financially backed by the GI Bill, qualified veterans flooded into the classrooms and seminars, together with current graduates of the colleges. We were older than the new BAs, and rather disoriented by the quick transition, but determined to make up for lost time. Everything seemed to be out of kilter. The whole place was not only crowded but competitive, and we lacked guidance. When I met my assigned adviser, Samuel Eliot Morison, he was still in his rear admiral's uniform, which did nothing to steady my nerves. Edwin Reischauer, who I had been aware of as a colonel in charge of the unit on radio intercept analysis in which I had worked, I met again as a Harvard professor of Japanese history. Mason Hammond, who had been a leader of one of the teams reclaiming confiscated art from the Nazis, was my teacher of Roman history. There was some, but not much, dormitory space, and I found myself scrounging for housing. All of this would eventually settle down, and a civil academic life would emerge. But it was in these confused conditions, with much of my world swirling around, and opportunities for studying history appearing left and right, that I decided on the principles that I would try to follow in what I would do. I remember writing them down on a tear-off calendar page, since they were brief and could be easily stated.

Having lacked books in the army, and without university catalogs or advisers of any kind, I could not at that point decide on specific subjects or problems to study, but it was possible at least to identify the general principles of what mainly interested me in studying history and that in one way or another I would later find specific ways to pursue. It came down to three kinds of interests and connections. First, I hoped to be able to work on the early modern period of Western history, where one could see the connections between a distant past and an emerging modernity. Further, I aimed to understand, in studying the past, something of the connections between ideas and "reality." And third, I felt committed to exploring the connections between America and Europe, in whatever sphere. All of that classified my subject, for administrative purposes, as early American history. On the books I had become an American "colonialist."

It was certainly a large enough subject, stretching from Columbus to Washington and involving, I would come to realize, aspects of the history of four continents. But when I came to study what had been written about any major part of this vast subject, and when I heard the current lectures about it, my soaring expectations pretty much collapsed. There were relevant narratives but no incisive analysis of the patterns of daily life and thought. There were accounts of wars and cultural and political clashes but no explanation of purposes, personal motives, and ramifications. And the whole subject was a teleological tale ending inevitably in the revolutions of the late eighteenth century, which were to be explained either as the product of Enlightenment ideas or as the product of economic forces with respect to which ideas were epiphenomena. Both, I knew at the start, were unrealistic. The early modern world, as then portrayed, seemed wide open for deeper study and reconsideration.

My encounters with my teachers were curious. Aside from Charles Taylor—the French medievalist whose excellent courses led me into that distant world and into the great school of medieval French institutional and intellectual historiography—my teachers were Morison, the Americanist Paul Buck (then doubling as provost of the university while President Conant was in Germany), and Oscar Handlin, the newly tenured young historian with credentials also in psychology and sociology. The Americanists' courses taught me little, but I learned a great deal from studying their thought in action and the books and papers they were currently producing. From Morison I learned how a large subject could be organized for clear exposition. His multivolume history of Harvard in its first two centuries, in addition to the learning it reflects, is a masterpiece of logical and clear exposition—it is as persuasive and informative today as it was when it was published—and I marveled at the cogent organization of the masses of information in his fifteen-volume history of the United States Navy in World War II. All of his books were written in an unstrained, almost casual way that carried the reader along easily. From Buck I learned the basic requirement for good teaching: to somehow find the student's instinctive, natural point of interest, encourage him or her to see its possibilities, and then leave the student alone to do what could be done. From Handlin I learned that history is a form of intellection, a mode of understanding the world, past and present, and that emergence and evanescence are the keys to past, as they are to present, experience.

For all my admiration for Morison, I never was able to stir his interest in what I was doing. In part that seemed to have been the result of my apparent resemblance to an undergraduate he knew who was active in the Harvard yacht club. At times when I would stop by to see him he would begin by asking me how things were going with the yacht club. Since the closest I had ever been to a yacht was a troop ship, I found this disconcerting and reintroduced myself. When he went on leave for a term in Hawaii to work on his naval history, I took the opportunity to switch my adviser to Handlin, establishing a relationship both intellectual and personal that would last until Handlin's death in 2011.

The two men taught me something else. They could not have been more different, which struck me vividly when, as a new faculty member, I sat with them at department lunches. I often mused about this. Both were accomplished and well-known historians, and both, curiously, had written their dissertations on a similar place and time: Boston in the early nineteenth century. But Handlin's book was on Boston's immigrants, especially the Italians, while Morison's was a biography of his great-great-grandfather Harrison Gray Otis, one of the wealthy Federalist leaders who in 1814 threatened to lead New England to secede from the Union, in opposition to the Republicans' embargoes. Handlin's sources came from the Boston archives, newspapers, and public reports; Morison's came in large part from two collections of his family's papers to which he had private access. In his recollection of his Brahmin boyhood, Morison described life on Beacon Hill and the etiquette of formally dressed young men leaving calling cards at homes they sought to visit, and happy summer days sailing off Northeast Harbor, Maine. After studying at St. Paul's School, he went on to Harvard College and then spent a year at the Sorbonne. Handlin recalled playing stickball in the streets of Brooklyn. He would in time reject the schooling of the yeshiva, devise his own education in the reading room of the Brooklyn Public Library, and go on to Brooklyn College. Socially the two were utterly distant, and intellectually they came from different worlds. But they were respectful and cooperative colleagues in the work of the history department. I thought about this strange convergent relationship—it was impressive, however unlikely—and I thought that I would someday write about it. The closest I have come was what I could sketch in the obituaries I wrote of these two teachers, which I append at the end of this retrospect.

Neither directed me to the main substantive subjects I would study, teach, and write about. In retrospect, everything I have done in history can be seen as following the principles of my main interests as I had defined them in 1946. But I was never tightly bound to them. Though they were always in the back of my mind, much was determined by the state of the existing literature as I found it, by encounters with other historians, by the discovery of problems I had not expected, by random reading, and by the personal situations I found myself in; and I always felt free to follow the dramatic human stories I encountered—

the struggles and passions of aspiring people, some ordinary, some gifted, some inventive and creative, some despairing, some hopeful.

My procedure in research and writing followed a pattern too. I found myself involved in a series of projects. In each case I wrote a main publication and then worked further around the margins and implications in lesser publications until I had little more to say. And in almost every case I discovered, unexpectedly, within the plentiful data, one or more obscure documents or individuals that in themselves, in some peculiar way, illuminated the greater picture. I did not search for these uniquely revealing lives and documents: they simply came to hand. But I found them to be vital encapsulations of what would become major developments in the emergence of modernity. The chapters that follow are organized around a succession of such small, strange, obscure, but illuminating documents or individuals. Each chapter focuses initially on one such datum and then explores its meaning for the world at large.

Thus the first chapter is devoted to the extraordinary will written in 1653 by a tormented Boston merchant caught in a double bind between capitalist avarice and constrictive piety. It is a document I first discovered in the 1950s and later published in modernized form. It is here presented analytically, to show the myriad details of the merchant's private life and the agonized strains of his inner voices.

The second chapter centers on a village census compiled by an obscure preacher in seventeenth-century Nottinghamshire and its immense, transcultural ramifications for the study of family life and education in the broadest sense. Its significance is heightened by contrast with both the eighteenth-century village censuses recently discovered in the tower of an ancient castle in Austria, and the records of a newly settled Massachusetts town of the same era.

The third chapter is an exploration in three parts of how deep into popular culture the ideology of the American Revolution penetrated—as seen, first, in a naïve tradesman's scribbled comments on Boston's newspapers of the early revolutionary years; then in the sudden outburst of an otherwise unknown provincial preacher who unconsciously, it would seem, connected contemporary politics with the Bible to form a powerful argument for American rights that more famous and sophisticated writers would later echo; and finally in the crude but astonishingly knowledgeable and incisive responses of obscure Massachusetts villagers to a draft state constitution submitted to them for their approval in 1780.

The fourth chapter concerns the creation, in the wilderness of early eighteenth-century Pennsylvania, of an entire religious community—a cloister—created by a charismatic, uneducated German Pietist. The community became famous, even among the cognoscenti of the European Enlightenment, not only for its recondite theosophy, its celibacy, and its spartan lifestyle, but also for its production of brilliant graphic art and its strange but enchanting vocal music, which proved to be one of the keys to Thomas Mann's great novel *Doctor Faustus*.

The final chapter finds in the organization of a single seventeenth-century family's small, provincial transoceanic trading network a simple model of what would become, a century later, the vast latticework of economic, political, and cultural entanglements that spanned the four continents of the Atlantic world.

Thus a retrospective of sorts—not an exhibition of unrelated essays but successive expressions of my search for understanding something of the origins of the world we know. And throughout, I have tried to preserve tales of some of the more remarkable people and places of the past that I've visited and some of my efforts to get the stories straight.

The *Epilogue* is a collection of comments on the elusive nature of history—not, together, a "philosophy" of the subject, just cautionary notes by a practitioner.

The *Appendix* is a testimony to the two extraordinary historians, mentioned above, my teachers one way or another, whose differences could not have been greater but who equally made the past come alive.

I

Keayne's Will, "All of It Written With My Owne Hands"

PURITANISM'S DOUBLE BIND

Puritanism, in the 1950s, had become a major academic concern not only for students of religion but also for those of literature or cultural history. What intrigued me was not the theology or literary influences involved but the relation of the Puritans' ideas and beliefs, derived from European sources, to the history of economic growth. Max Weber's famous articles (1904–05) that became *The Protestant Ethic and the Spirit of Capitalism* had touched off a huge debate on the cultural determinants of economic growth, all of which I studied from every source I could reach: works by Troeltsch, Groethuysen, Roberston, Halbwachs, and above all R. H. Tawney, whose *Religion and the Rise of Capitalism* made a deep impression on me. I knew what the core issues were. I agreed with Tawney that Puritanism in its initial form was a system of constraint on early capitalism as well as a powerful incentive to economic ambition. But how could that be proved? Europe's socioeconomic world was too complicated, too many strains flowed through that complex of trade and religion to see cause and effect with any clarity. But in early New England, where Puritanism was pervasive and the economy was constructed anew, the influences would be more visible, free of conflicting forces. The result was *The New England Merchants in the Seventeenth Century* (1955).

What strikes me now is not only the effort I made to comment usefully on the Weberian thesis but also the ramifications that developed in unexpected ways. The story that emerged as I traced the New England merchants' lives across the century was not only about the effect of religion on the economy but also about the lack of status distinctions within this provincial merchant community. This emerged in a spin-off study, written in collaboration with Lotte Bailyn, *Massachusetts Shipping, 1677–1714: A Statistical Study* (1959), which involved what I believe was one of the first efforts to use computer-derived statistics in modern historical study. In truth we had no computer, nor did anyone else at that time. (Thirty years later I would have full use of a modern computer to produce *Voyagers to the West.*) What we did have, for the study of ship ownership, was a massive, clanking, rattling tabulator, available to us only at night in the school of education. Into that machine we fed hundreds of punched cards that carried the data and that we programmed by inserting wires into a removable panel. Our late-night sessions struggling with the tabulator hovered between hilarity and hysteria, but with the kind help of a visiting Japanese professor of statistics who came around from time to time, we got the book out. I could not omit mentioning in a footnote, if only as a caution for others, the misfortune we had with a bent wire in the metal brush over which the punched cards flowed. Its rogue contacts led us to compose a miraculously revealing table, which, after discovering the wayward wire, regretfully, we had to discard as junk.

But of all the spin-offs of the *Merchants* book, the most important was my discovery, in a volume of miscellaneous documents collected by the town of Boston in 1886, of the astonishing, 48,000-word last will and testament of a tormented Puritan merchant named Robert Keayne. The text is literate but lacking in punctuation, clotted with ampersands, tangled with parentheses, qualifying clauses, excisions and amendments, and the spelling is random throughout. But when punctuated and clarified in modern prose it is vividly, brilliantly illuminating of the entire inquiry that Weber had provoked.

I first described it in a biographical essay with comments and worked some of it into the text of *The New England Merchants*. In 1964 I was able to publish the entire document, clarified and modernized, in booklet form, which has proved to be useful to historians and others interested in Puritan culture. I describe it here analytically, in modern form, with stress on the dilemmas, the double binds, that beset the inner life of that avaricious but profoundly pious tradesman.[1]

ROBERT KEAYNE, "CITIZEN and merchant tailor of London by freedom, and by the good providence of God now dwelling at Boston in New England," sat down, on June 1, 1653, at the age of fifty-eight, to write the final version of his "Last Will and Testament." He began pragmatically.

> Considering that all flesh is as grass, that must wither and will return to the dust, and that my life may be taken away in a moment, therefore that I may be in the better readiness (and freed from the distracting cares of the disposing of my outward estate, which commonly follows the deferring of it, while the time of sickness or day of Death, when the mind should be taken up with more serious and weighty considerations) I do therefore now in my health make ordain & declare this to be my Last Will and Testament and to stand and to be as effectual as if I had made it in my sickness, or in the day or hour of my death.

Since he was a rich man, by early New England standards, he had much property to dispose of. (He estimated his total value at £4,000, in real estate, mercantile assets, the contents of his "shops in Boston," household goods, cash, debts owed him, and "2 negros and a child negro"; the later probate inventory would total £2,569.) But he had much more on his mind than property. He had grievances, resentments, and injustices he needed to explain—libels and misunderstandings he had endured, deliberate slanders and attacks on his reputation that had dogged him for years. Above all he had the heavy burden of justifying his life in business to a loving but severe God whose approval he had sought all his life, through prayer, through biblical study, and through his personal behavior.

As he wrote, day after day, week after week, he found more and more things to say. The weeks became months. By August 12 he had written thirty-four pages. Reluctantly, three months later, on November 14, he signed and sealed the Will. It filled thirty-six pages "written full on both sides" (that is, he had folded each of nine large sheets once to form four pages). Then, as he had thought of other worthy benefactions that he had neglected, he had added a new sheet (thirty-seven) to include them. Finally, on December 28—six months after he had begun—he signed and sealed the codicil, and the will was complete.

He knew that what he had written was

> somewhat contrary to the nature of a will, yet I am willing to leave this upon public record as a just defense for myself knowing that a will will be read and made known and may be p[er]used, searched, or copied out by any other when other writings will be more hid and obscured.

And he knew the weaknesses of what he had written. His readers, he wrote, "may meet with some tautologies & some things that may be mentioned twice or thrice," which they may attribute to "an unsettled mind or weak or wavering judgment as if I were not compus mentis." They should impute such things to "the weakness & shortness of my memory, the [will] not having been written at one time or on one day . . . but at several times as I had leisure & opportunity to carry it on." As the writing had gone on, he had recalled things he had written

Robert Keayne

Robert Keayne's signature, as it appears at the end of his will.

earlier in the will that might not have been expressed properly or with enough emphasis, and so, without turning back to revise them, he had written those passages again in fuller, clearer form. He knew too that some words or expressions would no doubt "seem to jar or differ." They could be reconciled, he wrote, in the context of the will as a whole. Also he had suffered "a fit of sickness or weakness" that had slowed him down in the months of writing, and he had felt the need to hurry at the end to get everything in while he could. He hoped that his readers "will make a favourable construction of all things contained in [the will]" and that the defects in what he had written would be attributed to "human frailties & weaknesses" and might "justly call for a mantle of love to cover them."

There were other merchants sympathetic with the Puritan cause who joined the exodus to the refuge in New England—a dozen or more in the first decade of resettlement. We know their names and something of their economic fortunes in America, and we can trace their dutiful adherence to the Puritans' church and the positions they took in the searing theological controversy that scorched the fragile community before the first decade was over. Some, in the rush to create and to profit from a new economic subsystem in North America, had advantages that Keayne never had. Besides capital and experience in overseas trade, they had contacts abroad—siblings, partners, collaborators—located in England and throughout the emerging Atlantic world. Their enterprises would become elevated to a plane of complexity and entrepreneurship more sophisticated and profitable than Keayne's. Puritans they were, but religion did not consume their lives. None were as passionately devout as Keayne had always been.

In London as later in Boston he had been zealously faithful to his church and to his religious obligations. A Puritan sympathetic to the plans for escape from persecution in England, he had invested in the Massachusetts Bay Company by 1634 and had helped organize the transfer to America. Above all he had been faithful to his "deare & reverend Teacher," the Rev. John Cotton, whose sermons and biblical commentaries Keayne recorded year after year in hundreds of pages of minuscule notes written first in England and then in New England. And for all of this he had indeed been rewarded—at least in outward terms.

A butcher's son in Windsor, he had had "no portion from my parents and friends to begin the world withal." He had had to fight his way upward in the bustling world of London's Cheapside, Cornhill, and Leadenhall district, the tradesmen's core of London, with all its twisting alleyways crammed with shops and small-time manufacturers, its streets crowded with buyers and sellers seeking advantage. Despite all the difficulties in getting ahead in this fiercely competitive atmosphere, Keayne had risen quickly. At age twenty he had been admitted to the Merchant Tailors guild. Two years later he had married, advantageously, a sister of the eminent preacher John Wilson. By then he was called "gentleman," had been granted the freedom of the city of London, and had been accepted as a member of the high-status Honourable Artillery Company of London, which stimulated a lifelong interest in the military arts. He had also acquired a reputation for hard dealings in business, for covetousness if not greed.

All of this—his affluence, his deep piety, and his notoriety—came with him in 1635 when, though a well-established forty-year-old man of means, he and his small family gave up everything in England and followed his spiritual guide, the Reverend Cotton, to the Puritan refuge in New England.

It was an open field for his talents. Given on his arrival in Boston a substantial land grant for his support of the Puritans' project, he began a series of real estate transactions while developing his merchandising business in Boston. Soon he moved on to investments in shipping.

When the first immigrants' initial capital ran out he became a money-lender, in effect a local banker. But none of this constrained his religious zeal, which became publicly notable. Known to have "come over for conscience's sake, and for the advancement of the Gospel here," he became conspicuous for the regularity of his attendance at church services, his dutiful involvement in the church's everyday affairs, his tireless note-taking at Cotton's sermons and commentaries, and the benefactions he gave for public causes.

Public service followed. He would serve as Boston representative to the General Court in four sessions before 1640 and four sessions in 1648–49. He was elected Boston selectman five times before 1645, and on various occasions he was chosen overseer of the highways and a judge on "small causes." As commissioner of Boston's fortifications and the founder and captain of the colony's Ancient and Honourable Artillery Company, he became the authority on all things military and the benefactor and manager of the Artillery Company's training and engagements.

But all was not well in his life in New England. He was not liked, and when misfortune struck, he found he had few sympathizers or supporters. And misfortunes did strike, again and again in his eighteen years in the Puritan colony. In 1639 he was charged with "taking above 6 pence in the shilling profit; in some about 8 pence; and in some small things, above 2 for 1." The case touched off a fierce discussion in the General Court, recorded in detail by Governor Winthrop. The town deputies echoed the great "cry of the country . . . against oppression," and the elders and magistrates, having "declared their detestation of the man," listed aggravating circumstances. Keayne, they noted, was

> an ancient professor of the gospel and a man of eminent parts [i.e., ability]; wealthy, and having but one child; having come over for conscience sake; having been formally dealt with and admonished both by private friends and also by some of the Magistrates and Elders, and having promised reformation; [and] being a member the Church and Commonwealth now in their infancy.

In the end, the deputies and the magistrates split on the question of punishment. The latter found and listed six extenuating circumstances, and the result was a severe censure, but the £200 fine proposed by the deputies was reduced to £80.

Then the church entered. After debating excommunication on the ground of I Cor. 5.11, the elders, supported by the silent approval of the present members, settled for a blistering admonition, accepting Cotton's argument that the merchant had not sinned deliberately "against his conscience" and throughout his "whole conversation, but had made an error in his judgment, being led by false principles." Keayne was then reconciled to the church, but only after making a "penitential acknowledgment" of his sins, with tears and his promise of satisfaction to those he was said to have offended. But his troubles were not yet over. To compound his misery, Cotton took the first occasion to expand on five false principles of trade, and four correct rules, all clearly evoked by Keayne's errors and directed to him in the first instance.

All of this, Keayne wrote in retrospect, was the very "grief of my soul." But there was more to come. Three years later, in what Winthrop correctly called "a great business upon very small occasion," he was charged with having stolen and killed Mrs. Sherman's stray sow. The allegation was twice easily refuted, with court costs awarded to Keayne. He then promptly countersued for slander and won a judgment of £20. But Keayne, Winthrop wrote, "being of ill report in the country for a hard dealer in his course of trading, and having been formerly censured in the court and in the church . . . carried many weak minds strongly against him." He was indeed, Winthrop thought, worthy of blame, but to be fair, "he was very useful to the country both by his hospitality and otherwise. But one dead fly spoils much good ointment." The magistrates, though a minority in the General Court, vetoed the deputies' vote against Keayne, which set off a resumption of a struggle between the two groups that ended with the magistrates sitting separately, their "negative voice" intact.

There seemed to be no end to Keayne's travails. Though appointed to many public service committees on matters of finance and land boundaries, he was fined for an absence from his judicial post and barely escaped a second fine for responding to that charge sarcastically. In 1650 and 1651 he clashed with the Rev. John Eliot, the famous missionary to the Indians, who authorized his Indian praying town, Natick, to expand on to a seventeen-hundred-acre tract that Keayne and others had bought in 1649 and that Keayne had surveyed and bounded. Eliot, Keayne wrote, had sought "to pluck it out of our hands . . . for his Indians," though there was land enough granted to Eliot's cause by the General Court. But Keayne was helpless to overcome Eliot's "very unsavory & oppressive" act. "If the lion will say the lamb is a fox," he wrote, "it must be so, the lamb must be content to leave it." He could only strike from his will his planned donation to Eliot's "great work" and leave behind a request to the church elders that they not be "too stiff & resolute in accomplishing their own wills & ways" and "yield in civil & earthly respects" lest by too much stiffness "they hinder many good works that may be profitable to themselves."

Finally, a year after that unseemly dispute and a year before he began writing his will, Keayne fell into utter disgrace for having been found guilty of "drunkenness" and having been found "three times drunk and to have drunk to excess two times." For this he was fined 36 shillings, 8 pence, and charged 55 shillings, 2 pence, in court expenses. Keayne did not contest the verdict and resigned from his judicial post. The court agreed, "as judging him not meet to continue therein."

This tale of Keayne's misfortunes has long been known, but the deeper history of his career and the source of his misfortunes are not to be found in the narratives of his troubles. They lie buried in the workings of his inner life, which he revealed unwittingly in the will—the *Apologia*—that he left behind.

The will is ostensibly a list of his instructions for the distribution of his property that he wished his executors (his wife and his son Benjamin) to carry out with the advice of overseers he appointed. And his benefactions were many and exceedingly complex. The major division of his assets was threefold: one-third of all his property to his wife; one-third to Benjamin; and a third part for himself to distribute in benefactions of his own desire. But the first two were surrounded by networks of provisions for the further distribution of his wife's and son's thirds when they died and then by default provisions at the tertiary level, some of which he assigned to Harvard College. His own direct gifts were similarly surrounded by complex provisions to cover every contingency he could think of.

His main personal gifts were set out at the beginning: £300 to the town of Boston for the construction of a conduit for the town's water supply and for the construction of a townhouse built over an open-air market, to include a library, a granary, an armory, and a handsome gallery for the elders to meet and confer in and for scholars to work in.

But he leaves nothing to chance. He specifies precisely where the townhouse and its market are to be located and the books of his own to be given to the library (selected by the Reverends Wilson and Norton), particularly his "divinity books and commentaries" and his own "written sermon books . . . all English none Latin or Greek." If his £300 is not enough for his proposals, the town or other charitable people will have to make up the difference, and the construction must be completed within a specific time period or the gift is rescinded.* If that happens, if the town fails to follow through on the details of this bequest, he redirects the entire gift to Harvard College (which he also otherwise provides for). He then carefully stipulates how, if that happens, the college was to proceed. On the one hand, he confesses that "I have little insight in the true ordering of scholars and other things thereto belonging in a college way

---

* In fact the building of the townhouse, completed in 1660, cost 700 pounds, the difference made up by contributions of 175 people. Plans for the conduit were abandoned in 1671–72, the project having "not proved so useful as was expected and desired." Josiah H. Benton, *The Story of the Old Boston Town House 1658–1711* (Boston, 1908), 56, 58.

Keayne's townhouse, sketched from the surviving building plans.

    & so possibly may dispose of my gift where there is less need & that it may do more good if it had been employed in some other way, I am willing to refer it to the President, Ffeofees, & Overseers that are entrusted with the care & ordering of the College & Scholars or Students, with the things thereto belonging.

But having said that, he then adds that his gifts are *not* to be used for "buildings or repairs of the College" but for the help of such

    poor and hopeful scholars whose parents are not comfortably able to maintain them there for their diet & learning or for some addition yearly to the poorer sort of Fellows or Tutors whose parents are not able nor themselves have not the ability nor supplies otherwise to defray their charge and make their studies comfortable.

Similarly, he makes clear that his gift to the support of a free school was not for general purposes but "to help on the training up of some

poor men's children of Boston (that are most towardly & hopeful) . . .
not only in the Latin tongue but also to write and cipher."

In every point in the listing of his gifts he tried in every way he could
to micromanage and control into the future their intended uses and to
explain the reasons for the gifts.

Since he could not anticipate whether the town would fail to fulfill the precise terms of the £300 gift and because Harvard might
not inherit that sum by default, he makes an additional gift of £100
to the college, this from what he had once set aside for the Indians.
He then points out to the college that £100 "will purchase twenty
cows & those cows will be let for twenty pounds a year & the stock
still preserved." That putative annual income, if carefully managed, "I desire may be distributed & disposed of to the best good of
the scholars as I have heretofore proposed"—unless, that is, other
equally contingent provisions for Harvard came through, at which
point the £100 "shall become void."

When he leaves gifts "to my three Negars" (Angola, 40 shillings,
Richard, 40 shillings, and 20 shillings to Richard's wife Grace), all of
whom have been "diligent & careful in their business & serviceable"
to him, he writes that the gifts should take the form of "some young
heifers to raise and [be a] stock for them" even if they were sold away,
and he designates Richard's daughter Zipora to be her father's legatee.*
When he leaves the shoemaker Reynold 20 shillings, he makes clear
that it is for the word "that he spoke publicly & seasonably in the time
of my distress & other men's vehement opposition against me."

When he donates 10 pounds (in cows) each to his brother-in-law
Mansfield's children, he devotes three full pages of the will explain-

---

* The fortunes of Angola and his family—wife, son-in-law, and granddaughter—have
been traced in remarkable detail through twenty documents in the Massachusetts public
records. Having bought his freedom by 1661, Angola died in 1675, leaving an estate worth
approximately £45, £30 of it in "a dwelling hous and land adjoyned." Melinda Lutz San-
born, "Angola and Elizabeth: An African Family in the Massachusetts Bay Colony," *New
England Quarterly* 72, no. 1 (March 1999): 119–29.

ing why he leaves not a penny to Mansfield himself. He had been supporting his "unworthy & unthankful brother [in-law]" for years—got him out of prison, paid his debts, set him up in trade, paid for his clothes and other necessities, and covered all his expenses for his voyage to America. All of this had been repaid with "quarrelsome lewdnesses . . . distempered carriages & unworthy behavior." An idle, drunken conniver, Mansfield, who now lived with Keayne and disturbed the family, tried to extract "a maintenance out of my estate" and "would have cut my throat with his false accusations if it had lain in his power."

But more detailed than his condemnation of Mansfield were his meticulous efforts to protect the future of his beloved granddaughter, Anna, to whom he left the very large sum of 900 pounds. She was the daughter of a broken marriage: Benjamin had married and divorced the high-born Sarah Dudley, who had proved to be an adulteress given to "irregular prophesying in mixed assemblies" and was excommunicated by the church for "odious, lewd, and scandalous unclean behavior." Keayne realized correctly that Anna would in some sense be his ultimate beneficiary and he feared for her education, her spiritual well-being, and the security of the wealth he would leave her. So he struck her wayward mother from any possible benefits from the will and forbade her from having any role in Anna's upbringing. If Anna, refusing to follow her father's and the overseers' advice, succumbed to Sarah's "insinuations . . . out of natural pity or respect to her mother," she too would be struck from the will, save for what would be needed for her maintenance and education. In that case, Benjamin would inherit his daughter's portion or if he was then dead, his other children would receive Anna's bequest, or if they too were dead or otherwise absent, Harvard College would be the recipient, on the terms previously described.

Anna, he wrote, was not to be sent to board elsewhere for her elementary education and training but was to be instructed by her father and grandmother and thereafter by a godly family "where she may have her carnal disposition most of all subdued & reformed by strict discipline," and who would "provide some fit & godly match proportionable to her estate & condition." They were to see to it that she did not throw herself away on "some swaggering gentleman . . . that will look more after the enjoying of what she hath than living in the fear of God." If her grandmother and father were both to die before the girl was fit to receive her portion, he desired the Wilson family, his in-laws, to take charge of her protection and education for the good of her soul.

But try as he might, Keayne could not control the future in this case as in others. He would have twisted in his grave within a year of his death had he seen Anna's disastrous marriage, at age sixteen, to a scheming, impotent English real estate dealer associated with a couple of adventurers, to whom her grandmother, Keayne's widow, had transferred her rights as executrix of the will. Perhaps even worse to him might have been the sight of the extravagances of Anna's later settled life as the wealthy Madam Paige, riding through Boston's streets in her private carriage attended by black servants in livery and hosting famous dinner parties.

The original executors of Keayne's will being dead, his wayward granddaughter, Anna, and her husband, Nicholas Paige, were made administrators, in 1683, of the ultimate disposition of the will, under bond of $1,000 (New England money).

He would fail, too, in his elaborate provisions for the Artillery Company, which he had founded. His bequests for its development filled ten pages of the will. He wanted the company's arms to be stored in a safe "magazine" in the townhouse, and he set aside 5 pounds for pikes and bandoliers for members who came for training from outlying towns. But the major provision was for the construction of a firing platform for two pieces of ordnance, one large, one small. The platform was to be "planked underneath" and protected by "a shed of boards raised over it" for protection from rain and the sun. And there must be, at a convenient distance from the platform, a "butt or kind of bulwark" of raised earth or rising ground to receive the practice shots of the ordnance. (The company itself might well devote two or three training days to digging up the bottom of a hill to form the butt.) All of this would provide training for the members in the art of gunnery—"to traverse, load, mount, level, & fire at a mark." Most of the bullets fired, he thought, could be recovered in the butt and reused. But to be sure about the ammunition, he bequeathed to the officers of the company "two heifers or cows. . . . to be kept as a stock constantly, & the increase or profit . . . to be laid out in powder or bullets."

But his enthusiasm for this seemed not to have been reciprocated. The Artillery Company's application to be made a corporation had been flatly rejected by the colony's council. Citing the examples of the Praetorian Guard in ancient Rome and the Templars in Europe, they declared that it would be dangerous "to erect a standing authority of military men, which might easily, in time, overthrow the civil power." The company as such was approved, but "subordinate to all authority"—a view and doctrine that would resound through centuries of American history. More important, he had been annoyed and deeply disappointed by "the small attendance of the [members of the] Company & the declining of it daily," though he could imagine perfectly good drills carried out by only twelve men set in two files six or eight deep. They could perform "facings, countermarches, wheelings, yea such variety of forms of battles . . . & firings & charges as should be not only delightful but very useful & gainful." Still, there was a chance that the company might fail. If that happened, Keayne ordered the two cows to be returned to his executors or overseers at "the just value that they were worth at the time of their first delivery."*

---

* Keayne's Artillery Company survived, not as he had conceived of it, but as a social organization of some distinction. Active especially in the 1920s, the company, whose

In one area his accounting was particularly difficult and brought up sensitive issues of conscience. Beginning in England and continuing in New England, Keayne wrote, he had set aside weekly one pence out of every shilling earned in trust for a poor fund. From this fund, which amounted to 50, 60, or 80 pounds at any given time, he had granted sums to "any poor godly Christian or minister in need." But he had also used the poor fund for ventures at sea in order to enhance the balance of the fund. And in addition, he now confessed, he had used the fund from time to time for his personal benefit. He had borrowed from the fund when he had fallen into debt, promising to repay the poor fund when his financial situation improved. But in recent years he had not been able to contribute on a regular basis, and he now figured that he owed the poor box 100 pounds. But recalling all "that help & supply I have received from it in times of my own need," he now increased the grant to the poor fund to 120 pounds.

What emerges from this maze of benefactions and the contingent provisions surrounding them is a mind instinctively, passionately devoted to the control of the world it could reach. Everything had to be specified, every contingency anticipated, and every effort made to provide for control of the layers of default outcomes that might emerge. There was nothing abstract or theoretical about any of this. He was bound by concrete reality, and he pointed his heirs and their overseers to the whereabouts of all of the many accounts of his assets in which could be found the results of the rational organization of his life.

He explained that his executors and overseers would find, at designated places, three debt books, several shop books and books of account, a day book, a receipt book, a pocketbook for daily or weekly expenses, a book listing his debt accounts, a long white book containing bills, bonds, and receipts for land transactions, two secret

records are intact, established plaques to Keayne's memory, including one in downtown Boston, celebrating Keayne for his contribution for a town library, a "free schoolmaster," "introducing pure water to Boston," and for Harvard College.

cash boxes in his "closet" in Boston whose contents he recalled to the penny and which could be opened, he explained, "with any ordinary pin or needle thrust into a small pinhole . . . against a piece of steel which easily will give back," a leather letter case, several piles of loose papers, two "number books" begun "when I kept shop in London" and continued in New England but now no longer used, and above all his "inventory book." This "long paper book . . . with a white parchment cover" was the key to all the rest. In it, he explained, are "the particulars of my estate . . . with all that I owe and all debts that are owing to me is briefly set down under my own hand which will be a direction to my [executors and overseers] in all my affairs." It was, he repeated, "a breviat of my whole estate from year to year & shows how the Lord is pleased either to increase or decrease my estate." Though it omitted "household stuff, moveable goods & such," it contained all the particulars of his

> housing, lands, rents, debts, cattle of all sorts, farms, with some plate, jewels & some particular chief things with their several prices and valuations with a particular of all the wares and commodities & corn that I had to sell at the time of my casting up . . . with the names, quantities, prices, & sorts of them all as also a particular of the charges that I have been at yearly in building, house-keeping, apparel, servants & workmen's wages both at my farm & at Boston & whether I gained or lost by my estate that year.

Driven to succeed in his life as a merchant, he knew he had dealt rationally and logically with his business affairs and had managed them well. At the least his business life will testify to the world, he wrote,

> that I have not lived an idle, lazy, or dronish life nor spent my time wantonly, fruitlessly, or in company keeping as some have been too ready to asperse me, or that I have had in my whole time in Old England or New many spare hours to spend unprofitably

away or to refresh myself with recreations except reading & writing hath been a recreation to me.

But sheer diligence and the careful use of the time allotted to him were in no way sufficient proof, even to himself, of the depth—and weakness—of his piety. A familiar form of calculation carried over from his business life would have helped him, he believed, over the years.

> Yea more happy would it have been for me if I had been as careful & as exact in keeping an account of my sins & the debts that I owe to God & of that spiritual estate between God & my own soul & that I could as easily have made it appear to others or to myself when I gained or when I lost & to have taken as much pains this way as in the other.

But whatever the calculation, he knew that no action of his, however benevolent, however pious, could bring him closer to salvation. The utter unfathomability of God's determination of who would be saved and who would not was the core of his religious belief, which spilled out in the opening paragraph of his will. There, at the start, he committed his soul to Almighty God, "a most loving father & merciful savior," who had saved him, like all mankind, from the misery and ruin of original sin and actual transgressions through "the precious blood of his own dear son & my sweet Jesus." He had been faithful to God and the church, renouncing all known errors, "all Popish & prelatical superstitions, all anabaptistical enthusiasms and familistical delusions . . . and all old and new upstart opinions, unsound and blasphemous errors and other high imaginations." Above all, he wrote in this confession of his faith, none of this correct behavior would save him in the end.

> I do further desire from my heart to renounce all confidence or expectation of merit or dessert in any of the best duties or services

that ever I have, shall, or can be able to perform acknowledging
that all my righteous sanctification and close walking with God,
if it were or had been a thousand times more exact than ever yet
I attained to, is all polluted and corrupt and falls short of com-
mending me to God in point of my justification, or helping forward my redemption or salvation, and deserve nothing at God's
hand, but hell and condemnation.

Yet, though no amount of holiness would guarantee his salvation,
such was the paradox of Calvinist theology that correct behavior, the
holy life, "may not be neglected by me without great sin." Sanctification (good works, pious behavior) "are ordained by God for me to
walk in them carefully." So renouncing all confidence that anything
he did could assure his salvation, he could only pray to God through
Jesus Christ that his sins might be pardoned and his soul would find
redemption.

Such was his formal credo. He repeated it in various places and in
various ways as he wrote. But it was not the only evidence of his religious zeal nor in its formulaic wording the most impressive. More
important was his faithfulness to his church and to his powerful pastor,
John Cotton. Beginning in England and continuing in New England,
he made a habit not only of attending every church service he could
but of taking full notes on Cotton's sermons.

How many books of sermon notes he filled with his cramped, minuscule, scarcely readable script is not known, but three of them, covering
the years 1639 to 1642 in New England, survive. The third, of 584 pages,
is devoted to the years 1639 to 1640, tumultuous years in Keayne's career,
when he was deeply engaged in his own personal problems. Everything
he could record of Cotton's words is written out, as far as one can tell,
verbatim: the expositions, the doctrines, the uses, the questions, and
the answers, as well as the multitude of biblical passages and citations.
He could never forget his debt to Cotton's teaching. The great pastor

A portion of a page of Keayne's notes on John Cotton's sermons.

having died in 1652, Keayne bequeathed to his widow 3 pounds "as a
testimony of my respect unto her husband."[2]

He was careful to explain that his small library had a number of
works on religion, which he noted to his executors: divinity books,
commentaries, and "written" and printed sermon books. But far
more important were his "3 great writing books which are intended
as an exposition or interpretation of the whole Bible, as also a 4th
great writing book in which is an exposition on the Prophecy of Dan-

iel of the Revelations & the prophecy of Hosea." These large books he valued above all of his other writing. They were worth "all the pains & labor I have bestowed on them, so that if I had £100 laid me down for them to deprive me of them till sight or life should be taken from me, I should not part from them." Unfortunately these four great books were unfinished, and he asked his executors to see if they could find "some able scholar or two that is active and diligent & addicted to reading and writing . . . to carry on the same work by degrees, as they have leisure and opportunity, & in the same method and way as I have begun."*

Keayne's stated religion was mainstream Puritanism—or so it would seem. It conformed to the theological principles of the "non-separating" New England version of the Church of England's Calvinism, and he had forsworn all deviance from it. But Puritanism was no fixed set of doctrines. It was an unstable cluster of associated beliefs that sent out sparks in all directions, some of which took fire as distinct variations that threatened the integrity of the core version. Among the most extreme and notorious of such heresies were the beliefs of the Dutch "familists," the Family of Love, who preached easy routes to Heaven by radical spiritism, "free grace," ecstatic, direct unions with Christ without intermediation by church or clergy. The antinomianism that threatened the stability of the Bay Colony in the crisis of 1637–38 was a local, modified version of this popular and, to the authorities, dangerous heresy. One of the most blatant versions was "Grindletonianism," and it played a surprisingly important role in Keayne's otherwise orthodox spiritual life.

---

* "Books" to Keayne meant not only printed volumes but handwritten texts as well. "Scribal publication," David Hall explains, was common in Keayne's time, and such "written" books, often bound, were treated "with as much care as . . . any printed books." They were especially versatile and could more easily be confined than printed books to circulation only among specific people, especially those engaged in "illicit or controversial" issues. David D. Hall, *Ways of Writing: The Practice and Politics of Text-Making in Seventeenth-Century New England* (Philadelphia, 2008), 31, chap. 2.

Centered in and around the obscure village of Grindleton, on the Lancashire-Yorkshire border, the few "Grindletonians" were led in the early seventeenth century by the eccentric but charismatic preacher Roger Brereley (or Brearley) (1586–1637). He had long been notorious in church circles and mocked by orthodox clergy for his alleged "antinomian mysticism" and his dangerous, Quaker-like spiritism that relieved believers of all doubts as to their salvation. One declared that if Brereley's teachings were well learned, "it were not matter if the Bible were burnt." In 1616 Brereley had been interrogated by the York High Commission, charged with adherence to fifty listed errors. His repudiation of all such deviations from true doctrine and his promise of good behavior in the future did nothing to stem his work or influence, which reached into New England.[3]

The Puritans in New England knew about Brereley and his ideas, especially as exaggerated in their radicalism by his followers in northern England. Boston's sternly orthodox heresy hunter, the Rev. Thomas Shepard, who sniffed out lurking spiritism even in the most austere and highly respected mainstream Puritans, confessed that he knew these misguided people and their "superlative raptures," only too well. He himself had once flirted with Grindletonianism and had wondered "whether that glorious state of perfection [that Brereley preached] might not be the truth." That mistaken experience had steeled his resolve to expose every suspect of left-wing deviations, and that included Keayne's beloved leader, Cotton. At the very least, to Shepard, Cotton's moderate left-leaning views, more responsive than most to the belief in the unmediated grace of God that might bypass both the church's mediation and the strenuous labor of personal preparation, were suspect and led to a protracted public debate between Shepard and Cotton on theological principles that became magnified in importance as the antinomian controversy convulsed the colony. Cotton was fully vindicated and became the colony's leading cleric. But Shepard never slackened in his suspicion that Cotton's confession of orthodoxy was insincere. Governor Winthrop and the clerical establishment had no such doubts about Cotton himself, but they too feared the antinomianism that Cotton's protégée Anne Hutchinson brought into the colony. In the midst of the antinomian crisis they banned from entry into the colony "all such persons as might be dangerous to the commonwealth" and limited residence in the colony of any deviants to three weeks. For it was very probable, Winthrop wrote, that many of the dissidents who would be arriving had opinions "from Mr. Brereley his church."

How Keayne got hold of a copy of one of Brereley's sermons is not known. It must have been in England: such material did not circulate in the Puritan colony. Nor is it known how long he had it. But however it had got to him, it riveted his attention and moved him deeply. He described it precisely. His copy of Brereley's "treatise" was "a little thin pocket book bound in leather, all written by my own hand," and he bequeathed it in the will as a "special gift" to his son Benjamin. "I esteem it," he wrote,

> more precious than gold & which I have read over I think 100 & 100 times & hope he will read it over no less, but make it his constant companion, & that it may be as precious to him as ever it was & still is to me, to let anyone that desires have a copy of it I would not have him deny but . . . I desire him & hope that he will never part with it as long as he lives.

What it was in Brereley's treatise that so gripped Keayne's mind and imagination can only be surmised. The sermon was based, he explained, on "I Cor 11, 27, 28" which is St. Paul's comment on the Last Supper and his admonition that those who approach that sacrament unworthily "eateth and drinketh damnation." In any case, Keayne's fascination with this obscure document, however incongruent it might have been with his otherwise orthodox views, is testimony to his zealous search for understanding, his sensitive response to religious ideas, and the breadth of his religious sensibilities.

Such was Keayne's religion—reverential but high-minded, self-denying but aspirational, fateful but hopeful, demanding but forgiving. And it was forgiveness above all that he sought as he reviewed the events of his life and the record he was leaving behind. Forgiveness for his sins, but also for the sins of those who had fought against him. He could not forget, at this ultimate moment in his life, the mortification he had suffered at the hands of his jealous, mean-minded, truth-twisting opponents during the years he had pursued his God-given "calling" in trade. Now defiant, he sought justice from a fair-minded God. As he thought back through the years, he instinctively relitigated the ancient controversies that had so unjustly wounded him. And in doing so he made clear the high tension that had always existed between his success in his "calling" and the constraints on the spirit that had inspired it.

Even as he wrote he could anticipate the "clamors & evil reports" that would be raised once his will became known. It would be said that the conduit, townhouse, and marketplace he provided for could not be built on the 300 pounds he had left for their construction. To this he replied that (1) by the time he died the town might well have begun the work on its own; (2) the last two houses he had built had not cost him as much as 400 pounds; and (3) if his gift fell short, the town and public-spirited people should make up the difference. More important to Keayne was the likely charge that he was doing this "only for my own ends & benefit . . . because I have so many houses & buildings there about . . . that [constructing the conduit] will be more beneficial to bring trade to my shops." To this he replied: (1) "there is nothing sinful or unlawful in Christian prudence" in preventing danger to the public whoever personally profited; (2) what benefit would he personally receive from the construction once he was dead? and (3) all the construction was to be built at "the heart of the town and many fair buildings and shops are round about" so that "the advantage & profit of it will redound to the whole town in general." As for his personal profit, "I having given over trade long ago, the nearness of the market [to his shops] is more chargeable than beneficial to me."

Such accusations were not merely hypothetical. They were based on the "discouragements, more than a few," that he had previously met with that had tied up "both my heart & hands from such testimonies of my love." "Those unkind and unneighborly discourtesies that I have more lately & formerly met with . . . I cannot easily forget, though I desire to forgive & from many in the Church especially in those times of my troubles . . . actions & proceedings I could never take as a fruit of there love to my soul as much as a fruit of their prejudice against my person. But I desire to requite their evil with good, & unkindness with kindness."

Still, whatever he did, the charges against him, he knew, would continue in the future as they had in the past, and he could not fail to respond while he could. Some, he feared, "shall wonder or demand why I have let alone all these gifts and good deeds mentioned in this Will till I die & have not done somewhat in my lifetime . . . when I might have seen the disposing of it my self & have helped to have set them on foot . . . & so have reaped the benefit of the prayers of the poor & the comfort of such good acts while I had lived." This, he felt, reached into the heart of his identity as a benevolent Christian, and he spent five full pages considering it and attempting to refute it.

It's easy for others "to carve large portions out of other men's estates and tell what they might or should do," but

> a man is best able himself to judge what he can do or what he can spare to this or that good work, better than others that know not his charge, straits, or occasions. . . . Neither do I think that God doth require a man to be so liberal in his life . . . as thereby to cast his own family into straits or wants or that shall disenable him comfortably to discharge his own debts or engagements. . . . Then there is no just cause of censure.

God, he insisted, does not demand that others should be eased and we grieved. But there are always some people who criticize what other people's actions achieve, ignoring their own defects or neglects, exaggerating what little they do and minimizing what others do. In any case, past, present, and future we are all one to God who accepts the will for the deed as if they were actually done. God had accepted David's desire to build a house for Him as if he had actually done it. Those who seek "outward applause & the praise of men more than of God" are the ones who do all in their lifetimes while those who do good work in their own lifetimes "but not known till after [their] death" are free from ambition and popular applause.

But this was not a matter he could leave to generalities. The truth was that when he had suffered the trouble and censure by the court, he had also suffered great losses on sea and land. "I was indebted near or altogether thirty hundred pounds, which was sufficient to have broken the back of any one man in the country . . . & so would have done me if God had not carried me through it beyond my own expectation or foresight." Upon his recovery he had first paid off his debts and then provided for his family, but not with "prodigallitie." For he considered it "untruthfulness to God" for someone blessed with a large and comfortable outward estate "to leave everything to his wife and children, . . . making them great & rich in the world, or to bestow upon some friends or kindred that it may be hath no great need of it & to dispose none or very little of it to public charitable or good works." Now that he was able "to breathe, as it were" through the great mercy of God, only now was he able to put his benevolent wishes into deeds. "These are the true reasons," he wrote, "why I durst not adventure upon such [charitable] works . . . not for want of affection or desire but for want of convenient opportunity and ability to act."

His intentions had always been clear.

It hath been in my full purpose & resolution ever since God hath given me any comfortable estate to do good withal, not

only before I came into New England but often since, to study &
endeavor both in my life & at my death to do what I could to help
on any public profitable & general good.

But his efforts to promote the good in New England had been
answered with "unchristian, uncharitable, and unjust reproaches &
slanders." And there was "that deep & sharp censure" imposed by the
court that he could never forget. The bitter events of 1639 were never
far from his mind—the complaints that hundreds of people knew were
based on desire for revenge made heinous and odious and carried on
with such violence and zeal as if some of the greatest sins in the world
were involved. His opponents would have utterly ruined him if they
could. All this for selling a good bridle for two shillings which now
would sell for three shillings, and selling six-penny nails for seven or
eight pence which now sell for much more, and selling "gold" buttons
at 2 shillings 9 pence per dozen. "These were the great matters in which
I had offended," though he knew well of

offenses, complaints & crimes of a high nature against God &
men such as filthy uncleanness, fornications, drunkenness, fearful oaths, quarreling, mutinous Sabbath breakings, thefts forger-
ies & such like which hath passed with fines or censures so small
or easy as hath not been worth the naming or regarding, which
I can not think upon but with sad thoughts of inequality of such
proceedings which hath been the very cause of tying up my heart
& hands from doing such general and public good acts, as in my
heart I both desired and intended.

But God's justice would prevail. Those who do little and undervalue
what others do, growing "proud & high minded," should know that
God could bring them "into a lower frame & put them into such a condition that they may stand in need of the help of as mean & as much
despised persons as myself before they die." The day will come, he

added, "when I & they, the judges & judged, shall stand naked before one throne, where there will be no respect of persons, when all sentences & the causes of them will be called over again before a greater judge & a higher tribunal than man's can be, where the accused shall have his just plea . . . & where the sighs of the oppressed & wronged will be heard & a righteous sentence shall pass . . . as the true nature of the case stands without prejudice or partiality."

He could not shake his bitterness as he compulsively returned to his time of troubles. I submitted to the unjust censure, he wrote, I paid the fine, but had been pursued with such fierceness "as if I had not been worthy to have lived upon the earth." In comparison with costs now, his goods and prices "were cheap peniworths." He had never deserved the treatment he had received, and he believed that many, both in and outside the court, had agreed with him. There had been, he knew, a great debate in the court over the imposition of the fine. It had passed by only one vote, he believed, and "against the desire & judgement of almost the greatest number of the chiefest & wisest of the magistrates & deputies." Even Governor Winthrop, though he was "rather against me then," had seen the injustice of the verdict. Shortly before Winthrop's death [1649], Keayne recalled, there had been a gathering of the elders and others, including himself, at Captain Tyng's house. There he had heard Winthrop confessing to the Reverends Cotton and Wilson that he had been troubled by the verdict in 1639 and "that it was needful & just to consider of that act again." Keayne had had the impression that the governor intended to move the General Court "to recall that censure." But since the governor had not mentioned Keayne by name, he had kept silent on that occasion. Three weeks later, however, Keayne paid a visit to the governor and asked him for specifics. Winthrop had then "more plainly told me his meaning." Keayne was therefore certain that if Winthrop had lived,

he would have used his utmost endeavor that my fine at least should have been restored back to me, & not only himself but also some others not only of the Magistrates but of the Deputies, yea some of them that were then against me, have said that they think the Court ought in justice to do no less then to give me money again.

His conscience to God and man was clear. He had been "humble & penitential" in all of these proceedings which called for "mercy & clemency." He knew the errors of his life, "the failings in my trade & otherwise," but was all this, which could be reasonably justified by the situation at the time, "such a heinous sin?" He had palpable indications that God did not think so. For despite his formal belief that one's behavior had no influence on God's determinations, it could not be meaningless that God had favored him in his outward estate, had turned the charges against him "to my good . . . [and] hath since carried me through many & great engagements with comfort."

As he drew to the end of the will, the enormity of what lay ahead bore in on him. What he was now writing, he realized, would be "my last words that will live to speak for me when I am dead & in my grave." He still felt that he had not dealt sufficiently with those who had sought "to load me with divers reproaches & long[ed] to lay me under a dark cloud." But there were deeper issues than these notorious controversies—issues that lay at the heart of his existence as both a successful merchant and a devoted Christian. As he contemplated the completion of the will and his own mortality he was filled with pride but overcome with guilt. He could not leave the dilemma unresolved, and in the final pages of the will he made a last effort to settle his doubts. He isolated three questions which, in seven pages of rambling prose, he sought, at that late date, to answer.

First, how could he have created an estate of £4,000 "with a good conscience or without oppression in my calling," especially since he had nothing to begin with? Of his first going to London he could, like "old Jacob thankfully say, with my staff came I over this Jordan & now the Lord hath given me two bunds" [Gen. 32.10: bands]. To have built an estate of £4,000 in forty or fifty years of vigorous trading, with "good credit & great esteem & respect," amounts to an annual average of only £100 "clear gains." An industrious and provident man who avoids middlemen and was careful with giving credit can easily earn £100 a year "above his expenses & a great deal more very honestly without hurting his own conscience or wronging those that he deals with." In New England he himself rarely earned £100 a year above his expenses, though he had never been a "prodigal spender," just as he had not been a "niggardly sparer in things needful," as his many account books testified. And further, as was well known, he had brought with him from England "two or 3,000 pounds in good estate."

Second, if he valued his estate at £4,000, why was it valued for tax purposes at only £1,000? No one, he answered, "is bound in conscience to make known his whole estate & suffer himself to be valued to the uttermost extent . . . if he can honestly prevent it." Nowhere in the world is this not true, except perhaps in cases of extreme national danger. In England, he knew, knights, aldermen, and merchants worth thousands, including land worth hundreds a year, are not taxed at half the true value of their estates. In New England, he wrote, he was paying in taxes three times what he would have paid in England. There he had never paid over £4 in any one subsidy (tax levy), and subsidies were rare. In New England, he wrote, we are rated every year, and in some years we have been taxed £20 to country rates. And third, most of his estate now lay in his farm, cattle, houses, and household stuff, none of which is ever valued at its highest worth. Neither God nor any Christian state "would have their inhabitants crushed or weakened by continual charge." They are to be "nourished & preserved in a thriving condition that they may live well & be still able to do good in their places for the carrying on of public charges."

With that, he moved on toward a scattered conclusion, concerned now that his enemies might in the end try to thwart his will by pretending that certain of his expressions in it were offensive and thereby seize parts of his estate that he thought he had secured for his wife and son. No one could express himself so warily, he wrote, that some wits could make what is good or harmless appear to be evil. He had seen it in England, where some with a "desire to fish away a part of a dying man's estate" did so by challenging certain expressions or bequests. Many had suffered in the Star Chamber and the Court of High Commission from deliberate efforts to interpret good actions and expressions as contrary to their meanings. He hoped that such a thing would never happen in New England, but "I know not how strangely things may alter nor who may get into places of power & authority between this & the time of my death, nor what pretenses corrupt or prejudiced men may make." If any such complaints were lodged against him or his will after his death with "any interest either to get any part of my estate . . . or shall be troublesome or vexatious to my executor on pretense of any fault or offence of mine," and if such charges were countenanced by the authorities, he declared it to be his "will & full mind" that all his bequests for general or public use—the conduit, the library, the granary, the armory, the firing range, the school, the college, the market house—"shall utterly cease & become void & of no effect."

But whatever happened, he wanted it known, as he had written at the start, that despite all the "deep sorrows and . . . hard measures" he had endured, it was "a great blessing & undeserved favor of God that he hath brought me hither to enjoy His presence in the beauties of holiness." Though there may be failings in both state and church in the colony, "for all men have their weaknesses," which require amending and reforming, he does "unfeignedly approve of the way of the Churches of Jesus Christ and the civil government" that had been set up here; indeed, the colony's government "is one of the best and happiest governments that is this day in the world."

TAWNEY, IN HIS lyric *Religion and the Rise of Capitalism*, introduced
the advent of Puritanism in these terms:

> On a world heaving with expanding energies, and on a Church
> uncertain of itself, rose . . . the tremendous storm of the Puritan
> movement. The forest bent; the oaks snapped; the dry leaves were
> driven before a gale, neither all of winter nor all of spring, but vio-
> lent and life-giving, pitiless and tender, sounding strange notes
> of yearning and contrition . . . while amid the blare of trumpets,
> and the clash of arms, and the rending of the carved work of the
> Temple, humble to God and haughty to man, the soldier-saints
> swept over battlefield and scaffold, their garments rolled in blood.

But the storm was not only a clash of power and authority but a
wrenching transformation at the deepest layers of culture. There is a
magic mirror, Tawney wrote,

> in which each order and organ of society, as the consciousness
> of its character and destiny dawns upon it, looks for a moment,
> before the dust of conflict or the glamour of success obscures its
> vision. In that enchanted glass, it sees its own lineaments reflected
> with ravishing allurements; for what it sees is not what it is, but
> what in the eyes of mankind and of its own heart it would be. . . .
> For the middle classes of the early seventeenth century, rising but
> not yet triumphant, that enchanted mirror was Puritanism. What
> it showed was a picture grave to sternness, yet not untouched
> with a sober exaltation—an earnest, zealous, godly generation,
> scorning delights, punctual in labour, constant in prayer, thrifty
> and thriving, filled with a decent pride in themselves and their
> calling, assured that strenuous toil is acceptable to Heaven.[4]

Consider the case, he wrote, of Mr. Robert Keayne; and he summarized the scandal of 1639 and Keayne's tearful acknowledgment of his

"covetous and corrupt heart." But not having seen the merchant's *Apologia*, Tawney could not have known how vividly Keayne's life illuminates the personal cost of Puritanism's zeal: the tense balance of one's inner life, the torment of cross-pressures, the double bind of ascetic acquisitiveness and the guilt that breeds paranoia.

Keayne's lamentations having gone unheard in his lifetime, the only recourse he had had was to speak from the grave, free of his burdens, safe from contradiction, his pride if not his soul redeemed.

II

Laslett's Clayworth: Andover and Heidenreichstein

THE VARIANT STRUCTURES OF FAMILY LIFE

On October 21, 1946, I bought a copy of volume three of Werner Jaeger's *Paideia: The Ideals of Greek Culture* (New York, 1944). Why I did that, why I dated it, and why I read it with great fascination, underlining passages and writing in the margins, I cannot recall. I was then in my first year in the Harvard graduate school and at work on my first history courses, none of which involved Greek history or culture. But the result determined much of what happened five years later. By then, 1951–52, I was completing my dissertation and found myself favored with an invitation to teach courses on the history of education at the Harvard Graduate School of Education. Frank Keppel, the new young dean of the school of education, was determined to bring the work of the education faculty into the mainstream of what was developing in the faculty of arts and sciences. He had received a grant from the Ford Foundation to make two appointments, one in philosophy, one in history. For the former, Israel Scheffler was chosen, for the latter—by a process I never knew—myself.

The two or three years I spent in the school of education were a blessing. I learned something about teaching and lecturing (not always synonymous). I met highly motivated students with interests quite different from my own. And I had the opportunity to work with wonderful colleagues, above all with Scheffler. He was a fine intellect and an extraordinary person. He seemed to me to be what I can only call gracious, in a religious sense, and not because of his rabbinical credentials. He conveyed to me serenity and common sense, tough, sharp thinking, and a gentle attitude to the world and to everyone he encountered.

We met in very active, sometimes tense, faculty meetings, and we worked hard, in that crumbling red brick building (about to be demolished). For me, who knew little about the history of education or of the field's bibliography, it meant months of total immersion in the literature of the subject, lecturing twice weekly on what I was myself just learning. And among the things I learned was that the literature of the subject was stuck in a what seemed to me to be a Whiggish anachronism shaped by generations of education historians eager to trace the train of events that led inevitably to the triumph of contemporary schooling and pedagogy. As I went deeper into that rich, important subject, I began to conceive of it as a major part of America's evolving society and culture. And that, suddenly, brought me back to Jaeger and the concept of *Paideia* not as pedagogy but as the community's culture and its transfer across the generations.

The result, bundling together a critique of the existing literature with an extended example of how the subject might develop in this more amplified way, was *Education in the Forming of American Society* (1960). I did not mention, in what I wrote, the concept of *paideia* and Jaeger's representation of the Greek philosophers' view of education. But I developed the idea, loosely modeled on Jaeger's, that one can understand the subject best when one sees its elaborate involvements with the rest of society and notes its shifting functions and purposes. This introduction to the book was followed by a substantive historical narrative that exemplified the basic ideas. But the prologue alone was enough to alienate the professionals in the history of education. For them the approach was mistaken and misleading—a view of education that brought their familiar, well-designed subject into an amorphous, untracked landscape lacking structure or direction in which education in any proper, pedagogical sense was lost. The reviews were numerous, and among the history of education specialists largely critical. Forty years later the book was still in print and still contentious. A survey of the entire history of the historiography of American education, published in 2003, devotes a chapter to "Why Bailyn was Right Despite Being Wrong."[1]

I was confident, however, of the theoretical approach, and my main problem was to work out a full historical narrative that exemplified these general views. I turned to the materials I knew best, covering the first two centuries of British life in North America. In that era a transformation had taken place in the forms of education, the key to which lay not in formal schooling but in the history of family life, the primal core of education, and also the community and the church. All of this had to be seen as vital parts of education, but the family, I knew, was the major force in the transformation narrative. And so I began a search for works on the background of family life at the start of British settlement. It led me eventually through strange passages of history, controversies, and confusions in historical interpretation, and documents from obscure English villages, Massachusetts towns, and an ancient castle in the Waldviertel district of Lower Austria.

What was family life among the early settlers? What was their inheritance, and expectations? The subject had been almost entirely neglected. The only largescale treatment of it I could find was Arthur Calhoun's three-volume *Social History of the American Family,* which had little to say about the earliest period, and its interpretation was superficial. Even Willystine Goodsell's *History of the Family as a Social and Educational Institution,* despite its promising title, was derivative and sprinkled with quaint illustrations. The best work on the early American family I could find was Edmund Morgan's *Puritan Family,* but it was limited to a distinctive region, as was his *Virginians at Home.* The subject finally came into focus for me when I turned further back in time, to the English background, and came on an essay by Peter Laslett.

Laslett, then a young historian at the University of Cambridge, had published in 1949 an edition of the royalist Robert Filmer's *Patriarcha* and other writings. *Patriarcha* was the classical argument analogizing the state with the primordial family necessarily dominated by a male head ruling women, children, and servants, his role descending by primogeniture. Filmer's tract had circulated in manuscript in the 1630s, and when it was finally published in 1680 it became widely distributed and influential as the programmatic statement of the supporters of the claims of James II to the throne. It also became the target of the Whig opposition, whose main counterstatement was John Locke's *Two Treatises of Government,* of which Laslett would produce a definitive, "critical" edition in 1960. In his lengthy introduction to *Patriarcha,* Laslett examined and interpreted the document in great detail, but his interest went beyond the text to the historical context from which it had emerged. Was Filmer's actual social world consistent with his patriarchal view of the political world? In 1948 Laslett published an important article, "The Gentry of Kent in 1640." In Filmer's native Kent, he stated, "the unit of the county community at this time was the patriarchal household maintained by each recognized head of an individual family." These deeply rooted, stable, and elaborate households, which included kin in several relationships, together formed the county communities, which combined to form the overall community of the English realm. And not only England itself. England's county society, he found, was reproduced in early Virginia—"its attitudes, its literary interests, even its field sports [reappeared] in the swamps of the Virginia creeks." The colony's planter families illustrate "the immense strength of the family bond . . . there could be no more vivid illustration of patriarchalism at work."

Laslett's main purpose in writing "The Gentry of Kent" was to explore what might be called the sociology of Filmer's patriarchalism and through that, to sketch the basic social structure of the English landed realm. But for me it was the touchstone to understanding the role of the family as the traditional cultural context for education in the widest sense. Following Laslett's interpretation and combining it with other data on the early English family, I developed the idea of the family as a patrimonial group of extended kinship that reflected and reinforced the general structure of social authority.

> It was [I wrote] these patriarchal kinship communities that shouldered most of the burden of education. They were, in the first place, the primary agencies in the socialization of the child. Not only did the family introduce [children] to the basic forms of civilized living, but it shaped their attitudes, formed their patterns of behavior, endowed them with manners and morals. It introduced [the child] to the world; and in so doing reinforced the structure of its authority. . . . What the family left undone by way of informal education the local community almost always completed. It did so in entirely natural ways, for so elaborate was the architecture of family organization and so deeply founded was it in the soil of stable, slowly changing village and town communities in which intermarriage among the same groups had taken place generation after generation, that it was at times difficult for the child to know where the family left off and the greater society began.

Such was the background, as I then understood it, of education in the first centuries of American history, and around it I wrote, in the substantive part of *Education in the Forming of American Society*, what I called "an essay in hypothetical history." Like all such projections, I wrote, "it may well prove to be wrong or misleading. But if so, its purpose will nevertheless have been served by eliciting the contrary proof, which, too, will tell a different and I think a more useful kind of story about education that those we are accustomed to hear."

The complex patriarchal structure that Laslett had described could not, I wrote, be maintained in a barren world. People struggled to sustain and reproduce the traditional forms of social order. Education was dislodged from its ancient position in the social order, wrenched loose from the instinctive workings of society, and cast as a matter for deliberation into the forefront of consciousness. Some of its functions were transferred from informal to formal institutions. Schools and formal schooling became more important, more an instrument of deliberate social purpose, as the traditional role of the family was jeopardized and reduced, despite extraordinary efforts to sustain it. Capital punishment, it was ruled in Connecticut and Massachusetts, was fitting for filial disobedience. Parents and masters were again and again ordered to fulfill their duties as guardians of civic order. But if the guardians failed, as they did in this difficult environment, who would guard the guardians?

It was along these lines, awakened by Jaeger and informed by Laslett's early work, that I sketched the transformative history of education over the first two centuries of British life in North America.

Then something unexpected happened, which turned the story around. While I was seeing my book through publication, Laslett was rummaging about in the Library of Congress and in 1959 stumbled on a 1910 reproduction of *The Rector's Book, Clayworth, Nottinghamshire*. The original—sixty-two leaves of parchment closely written on both sides, still kept in the Clayworth church—contained the records kept by the rector of this obscure village and parish on everything he felt was important in the years between 1676 and 1701. But what caught Laslett's eye, and what would lead to a proposed new way of understanding the whole of English social history, were two short censuses, each containing "all the names of the inhabitants of the parish by a yearly poll, and out of them to be noted the communicants at sacrament," one for the year 1676 and the other for 1688.

For Laslett, long interested in social structure, and aware of the current work of the French demographic historians in developing new techniques for reconstructing the organization of past households and

*Item 9 of the Clayworth rector's list of parish records, noting the "yearly poll"
that led Peter Laslett to his study of family structure in time past.*

families, the two Clayworth censuses—a total of only nine pages in
modern print—were startling, exciting, and inspiring. For he could see
from his first study of the information in Clayworth's simple censuses
that they could lead to the recovery of what he would soon call "the
world we have lost." In his first essay on the rector's censuses (1963) he
explained that they revealed a community far different from what one
would have expected and what he himself had described in his writings
on Filmer. Almost at a glance he could see that the village populations
were not stable and unchanging. By 1688, approximately 60 percent of
the population in 1676 had disappeared—not by death so much as by
outmigration and the arrival of new families. The households were not
complex but were mainly made up of nuclear, independent families
(man, wife, and children). They did not include extended kin (retired
seniors, in-laws, and other relatives), though they often included servants drawn from other families within the village or from adjacent
or nearby villages. As a result the living units were small: the average
household size over the twelve years between the two censuses ranged
between 4 and 4.5.

Implications and possible ramifications stirred Laslett's imagination. Chief among them flowed from the possibility that Clayworth
was not unique but typical of rural England, and if that were true,
England's social history before industrialization would have to be
rewritten. He received encouragement from the discovery of records

kept by another rector, of the parish of Cogenhoe (pronounced Cook-noe) in Northamptonshire, which includes "no less than six listings of the inhabitants, family by family and name by name, dating from the decade 1618–28." Laslett and his collaborator John Harrison were able to include preliminary data from those listings, and while they discovered differences from Clayworth, there were striking similarities. The composition and size of households and the mobility of servants were of the same order as Clayworth's.

All of this was illuminating, and it led to remarkable developments. Many more such parish records would have to be discovered and exploited. Ultimately Laslett would mobilize volunteers in a hundred or more villages to contribute to the database. The implications for understanding the social impact of industrialization on society would have to be re-examined. Industry could not have broken up large, traditional, stable families as was commonly believed: they had been nuclear and mobile for centuries before. And all this would have to be brought together with the findings of the French demographers. In a later study of Clayworth and Cogenhoe he added, for comparison, the records of two French parishes of the late eighteenth century, Hallines and Longuenesse in the north of the country, whose censuses were especially complete. There were certainly differences, he found, in the two sets of parishes, English and French, especially in the role of the servants. But the French parishes, he discovered, were of approximately the same size as the English; the French turnover rate was "not dissimilar" from that of the English; and in general, French rural society was organized in a very similar way to the English—"so much so that Longuenesse has been described as more English than an English village, at least in its family structure." In conclusion, Laslett wrote in this last iteration of the essay of 1963, "Clayworth and Cogenhoe can be taken as revealing to us some at least of the general features of Western society as a whole."

Within twenty-five years from the first publication on Clayworth, all those ramifications would be explored in institutional form by the

Cambridge Group for the History of Population and Social Structure, a research center created by Laslett in collaboration with the economic historian E. A. Wrigley and others. While voluntary scribes in a hundred or more villages around the country were producing for the Cambridge Group population lists like those of Clayworth and Cogenhoe, Laslett himself continued to develop the ramifications of his original findings.

Laslett's interest in the work of the French historical demographers broadened out beyond simple comparisons. They evoked for him the possibility that his findings might apply beyond the British world and even the French, to the other nations of western Europe and perhaps also those of Asia. In 1969, after having published a book (*The World We Have Lost* [1965]) based on the Clayworth material, and a general essay, "The Study of Social Structure from Listings of Inhabitants" (1966), he convened at the Cambridge Group an international conference on household and family in past times. He was careful to distribute in advance his own paper on the size and structure of English households to define the aims of the conference. He was gratified by the results. Three years later, in 1972, the revised papers, introduced with a ninety-eight page comprehensive essay by Laslett, were published as *Household and Family in Past Times*.

It is an impressive volume. In its six hundred pages it contains parallel findings on family structure from England, France, Italy, Corsica, the Netherlands, Belgium, Serbia, Japan, and North America. And while there were great variations among these different worlds that the twenty-three contributors to the book explored in detail, the general conclusion of it fortified Laslett's belief that small nuclear families predominated nearly everywhere in the many areas studied, that there was little evidence of extended families or large complex households, and further, that mean household size may have been more or less constant everywhere for centuries before industrialization.

Unfortunately for me, he began his long, comprehensive Introduction with a glance back at the misleading, erroneous interpretations that had preceded the revelation of Clayworth. He singled out two examples of such errors. The first was casual and confessional—his own interpretation of the social setting of Filmer's *Patriarcha*, which, he explained, had been "written in entire ignorance of what any set of domestic groups in seventeenth-century England actually consisted in." The second example was not, as one might have expected, his own—now repudiated—"Gentry of Kent" article, but, alas, my *Education in the Forming of American Society*, which had in part derived from it. And he quoted what he considered to be my unfortunate errors. In a rather complicated footnote he approved of my criticism of the existing literature on family history and conceded that, despite my mistaken view of the loss of family extension during colonization, I "may be quite correct in [my] claim that the eighteenth-century colonial American family was in a critical situation." But in any case, he wrote, all such misguided pre-Clayworth writings were not really about the size and structure of actual domestic groups. They were simply reflections of attitudes or sentiments about what families "must have been," not what in fact they had been.

But the world turns, and so do the fortunes of historical interpretations. In 1970, while Laslett's vast *Household and Family* was being prepared for publication, I met with him at Harvard. We chatted, as I recall, about common interests—he was an amiable, learned, somewhat eccentric man, more enterprising than one might have thought—and then I mentioned to him that I had been reading the typescript of an article called "The Stem Family and the Developmental Cycle of the Peasant Household: An Eighteenth-Century Austrian Example."

It was written by a German-born graduate student, Lutz Berkner, who had come to Harvard from Princeton, where he had worked with Lawrence Stone, a distinguished scholar who had had his own problems with numerical calculations in his native England but who had turned to the quantitative study of family life, sex, and marriage. Berkner, following that theme for his dissertation, had located a remarkable, utterly obscure set of documents. He had found, in the tower of an

The castle tower in Heidenreichstein.

ancient castle in the north Austrian lordship (*Herrschaft*) of Heidenreichstein, a census taken in 1763 that covered the 729 households in
the thirty-six peasant villages within that manor's jurisdiction. He had
selected 657 households for analysis and had gained the permission of
the manor's lord to study them. The lengthy article, which I passed on
to Laslett as we talked, summarized Berkner's findings. Based on the
censuses in Heidenreichstein's tower archive, his findings were utterly
at odds with what Laslett had written on the subject since Clayworth
and that he was then about to republish in amplified form in the multinational *Household and Family in Past Time*.

I do not recall Laslett's immediate reaction as he glanced through the
paper, but he must have been thinking quickly about ways of dealing
with this problem. For it was a problem. Berkner's obscure documents,
fortified by other material he had found in the lower Austrian *Landar-
chiv*, demonstrated that extended, or stem, families did in fact exist
in Europe, at certain times and in certain situations. Laslett's data,
Berkner wrote, were static, cross-sectional pictures taken at a particular time in a town's history. The fundamental fact, well established by

the anthropologists whom Berkner cited, was that families and households go through developmental cycles "as the individuals who compose them go through their life cycles." It is the stage in the dynamic intersection of the two—the cycles of individual lives and the cycles of families—that determine household size and composition at any given time; and the Heidenreichstein data made that vividly clear.

> The extended family is merely a phase [Berkner wrote] through which most families go. Since there is a good chance that the parents will still be alive, when a young couple marries, they begin their marriage in an extended family. In time the parents die and the now middle-aged couple spends their years in a nuclear family. When one of their sons marries and brings his wife into the household the family becomes extended again.[2]

When a census reveals a low frequency of extended families—and a high frequency of nuclear families—it is reasonable to conclude that the families are in the nuclear phase at the time the census is taken. The patterns are clear in the Heidenreichstein censuses. When the head of the household was relatively young—under forty—his parents would probably still be alive and his siblings young enough to still be at home, hence the unit would be a complete stem family. When the parents retired or died and the siblings left home, the unit would likely be nuclear: that is, parents and children alone. The likelihood of a high ratio of nuclear families was increased in the early modern period because of the high death rate, which made three generational families unlikely: few children would ever have known their grandparents. And the economy played a supporting role. Few properties were profitable enough to support three generations. Rich farms could support retired parents and be owned by young households with children. In Heidenreichstein only 15 percent of the poorer families were extended, while 34 to 42 percent of the richer families were extended.

Thus the presence of extended families "depended both upon the age of the head of the household and the size or value of the farms."

At this point in his paper Berkner had turned directly to Laslett's main conclusions. They were, he wrote, clearly unpersuasive since they did not take into account "the age structure of the population and the distribution of wealth." Furthermore, the populations that Laslett had examined were not, as Berkner's were, "peasants" (*Bauern*), that is, property-owning farmers with political rights in the village and economic privileges in the common lands and forests. England had been the first European country to have had a substantial decline in its freeholder population, and the proportion of extended families had declined as the proportion of freeholders had decreased—hence the predominance of nuclear families in the English village censuses. "Laslett's statistics may simply confirm that the shift from a "peasant" [freeholder or farmer] society had already occurred in England by the end of the seventeenth century."

Such were the opening pages of the article that Laslett read as we talked and that would be published with elaborate statistical documentation two years later.[3] The problem it presented to Laslett was obvious. His magisterial *Household and Family* was soon to appear in print, but there was still time to deal at least briefly with Berkner's conclusions while the big book was still in proof. So with Berkner's permission to refer to his article in its prepublication form, he inserted a few paragraphs and footnotes on Heidenreichstein since, he wrote, it was "the most conspicuous and best documented example so far to be recovered of a past European community exhibiting stem family features."

But in fact he had little to say beyond insisting that there were widespread *attitudes* toward extended families in the Austrian region that *appeared* to be unique, and declaring that "none of the facts we have cited makes it likely that the situation in Heidenreichstein can have been typical of any extensive region of Western Europe." No doubt Heidenreichstein had peculiar features, which he listed in a footnote.

But the problem persisted, and Laslett returned to it in several brief references later in *Household and Family,* and then, a hundred pages after his first comments, he tackled the problem more substantially. Fortified by many population tallies the Cambridge Group had accumulated, he selected two villages from a list of one hundred—Ealing (Middlesex) in 1599 and Arleigh (Essex) in 1796—which had "some resemblance to the Heidenreichstein pattern." Examination of these two villages whose families were ostensibly extended revealed the presence of only a widowed mother or mother-in-law and grandchildren with grandparents. "In neither case would it seem that a persuasive argument could be made for these details representing the residual survival of some complex familiar form like the stem family." The rest of his comments on Heidenreichstein were relegated to two dense, technical footnotes, one defending his earlier writings against Berkner's criticism, the other supporting his argument with references to data from other English villages and from Belgrade and the Japanese town of Nishinomiya.

Such were Laslett's responses to Berkner's "Stem Family and Developmental Cycle" which he was able to insert into the manuscript of *Household and Family* before publication. In the vast bulk of that multicultural book crowded with statistical tables and ideographs of family structures, Berkner's study was a small, fringe distraction, to be quickly refuted or simply ignored. "The wish to believe in the large and extended households as the ordinary institution of an earlier England and an earlier Europe, or as a standard feature of an earlier pre-industrial world," is, he repeated, simply a matter of ideology— ideology, not social fact. Still, Laslett had to admit, somewhat lamely, that the existence of Berkner's data and the possibility of similar discoveries, while exceptional and merely limited to particular localities, "certainly enlivens the whole issue of domestic group structure in Europe in relation to industrialisation."

But if Laslett thought that he had thus disposed of the problem Berkner had presented, he soon discovered otherwise. Three years after the appearance of Laslett's masterwork, Berkner published a blistering seventeen-page review of the book, entitled "The Use and Misuse of Census Data for the Historical Analysis of Family Structure." "This volume," he wrote, referring to *Household and Family*, "will undoubtedly be cited hundreds of times as having proved that the family has been nuclear in most Western societies in the past. In fact, it has done nothing of the sort." Though Laslett acknowledges objections to his definitions and methodology, "he continues to 'proceed boldly' along his course, noting the difficulties but not incorporating their implications into his scheme. There are also considerable discrepancies between what he says and what he does." The example he uses is so poor, Berkner wrote, it limits any conclusions he reaches. His census lists contain no mention of the ages of the household head. "Family structure is not a thing, it is a set of relationships, whether viewed in terms of actual or ideal behavior." There is no knowing what rules the English enumerators followed, and what their purpose might have been. In fact, Berkner wrote, the population lists that Laslett used "are simply not real censuses." And not only, he continued, were Laslett's rules of evidence inadequate, but they conflicted with his own definitions. In any case, his omission of all consideration of the surrounding circumstances of village life limited any conclusions he reached. "The organization of the household must be derived from the context of the society in which it is found," especially in making comparisons among such different worlds as Serbia, Japan, and Austria. Further, Laslett's pre-definition of the household "according to an English model . . . is inappropriate for comparative purposes."

There were other ways, Berkner wrote, than Laslett's to explain the numerical dominance of the nuclear family. Some of the contributions to *Household and Family* tried to discover significant differences in family life within regions and among social classes, "but unfortunately they are usually diverted by their obligation to fit the data to Laslett's questions." Following the kind of evidence Laslett asked for and the format he set out, the contributors to the book were "unable to find anything interesting to say except that their data did or did not fit with his findings about England." The imposing volume would have made more substantial contributions if the authors of the many essays could have used a diversity of approaches and asked a wider range of questions. What in fact had the volume proved? It simply demonstrated what sociologists and anthropologists had long known, "that at a given point in time the majority of basic residential units in any society will be composed of nuclear families. But this is not the same thing as saying that the nuclear family has dominated in most societies as the familial institution, which is what Laslett claims." Perhaps nuclear families really did represent the typical English household in the past. "But by ignoring any evidence other than censuses and by then analyzing households outside of their social context in terms of the narrowest definitions, no other interpretation could possibly emerge."

If Laslett replied to this diatribe, I have found no record of it. He continued to write articles and edit books exploring more deeply his now established view of England's and Europe's family and social structures, while Berkner, writing in German and English and mainly concerned with economic issues, went further in probing complex inheritance practices, proto-industrialization, "household arithmetic," land management, and the peasant life cycle in Austria and France.

These convolutions based on data from across Europe and especially from the castle tower of Heidenreichstein, I had been following step by step, discussing in classes and seminars what was becoming available, piece by piece. It turned out that there was great interest among young historians feeling their way into new and exciting areas, for such small-scale community studies—village histories—based on long-neglected genealogical data, local tables of vital statistics, demographic calculations, and privately printed family histories. By 1965 four major studies of family life in New England towns were in preparation, all of which would be published in the same year, 1970, and all of which took account in one way or another of Laslett's Clayworth and its sequels: John Demos's book on family life in the Pilgrims' town of Plymouth; Phillip Greven's study of population, family structure, and land in Andover; Kenneth Lockridge's history of Dedham; and Michael Zuckerman's *Peaceable Kingdoms: New England Towns in the Eighteenth Century*. The coincidence of the simultaneous appearance of these publications was so striking that within a year they were the subject of a penetrating comparative study entitled "The Morphology of New England Society in the Colonial Period."[4]

Lockridge, in his *A New England Town*, described Dedham in its first century as a "Puritan / peasant utopia" and more specifically as a "Utopian closed corporate community" in which the villagers founded a comprehensive social coalition that dealt with land, social regulation, morality, and membership, and that guaranteed its members equal access to all resources. He was aware not only of Laslett's writings on Clayworth and its ramifications but also the writings of Wrigley, Eversley, and the French demographers, but he did not engage with the issues that mainly interested them. Zuckerman worked at a more general level. His book was a sweeping interpretation of the culture of New England towns in the eighteenth century, centered on issues of concord and conflict. Demos had a more contextual and graphic view of the lives of Plymouth's people, writing in detail of their housing, clothing, and furnishings as well as of the structure of their households. Well aware of Laslett's findings, he provided demographic tables to quantify five chapters devoted to household structure. Years later he recalled his entry into research in family history that would eventuate in his book on Plymouth:

> The seeds were planted, innocently enough, long ago. I was a student, newly arrived in graduate school, groping to find a topic for a research seminar. My professor put the obvious question: "Well, what sort of thing are you interested in?" There was a pause; then, for reasons I cannot now recall, I mumbled the word "family" and asked whether that might make a "legitimate

subject of historical study." The professor's response was to open his desk-drawer, remove a small folder of typescript pages, and toss it in my direction. "Here," he said, "this paper came just the other day from some people in England. It's a bit of family history. Why don't you look it over; maybe you could try something similar." Family history: how odd the term sounded then. But, correctly applied—the paper was indeed about family life in the past, one of the first such attempted anywhere. And I knew at once it was for me.[5]

Though they all knew about Laslett's initial findings, but not the post-Clayworth turn his studies on family and community life had taken, they found his views, taken together, confusing. Demos, assuming from Laslett's earliest studies that extended families were ubiquitous in Europe, believed that Clayworth could only have been an exception, but one that was consistent with the families and households he found in Plymouth. Greven, in an essay of 1965, cited Laslett's "Gentry of Kent," his introduction to *Patriarcha,* and writings on Clayworth, and declared that family structure in Andover fitted none of those forms but was something quite unique. Two years later he had picked up more of the recent European scholarship on family structure, which seemed to make Laslett's major contributions even more contradictory. On the basis of evidence in Laslett's *World We Have Lost,* Greven wrote, "it is difficult to account for [his] interpretation of seventeenth-century English society in terms of its traditionalism, its patriarchalism, and its remarkable stability," which he had advanced "vigorously" if not always persuasively throughout the preindustrial era. The high rate of mobility Laslett had discovered in Clayworth and Cogenhoe in itself indicated, Greven believed, that his picture of the typical village communities "is seriously distorted." The problem with Laslett's *World We Have Lost,* Greven concluded, was his "failure to integrate the demographic data with the analysis of the structure of society as a whole." Like Berkner, he argued that studies of the family and the community should be directly related to developments in the larger context of economic and social life.

With this in mind Greven tackled the rich records of the town of Andover. What stood out most clearly, he found, was the importance of the transfer of property across the generations. It was there, in those many land transactions, that Greven found the key to the history of family life in this frontier town.

Andover's remarkable data allowed him to follow the careers of 28 founding families and the 247 families that descended from them in the three generations that followed—a total of more than 2,000 individuals. By studying that entire population, person by person, Greven sought to answer "one of the most crucially important questions that can be asked about the nature and history of the family: Did the structure and the character of families change through time and from place to place." The answer was yes:

> families did change, and patterns of family structure, patterns of relationships between fathers and sons, patterns in the transmission of land, and patterns in demographic experience all gradually altered in the course of the seventeenth and the eighteenth centuries. Because of these complex and almost continuous changes . . . one can describe the family as having a history. . . . To a considerable degree, these changes corresponded closely with the generational cycles that underlay some of the most fundamental rhythms of life in agricultural communities like Andover.

Of the fundamental rhythms of life in Andover, the most important was the control and distribution of land. It was the control of land that determined family structure and the relationships among its members. This was an altogether and surprisingly new approach to the problems Laslett had posed, and it could be understood only in the context of the town's remarkable history.

Andover was settled in 1646 by families from Hampshire, Lincolnshire, and Wiltshire. The initial group was granted joint ownership of a huge area, sixty square miles (38,400 acres). Each of the town's founders, mainly young and middle-aged men with young families, received a town lot and a portion of the first "division" of upland, graded in size and location according to rank and wealth, though within a narrow range. Even the smallest allotment was far more property than the new proprietors could have imagined owning in England. In a healthy environment, the families flourished. Though the men married late, as in England (at ages 27 and 28), the women married young and bore children at regular intervals—8.3 on average, of whom no less than 7.2 survived into their twenties. These figures in themselves are remarkable. But most remarkable, and most important of all the statistics Greven was able to establish, was the founding parents' longevity. It is scarcely believable. The average age at death of twenty-nine male founders was 71.8 years; the figure for twenty first-generation wives was 70.8 years. Twenty-two of the male first settlers died after the age of sixty (five in their seventies, six in their eighties, three in their nineties, and one at the age of 106). Many of the founding women were also long-lived: fifteen lived to be sixty or more, four died in their seventies, five in their eighties, one in her nineties, and one at one hundred years. Equally important for family structure was the longevity of their children—the second generation—born in Andover. Of ninety-two Andover-born men whose records are known, over a quarter lived into their seventies, 20 percent into their eighties, and 3 percent into their nineties. About 70 percent of the entire second generation of men lived to be sixty or more.

It was around these and related statistics that Greven wove his analysis of family and community life in Andover. The long-lived elders of the first generation were the authoritative heads of these proliferating families, and as owners of the land, they determined the portions the sons would receive. Since the gift or inheritance of a portion of family land was the basis for the sons' independent living, it determined the time of their marriages. The founding fathers presiding over growing families were in no hurry to give over portions to their adult sons since to do so would diminish their own security and family authority. There could be long delays. The sons did everything they could to hasten the gift of the portions due to them, some by guaranteeing care and security to the parents, others by buying their portions from their parents and thus providing means for their elders' subsistence. Eventually these inheritances in land would be forthcoming, but until then—and it could take many years—the original family was indeed extended and patriarchal. When the sons did break away they founded their own families, necessarily nuclear, and most often on family land in close proximity to the original household. When this happened repeatedly the result was a unique family structure, which Greven called "modified extended." These were kinship groups

> of two or more generations living within a single community in which the dependence of the children upon their parents continues after the children have married and are living under a separate roof. This family structure is a *modified* extended family because all members of the family are not "gathered into a single household," but it is still an *extended* family because the newly created conjugal unit of husband and wife live in . . . close proximity to their parents and siblings and continue to be economically dependent in some respects upon their parents. And because of the continuing dependence of the second generation upon their first-generation fathers, who continued to own most of the family land throughout the better part of their lives, the family in seventeenth-century Andover was *patriarchal* as well.

Because of the magnitude of the available land, this process could continue into the third generation of family heads who dealt with their sons as their parents had dealt with them. But as the third generation passed into the fourth, pressures were building up against this now venerable system. The population continued to increase, from approximately 435 in 1680 to 945 in 1705: a birth rate commonly averaged at forty-two per thousand (vs. 37.2 in Clayworth); unworked land was steadily decreasing in availability and increasing in value; and as settlement extended farther from the original household, the town's original common-field system of agriculture, which had helped to keep the community together, tended to erode in favor of detached independent farmsteads spread across the land. Thus began the transformation of the original system of community life. And it was intensified by a decision of the descendants of the original families in 1702 to divide all the remaining land among fifty-four families rather than to continue jointly to grant individual lots in occasional large "divisions" of the original township. The result was an outmigration of the later-born sons, who settled outside Andover where land was cheap, and an inmigration of substantial strangers seeking to buy land in a developed area. The outward migration was impelled in part by the common belief that progressive morcellation of the original land grants could not fall below thirty acres to remain feasible for prosperous farming.

But this transformation took place largely in the mid- and late eighteenth century, a century or more after the original founding. For the century before, "patriarchalism was the rule. . . . Whenever they could, fathers continued to exercise their influence over their sons by means of their control of the land which their sons needed. The delayed marriages and the delayed transference of land from fathers to sons combined to demonstrate the continued power which many fathers could exert over the lives of at least some of their sons." And often independent sons continued to live in a community in which their parents, siblings, grandparents, uncles, aunts, and cousins also lived, thereby involving them constantly with people who were related to them by birth and marriage. These communities, Greven noted, resembled Old World communities in which families had lived for generations in complex extended family networks.

In the back of Greven's mind, through all the research he did to produce his *Four Generations* and the earlier pieces, lay the distinction between nuclear and extended families. It was the formative question, however elaborated, and it derived from Laslett's discovery and analysis of Clayworth's two censuses in 1963. By the time Greven's and Demos's books appeared Laslett was at work assembling the essays for his massive *Household and Family in Past Time,* determined to explore at a global level the issues he had raised in studying families and households in Europe. He was aware of the work under way in New England and enlisted Greven and Demos to contribute to the big book. But their papers were distractions for them, and they left all the contentious issues behind.

In time the interests of all the contributors to the debate on family size and structure shifted. In 1976, at age sixty-one, Laslett turned to the problem of aging and the emergence of what he called the Third Age of Life. In a new research unit on aging at the Cambridge Group, he explored the character and consequences of the aging population and the emergence, in the first half of the twentieth century, of a retired population whose potentialities were yet to be realized. He explored that problem in *A Fresh Map of Life: The Emergence of the Third Age* (1989), a dense work of scholarship in which he revisited his earlier views of nuclear and extended families as the background for his current study of aging in modern industrial societies. All his late interests concluded with the creation, in collaboration with others in the Cambridge group, of the University of the Third Age, loosely affil-iated with an international movement for the education and engage-ment of retired members of the community. Britain's "U3A," as it was called, was, and is, a great success. Laslett knew it was a major achievement, and he recorded it as such, along with his co-founding of the Cambridge Group, in the inscription on his headstone in the Wolvercote Cemetery, Oxford.*

---

* The headstone is quite elaborate: "PETER / LASLETT / HISTORIAN / SOCIAL & POLITICAL / SCIENTIST / Fellow of / Trinity College / Cambridge / co-founder of the / Cambridge Group for / the History of Population / and Social Structure / co-founder of the / University of / the Third Age."

———

Berkner, writing in German and English, followed his descriptive studies of the Heidenreichstein archive with probes of complex inheritance practices, proto-industrialization, "household arithmetic," land management, and comparison of peasant life cycles in Austria and France. But then he turned his skills in demographic analysis to the statistical study of students in higher education—their access to post-secondary education, their persistence as students, their achievements, and their finances. Both Greven and Demos went further into interior states of mind and shifts in the life experiences they had touched on earlier. Greven wrote on childhood, on religious experience, on the meaning of the self, and on apocalyptic impulses. Demos turned to adolescence, fatherhood, and the deeper psychological dimensions of witchcraft. But as different as their later work was, all four had participated in a new and intense study of the history of families and households. In that twenty-five- or thirty-year period they had helped reset our understanding of some basic facts of early modern society.

So my search for the history of family structures as the context for education in the broadest sense came to an end. There is and has been no singular universal form of family structure, nuclear or extended or in some way modified. Families are dynamic organisms whose structures change with changing circumstances. Patterns exist, but only for a time and not exclusively. Laslett's villages of nuclear families coexisted with the extended patriarchal households in gentry establishments like Filmer's in Kent. In Heidenreichstein extended families predominated, but nuclear families existed too, among the lowest strata of society. Andover's "modified extended" families were created by the transfer of parcels of parental land to the next generation, whose families, initially nuclear, clustered in complex compounds contiguous to and involved in the parental home.

In none of these variations of family organization was education explicitly mentioned, but in all, education as *paideia* was intrinsically involved, conforming to the shifting contours of family life. As Jaeger wrote: it is "the particular ethos of each community which determines the education of its citizens [and] forms the character of every individual on its own model." And he concluded:

> all the leaders of Greek paideia . . . agreed in deciding that paideia should not be limited to school-teaching. To them it was culture, the formation of the human soul. That is what differentiates Greek paideia from the educational system of other nations.[6]

III

Harbottle's Index, Johnson's "Connection," and the Villagers' Theories of Government

THE PENETRATION OF REVOLUTIONARY THOUGHT

While the contentious debates on the structure of families and households were running their course, and in the years after Laslett's initial discoveries, I was deep in another major project that became my primary concern for two decades and that in lesser ways has continued ever since. I knew from the start that I would do what I could to understand the history of the American Revolution. It was the pivot on which the whole of American history and much of Western civilization turned. And it was a subject that satisfied all my major interests as sketched in 1946: it lay at the heart of the transition from a distant past to an emerging modernity; it involved the fusion of beliefs and ideas with political and constitutional reality; and it was a struggle between British North America and Britain that radiated out to Europe and the nascent states of Latin America.

But the history of the revolution as I received it was grossly simplified and mired in controversy. The Founders, some said, drove the revolution forward to protect their private interests, others that they sought to realize the idealistic goals of the eighteenth-century Enlightenment, and still others that the entire story would have to be rewritten to include the importance of hitherto neglected segments of the populations, especially enslaved people, sailors, and debt-ridden farmers. It was a confused picture, but of one thing I was certain. The beliefs and ideas of those who led the resistance to Britain and the construction of the new nation were not derived either from systematic, formal discourses or from crass self-interest. Their thoughts and motivations were bound in with a world view, an amalgam of fears and aspirations, a multitude of historical memories, especially of Britain's fortunes over the years since Cromwell's Commonwealth and the Glorious Revolution of 1688. All this, I felt, might be recovered, if at all, by analysis that was as much anthropological as historical.

Two events created the opportunity for me to find my way into this transformative passage of American, West European, and West African history. The first was an invitation by Prof. Howard Mumford Jones, then the general editor of the John Harvard Library series of reprints of influential publications, to edit a volume of the pamphlets of the revolution. The second was the developing scholarship of English historians on the political thought of the opposition ("country") parties' struggles in the early eighteenth century to oppose the government of Robert Walpole, ultimately to bring down his administration. As I gradually identified, collected, and studied the many pamphlets and went beyond them to the associated documents—the letters, newspaper pieces, sermons, and incidental literary writings of the revolutionary leaders—I began to see the outlines of a world view different from what I had expected, shaped by the living memories of the English "commonwealthmen" and by the tradition of liberal thought that went back to classical antiquity. The pieces seemed to fall into place in an emerging ideology that could account, in large part, for what people thought and did.

The first expression of what I had learned in many months of research was a projected four volumes of edited pamphlets, seventy-two in all, each with a separate introductory essay with full documentation. The first volume appeared in 1965. Its 750 pages covered only the first fourteen pamphlets, but it also included a long general introduction to the series as a whole, and that introduction, which I called "The Transforming Radicalism of the American Revolution," took on a life of its own. It grew to three hundred pages that incorporated all the results of my many long months of study. I knew as I wrote it that it had become the first draft of a book that explained not the revolution as a whole—that was never my intention—but the mindset, the ideology of those who led the colonies into rebellion and defined the contours of the nation that resulted. My task, which seemed at times overwhelming, was to bring together into a coherent whole all the elements of that distinctive world view, and I worked at it with concentrated intensity. The last chapter was written during a hot summer in Hanover, New Hampshire, and I recall the final pages sticking to my hand. *The Ideological Origins of the American Revolution* was published in 1967; an enlarged edition covering the debate on ratification followed in 1992; a fiftieth-anniversary edition appeared in 2017.

I had managed to put that book together from the multitude of sources available, but there were limits to what I could do. While the book was well received, various challenges soon appeared, among them the charge that the Founders, as I had described them, were the elites of the local communities and that their views were not necessarily the same as those of the free population at large. How widely did this ideology extend? How deeply did it penetrate? What were the views of those who reached different conclusions than those of the revolution's leaders? What was it in the structure of American politics that gave these English ideas a salience that was absent at home? To all these and other challenges, I replied in various ways. To explore the different political responses to ideas shared by England and its colonies, I wrote *The Origins of American Politics* (1968). And to analyze and explain the reasonable views of those who opposed the break with

England—the loyalists—I wrote a biography of Thomas Hutchinson (1974), the last royal governor of Massachusetts and the most articulate dissident to the patriots' prevailing views. Begun as a logical obligation, that account of the most despised but best informed loyalist became for me a tragic tale. Adrift in a storm of challenges to the established political ideology that he could not control or fully understand, Hutchinson sought but failed to be relieved of his official duties and then, when his plea to resign was ignored, struggled on until completely overwhelmed. His account of his final years in exile in England, neglected as a troublesome provincial and devastated by the agonizing illness and death of his daughter, was painful to read and difficult to describe discretely.

But the question of the penetration of the Founders' beliefs into the population at large remained to be answered. Some clues appeared in odd and remote places—in the political commentaries of a Boston tradesman; in the subtle conflation of politics and religion in the writings of an obscure Connecticut preacher; and in the thought of the ordinary Massachusetts villagers and townsmen responding to a proposed state constitution in 1780. These are all obscure local documents, none of them cited in the literature of the revolution, but all of them reflective of the Founders' vision.

On January 7, 1765, in the midst of the Stamp Act controversy, a Boston shopkeeper named Harbottle Dorr—Harbottle Dorr, *junior*, to be precise, for his father, a leather dresser, bore the same name—set aside the current issue of the *Boston Evening-Post* and began collecting copies of each of the succeeding issues of the *Evening-Post* or of the chief opposition newspaper, the *Boston Gazette,* or occasionally of the *Boston Post-Boy.* And not only did he preserve each week a copy of one or another—sometimes two—of these newspapers, but he commented on their contents in inked notations in the margins and between the lines, expressing himself pungently on the events of the time, identifying anonymous and pseudonymous authors, and clarifying obscure references in the public charges and countercharges. At times he referred possible users of his newspaper collection backward and forward in a maze of cross-references to documents and stories relevant to particular events and statements that were reported in the news. And he tore into inconsistencies and misrepresentations of the authorities, reinforcing the truth as he saw it and guiding the reader's thoughts into proper channels.

In three years he accumulated 789 pages of newsprint[1]—an unbroken run of annotated Boston newspapers from early 1765 to the end of 1767—and he put that large bundle aside as volume one. Two years after that, at the end of 1769, he had accumulated another 788 pages, and his ambitions had blossomed. To this second volume he added as appendixes a series of documents in the history of Anglo-American liberty—copies of Magna Carta, the Massachusetts Charter, the English Bill of Rights, a "Chronology of Arts and Sciences" (apparently a documentary history of British liberty), Governor Bernard's confidential letters to the ministry that had been surreptitiously obtained in England and published as pamphlets in Boston, and two other pamphlets of 1769.

These documents he repaginated to follow in order the page numbering he had devised for the newspaper texts, and then he went through the whole of the first two volumes carefully, correcting some of his original notes and cross-references and adding others. And he began at that point to *index* the volumes—to index not only people, places, and events but the important topics as he saw them, in categories that express his immediate response to and understanding of the events he was recording.

Indexing caused Dorr, as it has many others, a great deal of trouble. It is difficult to reconstruct precisely how he went about compiling the first index, but apparently he assumed that if he allowed one column of a three-column page for each letter, omitting J and V, and entered the items as they occurred, he would have no trouble. And so he ruled off three columns on each of eight pages with the intention of filling each column with entries for a single letter. But one column, he quickly discovered, did not suffice for the A's, and he was obliged to hunt around in later columns for space for the leftover A's, stuffing part of them halfway down the D column and the rest among the G's. The B's were even more troublesome, since he was obliged to continue them under the N's but then discovered that there were more N's than he had anticipated, so the N's that should have been where the homeless B's had come to rest had to be pushed off to the bottom of the X column, which fortunately was otherwise occupied only with a few stray P's.

By the time he began the index to volume two he was a grizzled veteran of the indexing wars, and he had learned caution. Now he doubled the allocation for the A's, ruling off two columns for that letter, only to run out of space before he entered such major items as: "Admiralty, vice, court of, new, first established in America"; "Ancestors, our, why they left their country"; and "American British colonies, always have been considered as (and are) free independent states." But he had apparently expected real trouble from the B's, ruling off no fewer than ten columns for that letter, creating thereby not only ample room for those entries but a generally useful catchall for all other leftover entries. If that was his strategy, it worked very well; he ran out of B's in the middle of the fifth of the allocated columns and in the empty columns before the C's he had space enough to put in all the extras that later spilled over from the P, R, T, and W columns as well as the held-over A's.

He had solved these organizational problems reasonably well by the time he turned to the third and fourth volumes, but alphabetizing remained a hardship throughout. It was not so difficult, perhaps, for the reader to figure out that the index entry "America will rise, and be a mighty empire, maugre all Great Britain can do to prevent it," should be put under the A's, since after all it was something about America, but how was one to index a story about a man who had a remarkable appetite by virtue of possessing three stomachs? Dorr decided to put that under the E's for "Eater." And do you put a news item about an *herb* guaranteed to turn things into *gold* under the H's or the G's? Dorr took no chances and put it under both. A rather mysterious entry entitled "*U*ps and Downs" was no doubt safe enough under the U's, though one would scarcely have had occasion to look for it there since it referred to a listing in parallel columns of the scandalous state of affairs in England ("The [King] *up* in the nursery . . . The [Princess of Wales] *down* on her knees . . . the Scotch *up* in the world . . . Virtue at [Court] kicked *down*stairs"). And a heat record could be entered under the H's not for "*h*eat" but for "*h*ottest day for 22 years past." But how was one to index the story of a German who was executed for endeavoring to ruin his country? (Under the H's, Dorr decided, for "*H*anged.")

For volume two, which marks Dorr's emergence as a documentary historian, he composed a title page and a table of contents. He began the title page modestly, presenting his work apologetically with the words, "This has a very deformed body, but a BEAUTIFUL SOUL," and explaining that on reviewing the marginalia and index he had found various misspellings "which I hope whoever peruses will have candour enough to excuse (especially) as the remarks &c, were made at my SHOP amidst my business, &c when I had not leisure to be exact." Then he turned proudly to the substance of the project.

Newspapers, he explained in this remarkable title page, contain not only the passing news of the day but "intelligence of the greatest moment." They were in fact commonly resorted to as repositories of records, and the information they contained was considered to be more authentic than that found in all but legal documents. Since people commonly threw newspapers away, and since "during the period of the following papers, transactions of the utmost importance respecting liberty in general have taken place, and are recorded in them," he had thought it worthwhile, despite the "considerable expence, and very GREAT trouble" it had cost him, to collect the papers that followed and to annotate them. He hoped, he wrote, "that in future they may be of some service, towards forming a political history of [this] country, during the shameful and abandoned administration of ye disp[otic]

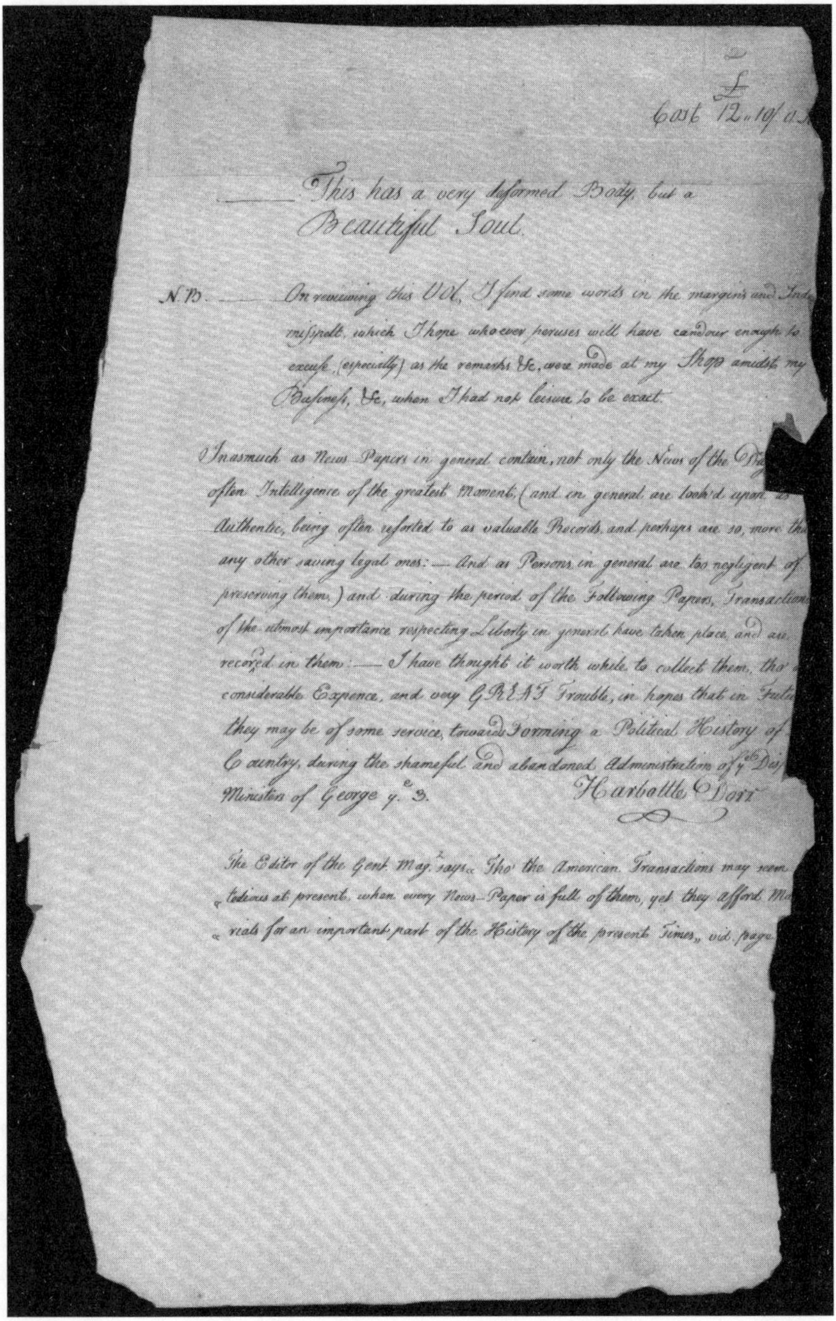

Cost £12..10/0

——This has a very deformed Body, but a Beautiful Soul.

N.B. —— On reviewing this Vol, I find some words in the margins and Ind misspelt, which I hope whoever peruses will have candour enough to excuse, (especially) as the remarks &c, were made at my Shop amidst my Business, &c, when I had not leisure to be exact.

Inasmuch as News Papers in general contain, not only the News of the Da often Intelligence of the greatest Moment; (and in general are look'd upon as Authentic, being often resorted to as valuable Records and perhaps are so, more tha any other saving legal ones: — And as Persons in general are too negligent of preserving them) and during the period of the Following Papers, Transaction of the utmost importance respecting Liberty in general have taken place, and are recorded in them: —— I have thought it worth while to collect them, tho' considerable Expence, and very GREAT Trouble, in hopes that in Futu they may be of some service, towards forming a Political History of Country, during the shameful and abandoned Administration of ye Des Ministers of George ye 3.

Harbottle Dorr

The Editor of the Gent. Mag. says,, Tho' the American Transactions may seem tedious at present, when every News-Paper is full of them, yet they afford Ma rials for an important part of the History of the present Times,, vid. page

Harbottle Dorr: title page of volume II.

ministers of George ye 3." And then he signed the page, with a flourish: HARBOTTLE DORR. But he could not stop. A citation seemed needed to validate on higher authority his claim for the value of the papers he had so carefully preserved. So he tacked on a postscript, quoting the editor of the *Gentleman's Magazine* to the effect that though American affairs may seem "tedious at present, when every news-paper is full of them, yet they afford ma[te]rials for an important part of the history of the present times." And then, in a fine little demonstration of the usefulness of his collection, he concluded: "vid. page [479]."

The title page finished. Dorr turned to the table of contents, and for that he poured out so powerful a stream of luminous prose that it broke through all the barriers of grammar, syntax, and simple order: it scarcely mattered that at one point, in his tumult, he wrote a parenthesis backwards-front. Volume two, Dorr wrote, contains

a full Account of the Jealousies, great uneasinesses, vast difficulties, and cruel TREATMENT of the COLONIES by the DETESTABLE ACTS of PARLIAMENT, granting duties on Tea, Paper, &c, and Establishing a Board of Commissioners of the Customs, &c, &c:—Together with excellent Essays and Letters.—GOVERNOR'S SPEECHES, Instructions to Representatives, RESOLVES of the House of Representatives, curious Anecdotes, &c, relative to the same. Also a full Account of the BRAVE, STRENUOUS, and NOBLE ACTIONS, of the Freeborn British Americans, in opposition to the said Acts and OPPRESSIONS, and in defence of their NATURAL, CONSTITUTIONAL, and CHARTER RIGHTS.—Likewise the remaining Letters of the Farmer, Journal of the Times, Essays against the establishment of Bishops in America, &c, &c, &c: Together with an appendix) containing MAGNA CHARTA, petition of RIGHT, Bill of RIGHTS, Charter of the Massachusetts Bay, Chronology, &c, &c,) And complete Index, with Marginal Notes and Explanations.

And then, still in full flight, he appended two sets of verses:

Our worthy fore Fathers
Thro' Oceans to Deserts for Freedom they came.
And dying bequeath'd us their Freedom and Fame.
All ages shall speak with amaze and APPLAUSE,
At the courage we Show in SUPPORT OF OUR LAWS.
To die we can bear, but to SERVE WE DISDAIN:
For shame is to FREEDOM more dreadful than pain.
   —Liberty Song

Is there a Power whose engines are of force
To bend the brave and Virtuous mind to Slavery.
NO! In the Drear and Deadly damp of Dungeons,
The Soul can rear her Sceptre, smile in Anguish, And Triumph o'er
OPPRESSION.
   —Gustavus Vasa

Thus the front matter for volume two was completed. The table of contents seemed a worthy model, and Dorr repeated it, with minor changes, in volume three.

That volume, covering the years 1770–71, contains 642 pages of newsprint and an appendix of four pamphlets, all annotated and cross-referenced. Volume four (1,061 pages of newsprint, with a title page almost identical to that of volume two) covers the years from 1772 to the siege of Boston (April 1775) with issues of the *Boston Gazette,* and thereafter to the end of 1776 with other Boston, Salem, and Cambridge newspapers. Eight pamphlets of the same years, four of them Massacre Day orations, were added to form Dorr's fourth appendix.

It is an astonishing archive, these 3,280 pages of annotated newspapers plus the appended documents and indexes, and it has come down to us almost perfectly intact. There is a slight indication that

Dorr at one point contemplated selling the collection since he carefully noted on the last three volumes exactly what the papers had cost him (between £12 and £16 Old Tenor for each volume). But if he had once entertained that idea, he apparently gave it up, for the volumes were still in his possession when he died, eighteen years after he completed the work. His executors estimated the value of "a number of newspapers, some bound" at 1 pound 16 shillings, but in fact they fetched 7 pounds 10 shillings when his property was sold.

One hardly knows where to begin in analyzing Harbottle Dorr's painfully composed indexes, his mass of marginal jottings, and the intricate network of cross-references that links documents, statements, ideas, and events in the four volumes to passages that precede and follow them. He was, after all, an ordinary tradesman, busy selling hardware and ship supplies in his shop on Union Street, near Dock Square, and in his private life he was no moral hero. During the war he did what he could to lay hands on the house and copper foundry of a loyalist who had fled, one Martin Gay, whom he had sued for ransacking his shop during the siege of Boston, though Gay's property, which adjoined Dorr's, was still occupied by the loyalist's helpless wife. "That republican, N[ew] E[ngland] puritanical Harbottle Dorr," Gay fumed in exile in Nova Scotia, "deserves a particular mark of infamy . . . for his unrighteous conduct in adding to Mrs. Gay's other afflictions." But Dorr's acquisitiveness did him little good. At his death in 1794 he left an estate that included gold buttons and buckles, half a pew in the New North Church, cash, and public securities. The total was valued at only £475 1s 2d, and he owed £151 4s 8d. The net balance was no more than the modest estate of a respectable Boston tradesman.

He did, it appears, have some marginal advantages. His father, the leather-dresser, must have been a somewhat bookish man, whose interests no doubt influenced his son. For while his physical property was consumed by debts, he left to his son not only a rather expensive

Bible but also thirty-three printed books and forty-four pamphlets as well: a small library that must have been selected with care. In all likelihood some of the publications were histories, for the sense of history the son acquired is something one learns early or not at all. Further, somewhere, if not at home, the son became acquainted with the apparatus of book publication—dedications, prefaces, indexes, and the rudiments of scholarly annotation. And he somehow had achieved an unusually high level of literacy. The extent of his vocabulary, the easy articulation of his emotions, and his fluent use of language as a force in public life were remarkable. Even his handwriting is impressive: slanting but graceful and regular, at times quite elegant, and clearly readable even when squeezed into the narrow margins of newsprint and into tight spaces between lines.

Despite all of this, Dorr remained an ordinary shopkeeper whose personal participation in the protest movement and the buildup to the war was unremarkable. He joined the Sons of Liberty, signing one of the earliest non-importation agreements (March 1768) and dined with the three hundred other Sons of Liberty at the Liberty Tree in Dorchester on August 14, 1769. Occasionally he wrote letters to the newspapers that reflect a deeper commitment. In one, written as "A Consistent Whig" in 1773, he criticized the clergy, "the mouth of the people unto God," for their "inattention to the calamities which threaten America," and he called for the convening of a colonial congress and the forging of a unified intercolonial policy of resistance as "the *most likely* method of obtaining *full* redress of all our grievances." But he never became an important political leader in Massachusetts, or even in Boston. He achieved the peak of his eminence in 1777, when, at the age of forty-seven, he was elected a town selectman, a post to which he was reelected eleven times thereafter; on the last occasion, in 1791, he led the list.

Yet there is something important in Dorr's amassment of the newspaper archive and in his strange index and his passionate commentaries. In the vast public literature of the colonies' break with

Britain—the hundreds of pamphlets, the innumerable newspaper columns, the published debates, and the state papers—the formal, public face of the struggle is clearly displayed. But the inner life of the true believers—the interior, private dialogues, the emotions, the fears, the resentments, the prejudices, the frustrations, and the hopes for the future—of devoted patriots caught up in the struggles of the resistance to British rule are hidden from view, until occasionally they appear, by chance, in strange and unexpected places. On such occasions the penetration of political thought into individual lives is vividly revealed. And nothing is more revealing of interior feelings, of private passion, than Harbottle Dorr's obsession with Thomas Hutchinson.

Many, like John Adams, were convinced that Hutchinson, governor of Massachusetts in 1770–74, was guilty of promoting Britain's impositions on the colonies and that he was a traitor to his native land. But no one was more virulent, or more bitter, in blaming Hutchinson for what was happening than Harbottle Dorr. He had grown up in the small provincial world in which the Hutchinson family had been accepted leaders time out of mind (Anne Hutchinson was Thomas's great-great-grandmother), and he must have seen the future governor frequently, heard him speak, and known of his public service and of his integrity in trade. But Dorr seems to have been gripped, obsessed, overwhelmed by what he took to be the malignity, the ineradicable evil of the man. All of his deepest fears, his visceral sense of outrage, and his passion for ultimate revenge came to focus on this single individual.

Dorr's index and commentaries catalog Hutchinson's errors, correct his supposed misstatements, and warn at every turn of his evil intentions. An anonymous columnist's claim that the colonies "had no *rights* of our own" is identified by Dorr in the margin as "Hutchinsonian doctrine." When a writer in the *Boston Gazette* wonders "if our governor is a *mere tool* of an arbitrary minister of state," Dorr instantly removes the doubt: "He certainly is one!" He footnotes a vague newspaper reference to government advisers known to be "supple eno' to bow the *knee of servility* to the tool of a tool of an haughty Thane"

The BOSTON Evening-Poſt.

Containing the freſheſt & moſt important   *Advices, Foreign and Domeſtick.*

JOURNAL of the TIMES.
vide [Continued.] *Page* 549

1769.
April 28.

AT the Superiour Court held at Charleſtown, application was made by the Cuſtom-Houſe Officers, for a full ſupply of Writs of Aſſiſtance, which were accordingly granted. By the late acts the officers of the cuſtoms are "empowered to enter into any houſe, warehouſe, ſhop, or other place, in the Britiſh colonies, or plantations in America, to ſearch for and ſeize prohibited or uncuſtomed goods."—A dreadful power indeed ! And if we can recollect inſtances of ſuch a wanton uſe of this power, even in Boſton, as that a magiſtrate ſhould be threatened and his houſe rummaged, by an officer in reſentment at his being fined for breach of law ; what may we not fear at a time when Spaniſh policy has been ſo far adopted, as that the moſt ignorant. hair-brain'd, and extravagant perſons in commiſſion on board the ſhips of war are converted into cuſtom-houſe officers ! As we on ye reflect, that the judges of theſe American courts, are appointed *during pleaſure*, and that one purpoſe for which money is to be levied upon the colonies by a late act is, that they may have adequate proviſion made for them, which is to continue, *during their complaiſant behaviour*, what an engine of oppreſſion may this authority be in ſuch hands ! We are well aware that writs of this kind, for ſearching houſes in England, have been granted under the ſeal of the Court of Exchequer, according to the ſtatute, which ſeal is kept by the Chancellor of the Exchequer : It ſhould however be remembered that the cuſtom-houſe officers, at home are under certain checks & reſtrictions, which they cannot be under here ; and therefore the writ of aſſiſtance ought to be look'd upon as a different thing there, from what it is here. In England the Exchequer has the power of controuling them in every reſpect ; and even of inflicting corporal puniſhment upon them for mal-conduct, of which there have been inſtances ; they are the proper officers of that court, and are accountable to it as often as it ſhall call them to account, and they do in fact account to it for money receiv'd, and for their behaviour, once every week. Do the officers of the cuſtoms here account with the ſuperior court, or lodge money received into the hands of that court ; or are they as officers under any ſort of check from it ? Will they concede to ſuch powers in the ſuperiour court ? Or does this court, notwithſtanding theſe are powers belonging to the Exchequer,—notwithſtanding it is ſaid to be veſted with all the powers belonging to the Exchequer,—and further notwithſtanding this very writ of aſſiſtance is to be granted as a power belonging to the Exchequer, will the ſuperior court itſelf aſſume the power of calling theſe officers to account, and puniſh them for miſbehaviour ? We know not of one inſtance of this ſort, but on the contrary, have we not ſeen not long ago, an inferior cuſtom-houſe officer, who has ſince ſwelled into a C——m——r of the Board of Cuſtoms, refuſing to account to any power in the province for monies receiv'd by him by virtue of his office, belonging to the province, and which we were then aſſured by the joint declaration of the three branches of the legiſlature, was unjuſtly as well as illegally detained by him ?

But notwithſtanding writs of aſſiſtance iſſued in Britain are guarded with ſuch reſtrictions, " The greateſt aſſertors of the rights of Engliſhmen have already ſtrenuouſly contended that ſuch a power was dangerous to freedom, and expreſsly contrary to the common law, which ever regarded a man's houſe as his caſtle, or a place of perfect ſecurity —If ſuch power was in the leaſt degree dangerous there, it muſt be utterly deſtructive to Liberty here. For the people of England have two ſecurities ; againſt the undue exerciſe of this power by the crown, which are wanting with us. —In the firſt place if any injuſtice is done there, the perſon injured may bring his action againſt the offender. and have it tried before independent judges who were *no parties in committing the injury*. —Here he muſt have it tried before dependent judges, being the men who granted the writ."

April 29. We are well informed, that the officers of the cuſtoms applied the laſt year to the chief juſtices or bench of judges, in ſeveral of the colonies,

for granting them writs of aſſiſtance but that thoſe juſtices from a tender regard to the conſtitution and the rights of American freeholders, did actually refuſe a compliance with thoſe demands. —— The C——f of the port of New-London in Connecticut, has lately applied a ſecond time to the ſuperiour court there for ſuch writs ; at the ſame time laying a letter before them, which he had received from one of the crown lawyers in England in anſwer to one wrote upon the ſubject, in which letter, a great compliment was paid to the chief juſtice of the Maſſachuſetts, for the proof he had given of a right underſtanding of the law, and of his zeal for his Majeſty's ſervice, by ſo readily granting thoſe writs upon the application made by the cuſtom-houſe officers ; and his example was recommended as worthy of their imitation. The court did not however, think proper to ſhow a like complaiſance, but choſe to refer this requeſt, to the conſideration of their general aſſembly at the approaching ſeſſion.

April 30. The quartering troops in the body of a town is ruinous to the ſoldiery as it is diſtreſſing to the inhabitants ; every day furniſhes out inſtances of their debaucheries and conſequent violences.

As an aged woman at the north part of Boſton, was ſetting the other evening in a lower room, having no perſon in the houſe with her ; a ſoldier came in and ſeeing her have a bible on the table before her ; he expreſſed his approbation of her piety and attempted a kind of expoſition upon ſome parts thereof, but ſoon dropping this diſcourſe, he acquainted her that he had a bad ſwelling on his hip, and ſhould be glad of her advice ; but while the good woman was attending to his relation, this abandoned wretch, ſeized her, by this ſhoulders, threw her upon the floor, and notwithſtanding her years, attempted a rape upon her, which was prevented by the reſiſtance and ſcreams occaſioned by his brutal behaviour ; he thought proper to hurry off, taking with him a bundle of ſhirts and other linen, which had been juſt before ſent into the houſe for waſhing, and ironing ; a buſineſs which the perſon followed to obtain a livelihood.

May 1. A captain of a veſſel lately arrived from Halifax, paſſing the ſtreets laſt evening, in company with two married women, were met by ſome ſoldiers, who immediately accoſted them in a rude indecent manner ; the captain tho't proper to inform them, that thoſe women were married, and alſo to reprove them for ſuch behaviour ; but for taking this liberty, he was preſently knocked down, and had like to have loſt an eye by a blow receiv'd.

May 2. On the other night paſt 11 o'clock ſeveral officers and one ſoldier, meeting with two of the towns watchmen, they began to curſe and damn them, and ſoon after the ſoldier ſtruck one of the watchmen, who returned the blow, which laid him in the gutter, then the two officers came up, and were as free with their blows as the ſoldier ; the noiſe and racket ſoon brought other watchmen to the aſſiſtance of thoſe who were aſſaulted, when one of the officers drew a bayonet, and damning them, ſaid ſtand off, or I will run you through ; the watchmen not being intimidated, gave him a ſtroke on the arm which obliged him to drop the bayonet ; when they ſeized him and carried him off to priſon, the watchmen were followed by another officer, with a drawn ſword or cutlaſs under his arm, but being told that if he did not leave them, they would endeavour to ſecure him alſo, he thought proper to ſheer off. Several officers came at different times, and offered the watchmen drink or money, if they would releaſe the priſoner, but to their honor they refuſed thoſe offers, & entered a complaint againſt them, to a magiſtrate the next morning.

Continued [To be continued.] *Page* 561

FIFTY DOLLARS Reward.

On the 15th 16th & 17th Inſt. many Panes of Glaſs in the Caſements of the Subſcriber's Dwelling-Houſe, were by ſome evil-minded Perſon or Perſons broken, to the endangering the Lives of his Family, and to his great Expence ; and as it is ſuppoſed there were ſome Accomplices therein. If any Perſon (even an Accomplice) ſhall give Information to him, who did it, and that he be Convicted thereof, ſhall be forgiven, and receive ſaid Reward from   John Box.

Boſton, June 19. 1769.

Province of MASSACHUSETTS-BAY, June 22. 1769.

Tueſday laſt a Committee of the Honorable Houſe of Repreſentatives, in General Court aſſembled at Cambridge, there waited on his Excellency the Governor with the following Meſſage ; being a Reply to his Excellency's Anſwer to their Meſſage of the 13th Inſtant, viz.

MAY IT PLEASE YOUR EXCELLENCY,

AS you have not thought proper in your Reply to the Meſſage of this Houſe, of the 13th Inſtant, to throw any Light on the Subject, or invalidate the Principles we therein advanced, your Excellency will allow us to conclude, that thoſe Principles were well grounded, and that there is no Reaſon for us to alter our Sentiments on this intereſting Point.

You are pleaſed to intimate that much Time and Treaſure has been ſpent in determining a merely ſpeculative Queſtion : The Houſe regarded the ſtanding Army poſted within the Province in a Time of the moſt profound Peace, and uncontroulable by any Authority in it, as a dangerous Innovation ; and a Guard of Soldiers with Cannon planted at the Doors of the State Houſe, while the General Aſſembly was there held, as the moſt pointed Inſult ever offered to a free People, and its whole Legiſlative. This, Sir, and not the Queſtion of your Excellency's Authority to remove his Majeſty's Ships out of the Harbour, or his Troops out of the Town of *Boſton*, was the principal Cauſe of the " Non-activity of the Aſſembly." Had your Excellency felt for the Aſſembly and the People over whom you preſide, even though you had ſuppoſed yourſelf not properly authorized, you would have employed your Influence, at leaſt, for the Removal of this Grievance ; eſpecially as His Majeſty's Council, as well as this Houſe, had before, expreſſed to your Excellency their juſt Indignation at ſo unprecedented an Affront. But inſtead of the leaſt Abatement of this military Parade, the General Aſſembly has been made to give Way to an armed Force : As the only Means in your Power to remove the Difficulty we juſtly complained of, your Excellency has ordered a Removal of the General Aſſembly itſelf, from its ancient Seat and the Place where the public Buſineſs has generally been done with the greateſt Convenience, Eaſe and Diſpatch.—It is with Pain that we are obliged here to obſerve, that the very Night after this Adjournment was made, the Cannon were removed from the Court Houſe, as though it had been deſigned, that ſo ſmall a Circumſtance of Regard ſhould not be paid to the Aſſembly, when convened by the Royal Authority, and for His Majeſty's Service in the Colony.

You are pleaſed to paſs a Cenſure upon this Houſe, in ſaying that, " you cannot ſit ſtill and ſee ſuch a Waſte of Time and Treaſure to no Purpoſe."—Thoſe alone are anſwerable for any Expence of Time and Treaſure on this Occaſion, who have brought us into ſuch a Situation, as has hitherto rendered our Proceeding to Buſineſs incompatible with the Dignity, as well as the Freedom of this Houſe.—No Time can neither be employed than in the Preſervation of the Rights derived from the Britiſh Conſtitution, and inſiſting upon Points which, though your Excellency may conſider as non-eſſential, we eſteem its beſt Bulwarks.—No Treaſure can be better expended than in ſecuring that true old Engliſh Liberty, which gives a Reliſh to every other Enjoyment. There we have the Satisfaction to believe are the Sentiments of our Conſtituents, to whom alone we are accountable how we apply their Treaſure : And we are fully perſuaded, from what we have already heard, that, notwithſtanding the apparent Deſign of your Meſſage to prejudice their Minds againſt us, what your Excellency is pleaſed to call our " Non-activity," will receive their Approbation, rather than their Cenſure ; for an entire Fortnight ſpent in Silence, or a much longer Time, cannot be diſpleaſing to them, when Buſineſs could not be even entered upon, but at the Expence of their Rights and Liberties, and the Privilege of this Houſe.

On Monday laſt a Committee was choſen in the Houſe to go to the Board, for any Letters or Papers they had received ſince the ſitting of the laſt General Aſſembly ; and on Tueſday, the Board ſent to the Houſe Copies of ſeveral Letters from his Excellency the Governor, and the Copy of one from General Gage, to the Right Hon. the Earl of Hillſborough, (which Copies the Board received ſometime ſince from England ;) together with two Letters from the Council to the Earl of Hillsborough, in Vindication of their own Character, and the People of the Province.

To be ſold by T. & J. FLEET and EDES & GILL,
The Caſe of *Great Britain* & *America*, Addreſſed to the
KING and both HOUSES of PARLIAMENT.

It is againſt the liberty of the ſubject, who hath a true property in his goods, which cannot be taken from him, without his actual or implied conſent.   Trial of HAMPDEN.

At the ſame Places may be had,
COPIES of ſeveral LETTERS from Governor *Bernard* to the Earl of *Hillſborough*, &c.

[handwritten marginal note at foot:] Charles Paxton a Commiſſioner. = Collector : Judge Hutchinſon — No Compliment to him; quite the reverse. as Coming from ſuch an Infamous Miniſtry, or their Tools * Judge Hutchinſon was the firſt who granted 'em in this Province, wh. made him obnoxious. & vide pa. 463 ... page 406. & page 603

[handwritten right margin:] vide pa. 552. (a) vid ye Commiſſioners Comiſſion. 253 ... Commiſſion pa. 253 (b) vid. Court of Admiralty pa. 109 & Judges Power & pa. 377. (c) vid Glaſs Act pa. 735 vol. 1. & vid. the Arrival of the Army & pa. 263. (d) vid. pa. 552. & vid. the Charter page 1077.

with the explanation, "Hutchinson (governor) is a tool to Lord Hillsborough, Lord Hillsborough a tool to Bute, and the Earl of Bute a tool of the Devil!" Dorr will hear nothing of Hutchinson's professed desire to promote the prosperity of his country: "words," he scribbles in the margin, "are but wind; actions speak louder." When Hutchinson as governor in a message to the House explains his aversion to unwanted, repugnant innovations, Dorr scornfully laughs in the margin, "Hah! Hah!" and to document the contrary, he triumphantly cites the governor's letters of 1768 supposedly recommending authoritarian changes in the colony's government. He jubilantly records a report that "Governor Hutchinson attempted to cut his throat"; explodes in the margins when the hated name appears—"vile hypocrite! and slanderer," "arch fiend," "traitor!"; and at one point writes simply, in smoldering indignation, "Oh the villian!"

Hutchinson had in fact assiduously sought the governorship, but after the Boston Massacre, in March 1770, believing that his appointment had not yet been signed by the king, he had written soul-baring, abjectly apologetic letters to his patron, the former governor, Sir Francis Bernard, and to the secretary of state, Lord Hillsborough, begging not to be appointed. "If I had more talents than I have," he had written Bernard, "yet I have not strength of constitution to grapple with burdens which . . . exceed beyond comparison what you met with. . . . [A] person of much greater weight than I" was needed, he had insisted. "I must beg you," he had written, "to make my most humble excuse or resignation from a sense of my utter inability to discharge the trust."

Among the eleven columns of entries under "Hutchinson" in the index of Dorr's third volume, following such entries as "Compared to King James" and "Would like to be made a baronet," is the comment "Wrote home desiring not to be appointed governor but always aiming at the chair." When in 1773 Hutchinson's supposedly incriminating letters to Thomas Whately were published by Benjamin Franklin to make Hutchinson the scapegoat for the ministry and hence give time for passions to cool and new terms of reconciliation to be devised,

Dorr tore into his copy of the letters (which he included as a pamphlet in the appendix of volume four) with a frantic pen. He scribbled curses in the margins, interleaved the texts of the letters with refutations, and directed the reader to what he believed was the truth through a complex series of cross-references to other documents in his monumental collection. His index contains no fewer than thirty references under the single entry "Hutchinson, Governor, his original traitorous letters," the last of which is: "an insinuation that he and [Lieutenant] Governor [Thomas] Oliver ought to have been immediately put to death on the receipt of their letters." And to be sure that this suggestion would not go undetected, he indexed it not only under the H's for *H*utchinson but also under the L's for *L*etters and under the J's for "*J*unius Americanus," the pseudonym of Arthur Lee, who had originally circulated the idea of a summary execution.

But what Dorr's outbursts and his interior turmoils reveal above all is his conviction that the government under which he lived and that Hutchinson dominated was corrupt and unworthy of public confidence. Personal observations, a multitude of writings, gossip, and everyday conversation had fused to convince Dorr beyond all argument that the public trust had been violated; that officeholding had become at the highest level a form of profiteering, at the lowest mere legalized thuggery; that the administration of law was unjust; and that government was callous to the needs of the people. The king, he wrote, calls America's legitimate resistance the work of a petty faction, but Britain's swarming "pensioners [were] more formidable to a free people than troops"; the king "sometimes grants pardons before conviction or sentence"; Lord Mayor Beckford was "suspected to have been poisoned"; the "corrupt Parliament [was] profuse of the nation's money"; the House of Commons was so foolish, so encrusted with tradition, that its Speaker "died because the House would not let him go to ease the calls of nature."

It was to Dorr a situation inherently revolutionary, in Robert R. Palmer's words, a situation in which confidence in the justice or reasonableness of existing authority is undermined; where old loyalties fade, obligations are felt as impositions, law seems arbitrary, and respect for superiors is felt as a form of humiliation; where existing sources of prestige seem undeserved, hitherto accepted forms of wealth and income seem ill-gained, and government is sensed as distant, apart from the governed and not really "representing" them. In such a situation the sense of community is lost, and the bond between social classes turns to jealousy and frustration.[2]

$$\sim$$

THE SEARCH FOR interior experiences—for sudden, unexpected signs, like Dorr's index and commentaries—of the penetration of revolutionary thought can never be systematic. One stumbles upon them in odd corners and in the interstices of standard discourses. Thus the role of the clergy in the mounting polemics of the early years of political resistance has been exhaustively studied. There is a library of documents and studies of the differing views of the ministry, from Jonathan Mayhew's *Discourse Concerning Unlimited Submission* (1750) to John Witherspoon's *The Dominion of Providence over the Passions of Men* (1776). But something strange happened later in the year in which Harbottle Dorr had begun his annotated newspaper collection.

An obscure forty-one-year-old preacher named Stephen Johnson, in the hamlet of Lyme, Connecticut (free population c. 3,500), suddenly broke his lifelong silence on public affairs and dashed off, and published, some 31,000 words on the problems of political liberty in general and the Americans' specific ideas and ideals that would dominate their thinking in the years that followed. But Johnson's surprising outburst took two quite different forms: first, a group of six newspaper articles on politics published anonymously in the *New London Gazette* from September 6 to November 1, and then on December 18 a remarkable sermon, *Some Important Observations*. The fusion of the two, written almost simultaneously, reveal not only the penetration of revolutionary thought in the mind of an ordinary preacher but the elevation of the entire political discourse to the realm of divine revelation.

The newspaper articles are entirely secular. They concentrate on the "evils apprehended from the late measures of the British ministry." Johnson attacked first Britain's claim that America was "virtually" represented in Parliament by running out the logical implications of that claim to the point of absurdity. *Why* were we virtually represented, he asked, and *how*?

> Whether . . . because the British Parliament are an assembly of men and of the same species with us, or because they are English men, as we are, or because they represent the nation from whence we descended, or because we are under the same king, or in what other view, is uncertain. In any of those (views) the boroughs and towns in England are as virtually represented in our General Assemblies as the colonies are in Parliament. And all the Jews scattered throughout the world would be as virtually represented by a meeting of the rabbis of Hungary.

Not one member of Parliament had the consent or vote of one American, and "five hundred noughts can never make an unit." And since America could in no way be represented in England, and in addition since the colonies had "by royal grant and compact certain privileges," they could not be governed in the same way that England itself was governed. To assume the opposite, Johnson declared, would lead directly to "self-repugnancy," a concept profoundly involved in the most subtle questions of British constitutionalism, which served in Johnson's essays as the ultimate form of refutation.

The concept of "self-repugnancy" was drawn on in a variety of forms in the *Gazette* articles as Johnson worked through the details of his arguments against the new regulations. If the aim of these measures was to raise a revenue, they would defeat themselves, for the colonists "cannot have money enough but for a short time to pay these taxes. . . . And what must be the consequence but [that] their lands, the dear patrimony of their fathers . . . must pass to taskmasters here, or to men of ease and wealth in Britain who have schemed them away for nought"—an eventuality Americans would never endure "till they have lost the British spirit." The result would be not only severe opposition in America but powerful resistance in England itself when trade, as it inevitably would, came to a stop, and "the [British] merchant, the husbandmen, and the manufacturer of every sort" realized the cost to themselves.

But the argument whose internal contradiction, its "self-repugnancy," Johnson demonstrated with the greatest zest and originality, was the claim that Parliament's power rested on the unitary and exclusive character of sovereignty. The concept of Parliamentary sovereignty when applied to the American colonies, he wrote, contradicted the initial premise of the argument advanced for it: that the colonies had rights subordinate to Parliament's. Since the purpose of all government was to "secure" the people in whatever rights they had, what Parliament in its sovereign power was attempting to do was to secure America's rights by destroying them, an action that "savors of contradiction and is plainly self-repugnant." To preserve something by destroying it, Johnson believed, was patently absurd.

His mind instinctively sought circularities, anomalies, and contradictions. Were the new regulations and taxes justifiable as *quid pro quos* for the protection England gave the colonies? **What protection**, Johnson asked, "past—or future—or present?" **Past?** "When our forefathers were few and poor and encompassed with innumerable enemies, they greatly needed help and protection, yet then . . . they were left unassisted to their own efforts and the protection of their God." Now that the colonies were numerous and strong, and "scarce an enemy dare lift up his head in all the land"—*now* there was "concern and bustle about it," for now there was wealth "to go into the pockets of placemen and stamp officers." As for England's expenses in the recent wars, they had long since been repaid—by the capture of Cape Breton by New Englanders, by direct colonial contributions, and by the vast acquisitions (Canada, Louisiana, Florida) that had accrued to England—to *England*, "and not a farthing to these colonies." **Protection in the future?** If the colonists' limited money supply was drained off by taxes, was "our protection and security against an invasion better in this situation than with our monies and all the profits of them in our own hands?" It would in fact "expose us to be an easy prey to any enslaving power that may invade us." **Protection for present needs?** What needs? Salaries of governors and common-law judges? "Gross stupidity and superlative nonsense."

Conceding that the crown had a legal right to collect "duties upon navigation," the only visible "need" for the internal taxation of the colonies, he said, was "to support arbitrary courts of admiralty and vice-admiralty and a numerous tribe of stamp officers and taskmasters, all . . . a dead weight upon an honest, industrious community." Or perhaps it was to support the 15,000 regular troops said to have been assigned to the colonies "to awe and keep them in order and make them to submit to these taxes, etc." But even the most craven sycophants of a power-hungry ministry should know that a standing army in time of peace was in flat contradiction to the principles of the British constitution—that it had led to the destruction of the liberties of Rome, France, "and many others"—that it had had catastrophic effects in England in the reigns of Charles I and James II—that it might well give rise to "a Caesar to break off our connection with Great Britain and set up as a protector of the liberties of the colonies"—and finally that it might "plunge us here and at home into a bloody civil war, the damage of which to the nation an hundred thousand hireling scribblers could not countervail."

The evidence of history, Johnson pointed out, was compelling. Assuming, as almost every writer of the time did, that "human nature [was] the same as in foregoing ages, and that like causes will have like effects,"[9] what, he asked, were the likely consequences of the new measures? Throughout history such grievances had caused "the most terrible civil wars and rivers of blood in England."

The pattern of these crises was only too clear. A ruthless gang of corrupt power-seekers panics a weak but liberty-loving nation with cries, first of nonexistent dangers, then of the immediate need for "better security and protection"; deliberately misinforms and deludes an essentially right-minded sovereign into building up instruments of power, and finally begins its assault on the most vulnerable member of the body politic, gradually working inward to the heart.

So in the present circumstances, Johnson writes, the ministry attempts to panic the nation with unreal dangers, among them the fear that the colonies were secretly plotting to throw off their dependence on England; then undertakes new programs—of trade regulation, of tax collection—to multiply the "places" at its disposal and to weaken the capacity to resist; finds excuses to station troops in America; deliberately misinforms the crown about conditions in the colonies; and step by step moves closer to its ultimate goal, the destruction of liberty everywhere in the British world.

Parliament, moving gradually "first on the colonies—then upon Ireland—then upon Great Britain itself," could destroy the liberties of England. But in the end, the effort, Johnson concluded, was not likely to succeed. For America would rise to its dangers and fight for its freedom—with two possible consequences. If the English people and their government responded wisely to the colonists' resistance, these early efforts of the ministry would be reversed, the chief manipulators cast out, and the country and its empire put back on their proper course. If the proper responses were not forthcoming, the result would be, not ministerial success, but "a very fatal civil war"—a "most unnatural war with the colonies," resulting not only in "the loss of two million of the best affected subjects" but also "one third, some say one half, of the profits of the national trade." He hoped, however, "in the mercy of God, things may never be pushed to this bloody! this dreadful issue! which must be attended with infinite ill consequences to the mother country and colonies, and, considering the advantage France and Spain would certainly make of such a crisis, could scarce fail of ending in the ruin of England and America." Americans must prevent it from happening not only by being generally vigilant at this early stage but by launching a specific program of action, which Johnson crisply outlined: investigation of the truth; petition for redress; propaganda to counter the misinformation ("printing and dispensing many thousands of tracts . . . it can't fail of a great and good effect"); and the organization of resistance on a continental scale.

Johnson's six newspaper articles, written and published in a short period of time in the fall of 1765, encapsulate almost the entire range of arguments and issues that would be discussed in the decade that followed. How did his fast day sermon, *Some Important Observations*, written at almost the same time as the *New London Gazette* articles, relate to the six essays? The relation of the two publications is important. Johnson's sermon connects the political arguments of the six essays to a universal language of the highest moral sanction. Setting out "to arouse and animate" his listeners, he associated the colonists' situation with that of the biblical Jews oppressed in Egypt, and he then probed in this cosmically dilated example "the general nature and consequences" of the category of evil the colonists were faced with.

The connection, the melding, of the biblical and secular historical worlds is continuous throughout the sermon, and it results in a shifting series of overlays—of individuals, events, and statements—the net impact of which is an unspecified yet comprehensive portrayal of seventeenth- and eighteenth-century problems in biblical terms. So the Old Testament Jews descended into Egypt in the condition of the Puritans escaping from Archbishop Laud: they were a "free people . . . they had a right to freedom afterwards, as they had done nothing to forfeit it, and no man nor nation had a right to take it from them." Then the image blurs in the confusing identification of Indians and Egyptians, but quickly refocuses on Pharaoh and the Stuarts. The Mosaic confrontation becomes the Exclusion Crisis, with Pharaoh exercising the Stuarts' dispensing power to his own inevitable doom, as once again "cruel oppressions prove the means of [a free people's] deliverance." The focus shifts ("so it happened in the case of Rehoboam's oppression of the ten tribes"), shifts again ("and it is possible that sooner or later it may happen to the British colonies"), and yet again (for "Rome fell by corruption"), and then settles into one of the great flights of rhetoric on the theme of corruption in the literature of the revolution:

> **If** the British empire should have filled up the measure of its iniquity and become ripe for ruin; **if** a proud, arbitrary, selfish, and venal spirit of corruption should ever reign in the British court and diffuse itself through all ranks in the nation; **if** lucrative posts be multiplied without necessity and pensioners multiplied without bounds; **if** the policy of governing be by bribery and corruption, and the trade and manufactures of the nation be disregarded and trampled under foot; **if** all offices be bought and sold at a high and extravagant price, which in the end must come out of the subject in exorbitant fees of office or lawless exactions; and **if**, to support these shocking enormities and corruptions, the subjects in all quarters must be hard squeezed with the iron arms of oppression—thence we may prognosticate the fall of the British empire—its glory is departing—the grand pillars of the state tremble, and are ready to fail.

The king is Pharaoh—the king is James II—Charles I—*Ahasuerus*, "when Esther must go in to petition the king (in a time of great calamity, great like ours, yea greater than ours)." The conflation is flexible. So "there arose a new king over Egypt, which knew not Joseph"—that is to say, who was "willfully ignorant, or very ungratefully forgetful, of the eminent services done to the nation by the Jews"—which is to say, ungrateful and forgetful "of the good services the colonists have done for Great Britain . . . services in which the colonists, at a vast expense of blood, toil, and treasure, have greatly contributed to the wealth, power, and glory of the British empire"—though Britain "knew not Joseph."

This fusion and magnification of the parochial political world into a mythic, dilated, divine universe allows Johnson to probe freely the hidden impulses and the ultimate dangers of the problems the colonists faced. Slipping easily from the biblical *ur*-world to present-day realities, he expounds at length on the innocence not only of "our gracious King (whom God forever bless)," but on Parliament and the British people in general, and fixes the blame for the present calamities on those latter-day Hamans, "the late British ministry" and their tools and hangers-on in England and America. Their ambitions are nothing new; such lusts as theirs are immemorial, elemental; and their techniques of corruption are as patterned as the movements of the tides. Inevitably they promote falsehoods calculated to panic the innocent; inevitably they raise the cry that a peaceful subordinate people plans to rise in rebellion. Thus Exodus i, 9, 10, ii: "Come on, let us deal wisely with them, least . . . when there falleth out any war, they join also unto our enemies . . . and so get them up out of the land." Here, Johnson writes, "here you have the grand, the whole strength of the enslaving cause; nothing can be added to it of any avail." For designers of "enslaving measures" needed then what they need now and always will need: a "colorable show of necessary, deep, refined policy," and they therefore devised the "plausible pretext of danger of Israel's independency." Some such "popular turns" must always be given to efforts of this sort, "otherwise they are so abominable to nature they cannot go down with a people of common sense and honesty." And so, educated by this "specimen of what has been commonly practiced by arbitrary enslavers in all ages," the colonists must be quick to respond to false accusations of seeking independence from England. They must be quick to point out that such dark and false prophecies of colonial independence, if acted upon, will inevitably become self-fulfilling, as they did in the case of the ten tribes, in the deliverance from Egypt—

" 'violent arbitrary oppressions has drove the oppressed into that state of independency which the oppressors feared and the oppressed by no means desired.' " Given a "wise, kind, and gentle administration of the colonies, they have no temptation to independency," but if "there be left to the colonies but this single, this dreadful alternative—slavery or independency—they will not want time to deliberate which to choose." Take warning in time, therefore; forestall the choice of such alternatives, and put to use the ample securities that are part of the "transcendent excellencies of the British constitution," the greatest instrument for the protection of freedom ever devised by the wit of man.

The sermon probes motives, explains tendencies, counsels action, on the basis not simply of reason and historical experience but of what are seen as the profoundest experiences of God-given humanity. It translates political arguments into cosmic imperatives, and freed thereby from the restraints of ordinary debate, it presents a magnified version of present problems that is at once clearer, less tractable, and politically more dangerous than what had appeared in the six *Gazette* essays.

Johnson's sudden publications in the fall of 1765 are the highlights of his public career. Little otherwise is known about him. A graduate in 1743 of Yale College, of which he became a Fellow thirty years later, he married three times, fathered eight children, was appointed pastor of the Lyme church in 1746 at the age of twenty-two, and served there until his death forty years later. In theology he was conservative, an adherent of the severely predestinarian New Divinity, publishing in the year of his death a 360-page treatise attacking Universalism and its core notion that the purpose of the moral world was the happiness of mankind. "It is God's will," Johnson wrote, that "fire and punishment" await the wicked "in the last day."

Legend has it that Johnson's remarkable outburst in 1765 was inspired by a neighbor of his, one John McCurdy. It may be more reasonable to suppose that Johnson's mind and imagination simply took fire in the

explosive atmosphere of the Stamp Act crisis and burned briefly with a
hard and brilliant flame.

~

FIFTEEN YEARS LATER, in May 1780, important documents of even
greater obscurity were being written by the townsmen and villagers
in Massachusetts. This was a perilous time in the fortunes of the state.
Massachusetts's constitutional structure, the foundation of public
authority, was in limbo. Since the destruction of the royal government in 1774, the Provincial Congress continued as before but without authorized foundation. All real authority had fallen to the state's
almost three hundred towns and villages, secure in their familiar
autonomy and tenacious of their powers.

It was in these circumstances that in 1777 the Commonwealth's
General Court hastily called a convention of the towns' representatives to produce a new state constitution that would reestablish public
authority on firm ground. A draft was sent back to the towns in 1778,
and a year later, amid a flurry of negative reactions, it was quickly and
soundly rejected. It was a crude effort, poorly conceived, internally
inconsistent, lacking a bill of rights, and unworkable. But all agreed
that some such basic document was needed, and with the towns' concurrence, a new convention was convened, made up of the towns' representatives. It was dominated by the state's most prominent public
figures, led by John Adams. Their charge was to bring forward a more
complete document incorporating the reactions that had previously
been expressed. On March 2, 1780, the new draft constitution, heav-
ily influenced by Adams, was submitted to the towns, villages, and
farming hamlets with the request that responses to it—approval, disapproval, or amendments—be submitted to Boston by June 7, 1780,
fourteen weeks after receipt. The convention would then tabulate the
popular votes, and if it believed that there was a two-thirds majority
for each provision, it would declare the constitution in force. If not, the

convention was authorized to amend the constitution to accommodate the towns' objections and then to enact the amended document.

No fewer than 278 communities complied. Their comments, scattered and diverse, were gathered in Boston. There some, probably a small number, were reviewed and then put aside with the other submissions. After an adroit, technically dubious interpretation of the varied returns from the towns, the convention declared that in one way or another two-thirds of the towns had approved all the provisions of the constitution, and on October 25, 1780, the document was put into effect. A century and a half later (1917) the long-since-forgotten responses of the individual communities were discovered intact in the state archives, and since then they have been published in modern form.[3]

These long-neglected documents are remarkable. They were written, often crudely, by the Commonwealth's ordinary people—not only the local lawyers, preachers, and gentry but the farmers, tradesmen, and craftsmen as well. The responses, however crude, are sophisticated in the knowledge of constitutional principles; some are sensitive to the exact meaning of words and concepts; and they are accurate in their assessments of the consequences that would follow from the enactment of certain provisions.

In form, they varied greatly. Some were simply numerical checklists of the votes on each clause of the proposed constitution. A few were wholesale endorsements of the document as it stood. But most challenged or amended specific items and explained the reasoning behind the recommended corrections. The responses are cordial even when critical, though one, from the river town of Northampton, is a seven-thousand-word treatise scouring and amending almost every provision in the constitution. It was written by an erratic but prominent radical reformer, Joseph Hawley, who privately believed that the constitution was "an unadvised, unconsulted, undiscussed, indigested, tautological, ragged, inconsistent, and in some parts unmeaning, not to say futile plan." But even his more moderate response written on behalf of the town is prolix. Almost all the towns' responses are brief though emphatic on sensitive points. The townsmen and villagers took their responsibility seriously and made clear, in various ways, what they approved of, what they hoped for, what they insisted on, and what the issues were that mainly concerned them.

There was much in Adams's constitution to consider. It was a sprawling, overelaborate document. It consisted of a Preamble stating the purpose and character of constitutions in general, followed by a thirty-article Declaration of Rights, and concluded with the basic Frame of Government. There were extensive chapters on each of the three branches of government, which enacted in great detail the resounding statement that appears, strangely, among the Declaration of Rights: that

> the legislative department shall never exercise the executive and judicial powers, or either of them; the executive shall never exercise the legislative and judicial powers, or either of them; the judicial shall never exercise the legislative and executive powers, or either of them, to the end it may be a government of laws and not of men.

Added at the end were chapters on miscellaneous matters. Among them were three sections confirming the legal status and existing rights of Harvard College as an "encouragement of Arts and Sciences and all good literature [for] the advantage of the Christian religion and the great benefit of this and the other United States of America." In all, the draft constitution, the product of seven months of work by the convention, fills twenty-seven pages of that body's *Journal*. It dwarfs the 4,543 words of the national constitution of 1787.

How much of this immense document the villagers read or had explained to them cannot be known, but behind much of the towns' most critical comments and suggested amendments was a latent and pervasive fear of domination—domination by whoever held power in any sphere, government, church, or militia. The town of **Windsor**, in the western Berkshire Hills, with a population of just over two hundred adult males, went to the heart of the matter. "It is not safor [*sic*] to put any more authority into one man's hand than what is of absolute necessity . . . two commissions of profit or honour is as much as is safe to be granted to one man." So the town voted to deny the governor the power to nominate all "judicial officers, sherifes, corriners etc. which power ought to be left with the people at large or with the representatives." For "if we should be so unhappy as to make choice of a governor who is badly disposed he may (by having this power) secure to himself his futer election . . . by disposing of commissions to his favorites." And furthermore, no governor can have as personal an acquaintance with every officer to be appointed as can those "who are daly conversing with them daly." Similarly Windsor refused to accept the idea that all civil and military officers should hold their commissions "without day." Their terms should be limited "to some sertain period for . . . there is many men in this state who have got commissions without the consent of the people, which is directly contrary to the spirit and meaning of this constitution." But like the great majority of the towns, Windsor directed its sharpest criticism to the third article in the bill of rights, which, they wrote, was "all bad."

Article three was about religion and the domination of the established church. On one point there was agreement among the towns of the Commonwealth: the constitution required all officeholders to be Christians. But town after town, with varying degrees of elaboration, insisted that the designation "Christian" was not sufficient. Officials, they demanded, must be *Protestant* Christians. For we are a community of Protestants, the fifty-four voters of **Sandisfield** wrote, "that are covenanting and emerging from a state of nature." As now written, **Greenwich** explained, the constitution would allow a Roman Catholic to be governor, "and we view it necessary to the preservation of a free government and security of the Protestant cause that no Papist should be admitted to a seat in the legislative or judicial departments."

Illuminating History

On that there was general agreement. The contentious issue, on which complaints were eloquent and solutions radical, was the de facto establishment of Congregationalism as the state's official church. The constitution continued the colonial system of requiring public taxation to support at least one Congregational church in every town, but with authorized exceptions for Baptists, Quakers, and Anglicans. The draft constitution dropped the exceptions. All towns were now required to pay taxes for the support of authorized religion, though the three groups of approved dissidents were permitted to use their taxes to support their own preachers as long as they pledged regular attendance at worship. If for whatever reason they declined to support their own church they would be taxed for support of the town's official church, as would all those who attended no church or belonged to sects not recognized by the state.

Here was a form of domination that many, besides those directly disadvantaged, were determined to oppose. "It is as much against the Quacors and Baptists principles," **Windsor** wrote, "to request any money to be paid to their own teachers . . . lays them under an absolute necessity of doing that that is against their conscince or to suffer their money to be paid to the town." **Adams** cast all of its sixty votes against article three, arguing "that no person or persons on any pretence whatsoever shall be compeled to attend on any public worship or to contribute to the supoart or maintain of any public teacher contrary to his or their sentiments." The newly organized town of **Lee** (still simply known as "No. 7") went to the fundamentals of the issue, anticipating by six years Jefferson's great Act for Establishing Religious Freedom and the concurrence of the state of Massachusetts by five decades. The village rejected article three by a vote of 13 to 5 "because," they wrote, "it is our opinion that the sevil [civil] law ought not to have any power to oblige any one to soporte the Gospel." Others agreed. **New Salem**: since "religion must at all times be a matter between God and individuals, then we see not the least propriety or fitness in the peoples investing their legislatures with any spiritual jurisdiction." And **Dartmouth**:

the legislature should have nothing to do with religion. "It is a matter that solely relates to and stands between God and the soul."

There were, of course, many towns that supported the constitution's provisions for state control of religion. Some sought even tighter restrictions in view of the spread of dissidence and denominations. At times, to support their fears of unlimited toleration, they evoked the images of the bloody upheavals caused by the Anabaptists in sixteenth-century Germany, and fresh in their memories were the religious turmoils of Massachusetts itself in its early Puritan years.

But it was not only religious restrictions that provoked bitter resentments and radical solutions. The proposed constitution restricted the right to vote for governor, senator, or representative to adult males who owned property that yielded £3 a year or that was valued at £60. This was 50 percent higher than the property qualification under the colonial charter. Those excluded, the convention had argued, were supported by their parents or were just beginning in business; or were those whose "idleness of life and profligacy of manners will forever bar them from acquiring and possessing property"—men, in other words, who would have less interest in protecting property "because they have less to lose." **New Marlborough**, a small village in the far southwest of the state 128 miles from Boston, was having none of this. The town voted 54 to 4 against "making money an essential qualification for a voter." Why? Because it contradicted the first article of the convention's own Bill of Rights, which echoed almost exactly Jefferson's words of 1776: "all men," the town wrote, "are born free and equal, and have certain natural, essential, and unalienable rights." **Stoughton** in the east was equally decisive. "The right of election is not only [a] civil but it is a natural right which ought to be considered as a principle cornerstone . . . for the frame of government to stand on." Nearby **Dorchester** went further: "every person who is free and twenty one years of age . . . having estate or not" should be able to vote for representatives. **Lee** stated that "we think it unreasnabul that any shud be taxed with out a vorse [voice] in electing." **Richmond** declared that property qualifications for voting "is an infringement on the natural rights of the subject and will exclude many good members of society"; other means could be found to exclude "bad members." They recommended that would-be voters obtain certificates from the towns' selectmen testifying that they were "good members of society and of sober life and conversation" and were willing to take an "oath of fidelity to the common wealth"; thus obtained, the privilege of voting would continue "till forfeited by misbehavior." The townsmen in tiny **Tyringham**, buried in the Berkshire Hills, were peculiarly eloquent in their view of suffrage. "Every male inhabitant that is free and twenty one years of age," they wrote, "shall have free liberty to vote . . . unless by some vicious conduct he has forfeited the same." For these are people who had voted themselves "independent of Great Britain" and had stood "forth in the defence of their darling rights and priviledges. They will not now give up so dear a priviledge which they have a right to." So **Douglas**, in central Worcester County, wrote briskly "that all rational men above twenty one years of age should have the privilege of voting . . . otherwise all men cannot be said to be born free and equal."

But it was left to the town of **Petersham**, a hamlet in the center of the state, to give all of the critical themes their full orchestration. On May 29 the town voted unanimously—24 to 0—to reject the constitution, then a week later wrote an explanatory "adress to the honorable convention as the sence of the town." They apologized for any errors they may have made in what they were submitting, but time had been short to "revise" so important a document as the constitution. In fact, Petersham's "adress," of some five thousand words, lost among the hundreds of replies sent to the convention, is the most original and penetrating critique submitted to the convention and also the most radically populist. Misspelled and crudely structured, the town's discourse went beyond the explicit issues of the state's proposed constitution to penetrate some of the most radical—for many the most disturbing—implications of revolutionary thought. It is perhaps not surprising that seven years later Petersham village became the site of

To the Honorable Convention of Delegates for forming a
Constitution of Civil Government for the State of Massachusetts the
Town of Petersham taking into their Serious Consideration the frame of
Government presented to them By your Honors Would ask your Candor
When we offer to your Consideration the following Remarks on the same
and Firstly we think the time given us For its Perusal much too short
Considering its Importance Therefore we hope if it should appear that
We have Committed any Errors we may have Charitable Allowance on that
Account.

The Consequence in the third Article of the Declaration of Rights we
think Does not answer to its Introduction Nor Coincide or flow from
the Second Article For if No person shall be Hurt Mollested or Restrained
in his person Liberty or Estate for Worshiping God in the Manner and
Season most agreable to the Dictates of his own Conscience and as you
Justly Say in your Address that Religion is a Matter Between God
and Individuals in such Case Can Individuals with safety Delegate
a Power to others to Be Judges for them of the proper Institutions of
Divine Worship and Be their absolute Dictators as to the times and
Seasons of such Worship We grant that the Happiness of a People And
the good order and Preservation of Civil Government Greatly Depends
upon Piety Religion and Morality But we Can by no Means Suppose
that to Invest the Legislature or any Body of Men on Earth with a power
absolutely to Determine for others What are the proper Institutions of
Divine Worship and To appoint Days and Seasons for such Worship
With a power to impose and Indow Religious Teachers and by penalties
and punnishments to be able to Enforce an Attendance on such Publick
Worship or to Extort Property from any one for the support of what
they may Judge to be publick Worship Can have a Tendency to promote
True Piety Religion or Morality But the Reverse and that such a
Power when and where Ever Exercised has more or Less Been an
Engine in the Hands of Tyrants For the Destruction of the Lives Liberties
and Properties of the People and that Experience has abundantly
Taught Mankind that these are Natural Rights which ought Never to
be Delegated and Can with the greatest propriety be Exercised by Individuals and by every Religious Society of Men Therefore we think the third
Article ought to be amended in the following Manner or in Some
Manner Similar Viz. as the Happiness of a people and good order
and preservation of Civil Government Greatly Depend upon Piety Religion
and Morality therefore it shall be the Duty of the several Branches
of Delegated Power Effectually to protect the People in the Exercise of
the Natural Rights of Conscience and of Worshiping God According
to its Dictates and by Example to Encourage those Natural and Christian
Graces and to Discountenance and Punnish Vice and to See that
                                                        Immorality

A portion of Petersham's response to the proposed state constitution, 1780.

a key battle in the rebellion of the disadvantaged led by Daniel Shays that shocked the state and the nation, drew George Washington back into public life, and helped shape the federal Constitution.

Petersham's report began with critiques of eight of the Declaration of Rights' thirty articles. The first was a flat condemnation of the third article, on religion. "Can individuals with safety delegate a power to others to be judges for them of the proper institutions of divine worship and be their absolute dictators as to the times and seasons of such worship?" Of course happiness, good order, and civil government depend on piety, religion, and morality.

> But we can by no means suppose that to invest the legislature or any body of men on earth with a power absolutely to determine for others what are the proper institutions of divine worship . . . and by penalties and punnishments to be able to enforce an attendance on such publick worship or to extort property from any one for the support of what they may judge to be publick worship can have a tendency to promote true piety religion or morality, but the reverse.

That power, wherever used, has been "an engine in the hands of tyrants for the destruction of the lives, liberties, and properties of the people." The townsmen therefore would amend the article by reversing the burden of the argument, to enjoin the leaders of government "to protect the people in the exercise of the natural rights of conscience and of worshipeing God," to encourage natural and Christian graces, and "to discountenance and punnish vice and . . . immorallity." All Christian denominations "shall be equally under the protection of the laws and no subordination of any one sect . . . to another shall ever be established by law."

Article four, establishing the state's sovereignty except for powers and rights delegated to the nation, needed a vital addition: "Viz, and no power shall be delegated to Congress incompatible with the freedom of this Commonwealth." Thus the freedoms guaranteed by the state would take precedence over national law.

To article five, on annual elections of the state legislature, the town added that the people at large ought to keep "in their own hands a power to recall their representatives at any time and to elect others in their stead."

A small verb change recommended for article sixteen would make a vital difference in the guarantees of liberty of speech, writing, and printing—it was not that these rights, they wrote, "ought" never to be restrained; they "shall" never be restrained. They recommended the same verbal change to article seventeen, on the guarantees for the "right to keep and bear arms for the common defence," but added a significant comment. The constitution's statement that since "in times of peace armies are dangerous," and therefore ought to be maintained only with consent of the legislature, was much too weak. So they added: in times of peace armies "shall not be kept up without there may be danger of invasion . . . And the executive power shall never make use of mercenary troops for the administration of civil government but shall have recourse to the people only for assistance." With article seventeen's conclusion that "the military power shall always be held in exact subordination to the civil authority and be governed by it," the town entirely concurred.

Article nineteen, on the right of people to assemble and petition for a redress of grievances, was clearly insufficient. What recourse would people have if they failed in their petition for redress? In that case, the town wrote, there should be a constitutionally authorized "coart of convention . . . to sit and to be impowered to act for that purpose."

They wasted no time on article twenty, which authorized the legislature to suspend laws or block their execution. That provision was dangerous, they wrote, and should be "expunged" from the constitution. For the power to suspend law "militates" against having "a government by laws and not of men . . . it must most surely introduce anarky or a government of men, and why should we open a door in our constitution for either?"

Their comment on article thirty, on the separation of powers, was an elaboration of a critical supplement to provisions of the constitution itself. They agreed with and copied verbatim the relevant passage in the convention's explanatory address to the towns that had been written in March 1780:

> The history of the rise and fall of the empires of the world affords us ample proof that where the same man or body of men enact, interpret, and execute the laws, property becomes too precarious to be valuable and a people are finally borne down with the force of corruption resulting from the union of those powers.

To this, the town added that if at any time an officeholder in any department was elected or appointed to an office in another department, he must, to avoid the corruption that follows plural officeholding, be obliged to choose the one and only department in which to serve. And in addition they noted that the exclusion of plural officeholding would open opportunities for "the rising generation to qualify themselves for office." Initial officeholding would give aspiring young newcomers to power "that useful learning ever requisite for the protection of the government of a free and happy commonwealth."

At this point the town turned from the Declaration of Rights to the Frame of Government. On this they had much to say, much to explore, in protecting the individual from the power of the state. They began with an attack on bicameralism, a concept to which Adams, the chief author of the draft constitution, was deeply committed and to which, seven years later, he would devote his three-volume *Defence of the [State] Constitutions of the United States*. There was no need to have two branches of the legislature, they wrote, the chamber of representatives and the senate. That arrangement doubled the entire election system at great expense and created a superior body removed from the people. Let there be a single election for a single body that would elect one third or half of its members "who may be stiled the Senate." It would sit separately and establish its own rules. The two bodies would have veto powers against each other. Irresolvable issues would be settled by the majority vote of a special "convention of the legislature" convened for that purpose by request. This would reduce the membership of the General Court, "render it more wieldy and fit for business and less expensive and burthensome to the people." And in this way the people would "be more likely to obtain the best, wisest and most virtuous legislative body."

Article two, on the veto power of the governor, they wrote, "should be totally expunged."

Article four, on taxes, drew a complex response. The town ruled out "duties and excises on the internal consumption, produce, and manufactures of the Commonwealth" as injurious to the happiness of the people. "Money thus raised is in great measure swallowed up in collecting and may be easily kept out of the knowledge of the people." They had no objection to levies on imported goods, but they preferred the "common method of raising money" by taxes "on poles and estates." The governor or lieutenant governor should have no role in tax collection or in creating new offices or departments, which should be done only by popular elections. In fact, the president of the senate could do all the duties assigned to the governor, and should do. In that way, much expense would be avoided and the people "saved from being droved into parties by the influence of rich and powerful men who will act in competition with each other for the obtaining the office of governor and their morals saved from the corruption that naturally flows from bribery and undue influence." Similarly there was no need for the General Court to be convened as a judiciary for the trials of errant officers. The superior court could serve as such a tribunal, in which the accused could be tried by a jury. "This will in some measure keep up and support the supremacy of the people."

At that point the town's well-organized, article-by-article critique of the proposed government was overwhelmed, and the comments came in a rush.

Travel expenses for representatives to and from the General Court should be paid by the state, to guarantee "full representation and prevent partial and ruinous measures from being carried into execution." The cost would be much less than "others pay in an indirect manner for the support of arbitrary power."

A specific day should be fixed for the election of representatives, thus avoiding the uncertainty and delays of waiting for the issuance of writs "as was the case with the people of Britain in King Charles the First's time."

Any qualified person should be eligible for election to the legislature:

> Riches and dignity neither makes the head wiser nor the heart better. The overgrown rich we think the most dangerous to the liberties of a free state, and we object against a discretionary power in the General Court to alter such qualifications in future.

People elected to public office "ought to return to private life at certain periods," and there should be election of local officers "at most in five years."

A specific provision should be made for the abolition of the slave trade, "a wicked and ruinous practice."

The entailing of estates should not be for any longer "than for one life only."

The processes of government should be transparent. Proceedings of the General Court should be open unless secrecy was absolutely required. Any member should have the right to have his dissent entered in the journals, and any five members should be able to demand for yea or nay votes, and those votes too should be printed in the journals so that the people "may be able to investigate the doings of the important servants of the publick."

The town thought it "too much" to give Harvard College an entire section of the constitution. That should be left to the legislature, which might well, in time, "find it necessary to curtail that rich and growing corporation least it should endanger the liberties of the Commonwealth."

As for amendments to the constitution: when a majority of towns thought it necessary, a court should be convened to propose amendments and also to sit as a trial court for "great officers of state who may have been guilty of male[i.e., mal-] administration or treason" and to ban such from ever holding office again. Such a court should in any case sit at least every thirty years and should know that the highest treason was to oppose the workings of the constitution either by arms or by any actions in the legislature itself.

Finally, the Habeas Corpus Act should never be suspended "by any power on earth." The danger of "any human beings" having the power of suspending the writ is far greater than anything that might arise from its use.

With that ringing pronouncement, amid clusters of smaller objections and suggestions, the town concluded its critique of the constitution. It was left only to apologize for the length and tediousness of what they had written and for any "arrogance" they might be charged with "by the great, the wise, and the powerful." They hoped that any errors they might have made would be overlooked; they wanted only to help perfect "this great work." They hoped that their suggestions would be accepted. If not, they would submit to the majority's views—except, they wrote at the end, for the "rights of conscience." *That*, they said, "we beg leave to reserve."

Petersham's commentary, hidden among the neglected bundles of the towns' responses, was unique in the breadth of its coverage, in its analytical acuity, and in its extraordinary devotion to protecting every shred of the individual's freedom against the powers of constituted authority. It is, in its rolling fluency, a radical populist tract that went beyond the more cautious imaginings of other searchers for enlightened reforms. It raised fundamental questions, some of which would not be resolved for generations, others that have never been resolved in the two hundred years that followed. In seeking solutions to their discontents, they anticipated a future political world far different from anything they had known.

IV

Beissel's Ephrata and the
Music of the Spheres

UTOPIAN FLOWERING IN
AN UNENCUMBERED LAND

Harbottle Dorr, Stephen Johnson, and the Massachusetts villagers—these were utterly obscure figures in the world at large, but what they thought and what they wrote illuminated the fervor of the revolutionary movement as few other documents could do. For me, their writings have been vital extensions of my main work on the revolution, which had been done in the 1960s and early '70s. With the publication of the Hutchinson biography (1974), I began to turn to another major project that had been brewing in the background—less public than the history of the revolution but of fundamental importance in the development of American life and society: *The Peopling of British North America*.

Who were the 2.5 million people who settled on the vast territory from the Atlantic to the Mississippi and beyond? Where had they come from, how had they lived, and what would they transmit to the future? Could they, or some of them, be identified as individuals? Could the origins of the enslaved population be traced—their way of life before and after their forced migration? And the native Americans—repressed, despoiled, and partially absorbed—could they too be described, their lives understood?

A vast subject, but the sources, the documentation, were available in abundance, the result of generations of archival research, newly available public records, biographical and regional studies of the indigenous and enslaved as well as the free immigrant population, and miscellaneous data on social and economic life. All of this might be drawn together to give an account of the peopling of British North America before the revolution, not in general terms but as far as possible in terms of the fortunes of identifiable individuals.

With a grant from the Rockefeller Brothers Fund supplemented by support from the National Endowment for the Humanities, and with the help of a remarkable research assistant, Barbara DeWolfe, who became more a collaborator than an assistant, I set out to write some part at least of such a comprehensive study. Along the way through a convoluted route, I found the strange but illuminating story that follows.

I had no clear design for the ultimate product, only a general sense of three large divisions: one on the late period, emphasizing the extraordinary surge in European immigration between the end of the Seven Years War (1763) and the beginning of the revolution (1775); then an account of the initial migrant population in the seventeenth century; and a third describing the increasingly complex population in the mid-eighteenth century with emphasis on the advent and settlement of the slave population (anticipated in the seventeenth-century volume), relations with the indigenous peoples, and the growth of a unique form of provincial urbanism and gentility.

Telling a large story in terms of identifiable individuals proved to be surprisingly feasible in writing the first volume, *Voyagers to the West: A Passage in the Peopling of America on the Eve of the Revolution,* published in 1987. It is a large book spanning two continents, but fortunately it had a singular documentary source that provided a multitude of well-organized details. The English government, its great leaders fearful of the depopulation of their estates, had created a register listing every person who left England and Scotland legally from December 1773 to March 1776 with personal information about each individual: place of origin, gender, age, occupation, family relations, and intended destination. Computer analysis revealed that 9,868 named individuals were voyaging from England and Scotland to the western hemisphere, of whom 8,869 clearly or probably intended to settle permanently in the mainland colonies. So detailed is the information in the register that some individuals and families could be traced from their English or Scottish homes to the specific places of their resettlement in America. Some individuals were so clearly described that I arranged for drawings of individual migrants by an artist familiar with historical material and able to depict the physical descriptions of individuals that had been recorded. (Unfortunately, by a misjudgment of mine, the artist's colorful and historically accurate portraits appear only in the hardcover edition of the book, not in the paperback.)

The sources for the volume on the earliest period—*The Barbarous Years: The Conflict of Civilizations, 1600–1676* (published in 2012)—had no register of people to work with. But a common theme was evident through all of the demographic material: the ever-present struggle of European settlers with the indigenous peoples—bitter struggles, bloody encounters, occasionally lightened by periods of negotiation and amity. All of this would have been continued and developed in the third volume, on the mid-eighteenth century, covering the emergence of a unique provincial society, still barbarous at the margins but complex in its "mixed multitude" of peoples from Europe and West Africa. Its growing gentility and self-confidence were poised precariously on the savagery of slavery, on the conflicts of religious sectarians, and on the capricious rule of European powers. There was no continental cohesion; the dominant subcultures were separately oriented eastward, through networks of associations, to the Atlantic homelands: the British archipelago, east-central Europe, and the western rim of Africa. But that volume remains unwritten. As time passed I became increasingly absorbed in identifying distinctive individuals whose

lives reflected important aspects of this swiftly developing and constantly changing world and whose surviving documentation allowed
one to search below the surface.

After three years of research, I thought I had enough to start with,
and I decided to sketch, in a working paper (1978) what I saw as emerging in the third segment.* I made no attempt in this partial overview to
cover the whole subject, only some of the significant lines of development. Among them was an influx to North America of the Protestant
Germans, a subject I had long been interested in. Some were attracted
to America by its reputation for religious toleration, some by hopes of
relief from poverty and the chaos of war, still others by the lures set out
by entrepreneurs seeking to populate and thus exploit large land grants
in the colonies.

I had been following in great detail the many careful studies under
way on the magnitude of this German migration and the many resettlement patterns. The numbers were impressive. Nearly 10 percent of
the total British mainland population, north and south, were Germans
or their progeny; by 1775 a third of the entire population of Pennsylvania were German speakers. Before the working paper could be complete, I needed to know more about this remarkable phenomenon than
I did and that I had discussed in the paper's notes (pages 143–47 in
the published version). In the summer of 1977 I went to Germany, settled down in the town of Meissenheim, close by my wife's stepmother's
family, and began a survey of the available local archives relevant to the
eighteenth-century migrations. The sources, I found, were overwhelming in the towns and villages throughout the Palatinate ("Pfalz").
They were scattered but identified to some extent by the "Heimatstelle
Pfalz," a migration research center in Kaiserslautern. I became a reg-
istered member of the center and took notes on its publications while
visiting as many of the Rhenish town archives that I could reach. I took

---

* The paper developed into a series of lectures published as *The Peopling of British North America: An Introduction* (New York, 1986).

back from the trip a mass of notes and also the beginning of a special interest in a subgroup of the German migration as a whole: the religious dissidents, the Pietists, the radical searchers for direct communion with God independent of the predominant Lutheran and other established churches. For everywhere in the Rhineland, I wrote in the working paper, the Pietist awakening created new radical movements, but they were movements whose European shapes were formed and whose European destinies were limited by the establishments in whose interstices alone these movements were able to grow. In the far western American marchlands, where there were no external controls, no central establishment, the results were altogether different.

And so I sketched in a few pages what I knew of the mystical sect of Johannes Kelpius, transported to Pennsylvania in 1694, and at greater length what I could then discover of the most dynamic Pietist movement of them all, the creation in Pennsylvania in the 1730s of the Ephrata cloister by the charismatic, God-possessed Johann Conrad Beissel. And thereby hangs this tale.

It happened that while writing the working paper, I was reading the English translation of Thomas Mann's great novel, *Doctor Faustus*. I knew Mann's writing well, and as I read the *Faustus* book, with the *Peopling* project in the back of my mind, I came on a passage that startled me. The exact wording was eerily familiar to me. I was certain that I had read those very words before, in a different context. But since what I was reading was an English translation of Mann's German, there was a problem. The translator could not possibly have translated these phrases from Mann's German into the exact English I knew. She must have copied them from the same English source I had read and that Mann must have translated into German. It took me a while to recall where I had originally read these words and phrases which Mann and his translator had taken over for the *Faustus* book. It turned out to be a contemporary's description of Beissel's strange, even weird music. I had found that description quoted in something I had recently read, and had remembered it. Mann, then living in Princeton, was designing the structure of the *Faustus* novel—the story of a doomed German musical genius, Adrian Leverkühn, whose creative brilliance, like that of Germany itself, would end in madness and demonic catastrophe. By chance Mann had found the same description of Beissel and his "spiritual music" quoted "in some magazine" he had picked up in Princeton,* and as soon as he read it, he later wrote, "then and there" he had decided to make Beissel's "naïve and dogmatic" music one of the conceptual keys to the novel. It helped solve the problem of the ultimate source of Leverkühn's extraordinary music.

How Mann "so slyly" (his words) worked the true story of Beissel's incredulous musical creations into the fictional life of Leverkühn, whose descent into madness occurs when Germany precipitated World War II, is a measure of the novelist's own genius. For the spirit of what Mann, in the words of his pseudo-narrator of the *Faustus* story, called the "arbitrary, ingenious musical activity . . . of that queer fish across the ocean" permeates the entire novel and helps make the narrative coherent.[1]

But in fact Mann knew little about Beissel's passion for music or his motivation in developing his own harmonic system and his own way of blending sound with the words of mystical and biblical texts. All that is part of Beissel's extraordinary life story and the history of the commune he created in the unencumbered land of Pennsylvania. I knew that tracing his story in any detail, fascinating as it was, would be a diversion from the main lines of the Peopling project. But my interest in him and his reclusive haven grew as I came to realize how vividly they illustrated a powerful theme in America's history. So I put aside

---

* The magazine piece Mann had stumbled on was Hans T. David, "Hymns and Music of the Pennsylvania Seventh-Day Baptists," *American-German Review* 9, no. 5 (1943). Mann had marked in pencil, we now know from the manuscript in the Mann archive, the description of Beissel and his music and must have given it to his translator to insert in place of his German translation of it.

the larger story to explore what I could of Beissel's life and achievements and the parochial world he inhabited.[2]

How Johann Conrad Beissel (1691–1768), son of an impoverished
baker in the obscure village of Eberbach, in the German Palatinate,
became the dominant leader of one of the most creative utopian communities in North America—its inspiration, spiritual guide, manager, composer, choral director, artistic promoter, hymnologist, and
theologian—can never be fully explained. But somehow, before he left
Germany for America at the age of twenty-nine, he had absorbed not
merely much of the intellectual content and passion of radical Pietism
and its occult associations but also the idioms of popular German
music and the cadences of its prayers and hymns.

Utopian ventures, perfectionist projects, were founded everywhere
in the western hemisphere in the early years of Europe's encounters
with the Americas. Some were modeled on More's *Utopia*, some on
the Jesuits' efforts to "reduce" native peoples to rigorously disciplined
villagers, some on the Puritans' passion to create a Protestant "new
Jerusalem," which would itself prove to be the source of an array of
minor Jerusalems scattered across the land.[3] But no other perfectionist project can compare with the originality and range of achievement
of Beissel's commune, which he called "Ephrata." Based on yearnings
for direct union with God, the Ephrata Cloister, under Beissel's leadership, developed its own distinctive mystical language, its own sym-
bolism and system of prophetic signs, its own architecture, its own
maxims, proverbs, and poems, its own elaboration of *fraktur* art and
book illumination, and above all its own unique form of vocal music,
which Beissel composed and trained his followers to sing with what
contemporaries described as unearthly beauty. At its peak in the mid-
eighteenth century, Beissel's cloister included a cluster of uniquely
designed buildings and some three or four hundred members organized by religious commitment, sex, and marital status, all of whom
were devoted to searching—through prayer, disciplined behavior,

symbolic ritual, study, music, and the manipulation of occult signs—
the heavenly mysteries in hopeful anticipation of the ineffable union,
the forthcoming marriage, with Jesus, ultimately with divinity itself.

All of this was eccentric and strange—the creation of an obscure
Pietist whose imagination, talents, and aspirations had flowered in
the unconfined spaces of Pennsylvania. But Ephrata did not remain
obscure. Its fame spread throughout the English as well as the German
population of Pennsylvania and ultimately throughout Europe. Voltaire heard of Ephrata from the Quakers during his stay in England.
Later, in his *Dictionnaire philosophique*, he wrote enthusiastically that
Beissel's sectarian society

> rejects the doctrine of original sin as impious, and that of the
> eternity of punishment as barbarous. The purity of their lives
> permits them not to imagine that God will torment his creatures
> cruelly or eternally. Gone astray in a corner of the new world, far
> from the great flock of the Catholic Church, they are, up to the
> present hour, notwithstanding this unfortunate error, the most
> just and inimitable of men.

For the Abbé Raynal this was exciting and important, and he amplified
Voltaire's jubilant description with greater detail, devoting four pages
of his famous *Histoire philosophique . . . des deux indes* (1770) to Beissel's mystical sect (which he called Euphrates) as a living example of
Enlightenment principles.[4]

When Beissel left Germany in 1720, he had given no outward signs
of extraordinary gifts (his musical experience seems to have been limited to playing the fiddle at social events). But in his formative years
he had found his way through the intense churnings of religion that
followed the devastation of the Rhineland in the Thirty Years War and
the scorched-earth invasion of French troops that had reduced much
of Beissel's world to ruin and its people to poverty. In Beissel's youth

the region's basic culture had been splintered, and he had in fragmentary ways touched it all: the powerful, destabilizing surge of Pietism within the established Lutheran and Reformed churches; the mystifying influence of Kabbalistic and Rosicrucian occultism; and the ecstasies of solitary seekers. All of this, with various degrees of intensity, reached Beissel and provided much of the intellectual and spiritual capital on which he would later draw.

Though we cannot trace the inner processes of Beissel's early development, there are accounts of his persona and character scattered through the history of the cloister, the *Chronicon Ephratense*, published eighteen years after Beissel's death by two former members of the cloister, Jacob Gaas and Peter Miller (Brothers Lamech and Agrippa). Beissel's presence in his later years, they wrote, was unforgettable:

> He was small in person, well formed and proportioned, had a high nose, high forehead and sharp eyes, so that everybody recognized in him an earnest and profound nature. He had excellent natural gifts, so that he might have become one of the most learned men if pains had been taken with his education. All secrets were opened to him. . . . He used to say it would be a shame for the human mind if it would be defeated in anything. He likewise was endowed with such a keen perception that he was enabled to discover with ease whatever might be hidden to others. But after he had dedicated himself wholly to the service of God these gifts were sanctified, and were used by him for the upbuilding of the temple of God in the Spirit.

Above all, they wrote, he was "an enemy of self-interest," always guided by the principle of "disinterested love." Such was his imposing presence, his saintly indifference to the cares of everyday life, and his authentic spirituality—yet also his tactless imperiousness in maintaining his personal dominance in his holy world that "we are naturally so

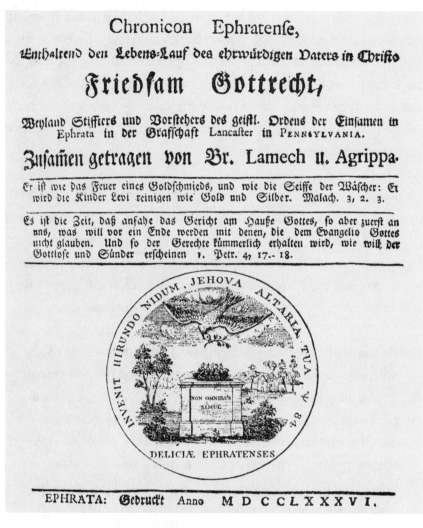

Chronicon Ephratenſe,

Enthaltend den Lebens-Lauf des ehrwürdigen Vaters in Chriſto

Friedſam Gottrecht,

Weyland Stiffters und Vorſtehers des geiſtl. Ordens der Einſamen in Ephrata in der Grafſchaft Lancaſter in PENNSYLVANIA.

Zuſammen getragen von Br. Lamech u. Agrippa.

Er iſt wie das Feuer eines Goldſchmieds, und wie die Seiffe der Wäſcher: Er wird die Kinder Levi reinigen wie Gold und Silber. Malach. 3, 2. 3.

Es iſt die Zeit, daß anfahe das Gericht am Hauße Gottes, ſo aber zuerſt an uns, was will vor ein Ende werden mit denen, die dem Evangelio Gottes nicht glauben. Und ſo der Gerechte kümmerlich erhalten wird, wie will der Gottloſe und Sünder erſcheinen 1. Petr. 4, 17.- 18.

EPHRATA: Gedruckt Anno M D C C L X X X V I.

Title page of the Chronicon Ephratense.

shy of him," Miller, who knew him so well, confessed, "that we always keep at a distance from him."[5]

But the self-creation of Beissel's charismatic presence had been a slow process. An orphan from the age of eight, with very little formal education yet acutely sensitive to ideas of any kind, he had moved from place to place, first among his older siblings, then as a baker's assistant to various employers in Eberbach. In those teenage years he developed an uninstructed skill in "mercantile calculation" (possibly related to numerology, which would later prove important for his theosophical views) while discovering his natural leadership capability. Above all, he experienced the first impulses of Pietism. In visits to the clandestine meetings of the Pietists he found a world of excited religiosity, a "religion of the heart," more fervent than anything he knew in the established church, more devout, more emotional and moralistic. There too he probably encountered not only Philipp Jakob Spener's *Pia desideria*, advocating small lay groups of the devout willing to live under clerical direction and thus emulate the Apostolic Church but also something of the teachings of Jacob Boehme, which would ultimately dominate his intellectual life. All of this, for the young Beissel, was enlivening. It stirred his imagination and engaged his emotions. But it brought him under the scrutiny of both church and state for defying the church and embracing Pietism. He left Eberbach as a licensed journeyman baker, singed by the fires of Pietism, seeking endorsements from bakers in various towns for advancement to the status of master baker.

In Strasbourg, a cosmopolitan intellectual and religious center, he went deeper into Pietism. He also discovered the even more radical world of the Inspirationists, whose holy status was validated by visions, miracles, and prophecies at the expense of established dogmas, clerical procedures, and reason. And more important, he found the Philadelphians, the mystic cult that was devoted to Boehme's theosophical writings on the experience of direct union with God and that exalted the spiritual importance of music.

But his commitment to the service of God was still uncertain, and in Mannheim he failed to maintain a careful balance between the world and the spirit. Too much of the former got him in trouble with his master's wife, as a result of which he fled the city and, significantly for his later doctrine of celibacy, "bade good-night to earthly woman." In Heidelberg he worked for a particularly indulgent Pietist master, whose female kin came to see in Beissel what one historian has called his "charismatic saintliness." There, the *Chronicon* authors wrote, he experienced "the first impregnation of a spiritual life . . . when the great weight of the spirit was laid upon him," and he cut all ties to the established church. At that point he became recognized as a Pietist intellectual, devoted to Boehme's thought, of which he learned more through the writings of Boehme's disciple and editor, Johann Georg Gichtel. He learned too not only of the underground radical conventicles associated with the Inspirationists and Philadelphians but also something about the mysterious and elusive Rosicrucians, supposedly a secret society devoted to the betterment of humanity, but in fact a succession of esoteric tracts that captured the imagination of meliorists in various parts of Europe. But at the same time as his secular fortunes rose (he became treasurer of the local bakers guild), so too did his dismay at what seemed to him to be the extravagant worldliness of his professional colleagues. His criticism of their excesses was sharp, and they responded by publicizing his secret life as a Pietist dissident no longer a member of the church, a charge that brought him before the ecclesiastical court. The result was banishment, not only from Heidelberg but from the entire region of the Electoral Palatinate.

He fled, a vagrant; suffered various illnesses; punished himself in penitence; and became more deeply immersed in theosophical writings. His wanderings brought him finally north to Schwarzenau, where a well-organized congregation of the German Baptist Brethren took him in. There he found like-minded meliorists, many of them Dunkers, some Inspirationalists, some Spiritualists, some Philadelphians. His friendships multiplied, deepened, and became collaborations. He and a small group of friends shared their views and religious passions and in time came to discuss a radical break, a fresh start, in a solitary world of their own, elsewhere—across the Atlantic, where they might live alone, free to worship as they pleased, to re-create the Apostolic Church, and to await the coming of the Lord. For their thought was permeated with beliefs in the imminent second coming of Christ and the millennium that would follow after the reign of the Antichrist.

Beissel and his friends knew little about America in general, but they did know something about Pennsylvania and its religious tolerance. What they knew was inspiring and attractive. They were told of the earlier pilgrimage to Pennsylvania of the revered Johannes Kelpius. A multilingual scholar in touch with the renewal of European intellectual life at the turn of the century, he had studied at the universities in Tübingen and Leipzig and was a *Magister* of the University of Altdorf as well as a Rosicrucian mystic devoted to that elusive society's mystical insights into the divine secrets of the universe. Beissel and his friends knew that Kelpius had led a devoted group of like-minded worshippers to Pennsylvania in 1694, a year in which, Kelpius's pilgrims believed, the Lord would reappear and usher in the end of days and the ultimate millennium. There, on a ridge near Philadelphia, they had built a log-walled monastery and a primitive laboratory, where they had conducted alchemical and pharmaceutical experiments aimed at eliminating disease and prolonging life indefinitely. And on the roof they had built a telescope, which they manned from dusk till dawn, so that in case, as they put it, the Bridegroom, Jesus, came in the middle of the night, their lamps would be prepared—which is to say, they would be prepared to receive the Deliverer. They called their group The Woman in the Wilderness, that is, the true Church, the saving remnant of all the world's corrupted churches. Its heart lay in a cave which they found in a nearby hillside. There Kelpius spent much of his later years pondering truths concealed to ordinary souls but in his ordeals revealed to him. For he had been convinced, from Revelation xii and other passages of the Bible, that the wilderness into which "the Woman" had fled was certainly Pennsylvania. It was here, he believed, that mankind would "find the dear Lord Jesus"; it was here that the true Christians, like wise virgins, should vigilantly trim their lamps, await the Bridegroom, and prepare for the heavenly consummation.

In all of this, music was essential. Kelpius was no composer; nor did he organize or direct musical activity. But in his own thinking and in what he wrote, he detailed the crucial meaning of music as a spiritual language in which mankind could transcend its pride, confusion, corruption, and religious contention and share in the unity of divine wisdom.[6]

The apocalyptic year passed quietly. Though Kelpius kept faith with his prophetic expectations many of his followers did not, and succumbed to the temptations of the profane world. The community had dwindled in numbers and much of its vitality had faded by the time of Beissel's arrival. But a few survivors of Kelpius's famous hegira were still there and carried into Beissel's time Kelpius's core beliefs: the certainty of the coming apocalypse; the need for holy sanctuaries in which individuals could exclude the mundane world and immerse themselves in devotion and the search for God's embrace; and the assumption that music was a language that transcended all mundane discourses and could help make contact with the heavenly sphere.

Beissel began his life in America by surveying what he could of religion in William Penn's tolerant province. The region around the recently founded village of Germantown, he discovered, though populated largely by members of Lutheran or Reformed churches, was dotted with clusters of German dissidents—radical Pietists devoted to the teachings of Spener and Boehme; Mennonites and Quakers originally led by the formidable multilingual humanist scholar and lawyer Francis Daniel Pastorius; Dunkers led by Peter Becker, an itinerant preacher and evangelist who employed Beissel briefly; and there were Schwenckfelders and Moravians.* In the end none of the scattered groups in and around Germantown, not even the rigorously ascetic, celibate, and communalist Labadists, satisfied Beissel's need for solitude and independence or provided the proper site for the development of spiritual expression. Two years after his arrival Beissel broke away from all of the groups and with a loyal young companion moved off to a tranquil forest site on the Conestoga frontier, where he built his

---

* Alderfer lists six religious communes established in America in 1662–1742. *Ephrata Commune*, table 2. But there were others, more ephemeral.

first habitation in America, a small log cabin, to serve as his private cell and a school for the instruction of the young.

But then, as his ideas and aspirations were beginning to develop, his personal attractiveness and distinctive passion were becoming evident, and he found that the solitude he sought could not be maintained. One after another searcher for divine revelation came to him, and his primitive habitation became a magnet for individuals from the German sects floundering in the confusion of competing beliefs. Beissel found strength in reaching out to others as an inspirational preacher while extending the range of his personal experiences. Just as the memory of Kelpius and the Labadists had shown him the way to a rigorous ascetic communalism, so the Baptist Sabbatarians convinced him of the validity of the Jewish Sabbath and led him deeper into the Kabbalah and medieval Jewish mysticism.

In the decade that followed, the pattern of his life was repeated again and again. As Miller explained to Benjamin Franklin, who at age twenty-four had been the Cloister's first printer,

> When he arrived in these parts of the world he cast his eyes upon a certain solitary place, in order to spend the residue of his days in an hermetical life, but he had not long tasted the sweetness of that paradisacal life in a retired solitude . . . before he was commanded by Divine Providence, who dictates all his resolutions, and to whom he stipulated an inviolable obedience to appear publickly. Thus pretty early the hermetical life was metamorphised into a monasterial one, and Ephrata designed at first for an Hermitage, has become now without any mans premeditation, the Camp of Solitary Congregation.[7]

Thus at first he would roam the region, from settlement to settlement, farm to farm, and cabin to cabin, preaching his own evolving doctrines, inspiring acolytes, gathering co-workers, and establishing himself as a charismatic spiritual leader among the Germans in the frontier region. But then, alone in an isolated cabin, he would seek to achieve the height of mystical theosophy in states of exaltation. It was in such retreats in the 1720s and early '30s, barely a decade since his arrival, that he produced the first of the many hymns he would eventually write, and conceived the first of the antiphonal choral works that in years to come would distinguish the Ephrata Cloister from the other Pennsylvanian German utopias.

As he felt his way forward, obstacles appeared on all sides: doctrinal differences among his followers; bitter competition for leadership; and fierce resistance by the surrounding secular world. Beissel's views on celibacy were particularly provocative. They led to rumors of free love among the brethren and of the seduction into the cloister of susceptible wives. Some of the Cloister's men were waylaid and beaten by nearby frontiersmen. At one point Beissel himself was assaulted at night and beaten "with knotted rope and leather thongs"; at another, an enraged husband dragged his wife from the Cloister repeatedly and attacked Beissel, the *Vorsteher* (leader), according to the *Chronicon*, "with the intention of taking his life." When later the husband heard that a "love feast" would be held at the Cloister, he and "another evil fellow" seized his wife and "tied her fast lest she should run away from him again." Fortunately the husband, consumed by "hellish brimstone," died before his wife, who happily rejoined the Cloister and led "an edifying life for some years more."[8]

But Beissel's magnetism, his saintliness, his endless charity for all mankind, his zeal in searching for ineffable goals, the uniqueness of his occult mysticism, and his self-discipline in living an utterly spartan existence—all of this continued to enthrall many of the rootless Germans longing for religious certainty, and especially the women, for whom celibacy could be liberating if not life-saving. Recruits flocked to Beissel as disciples, squatting in nearby empty cabins when they could find them, throwing together crude habitations on land to which they had no title. Gradually the scattered acolytes formed a congregation, distinct from the major groups in and around Germantown, with Beissel as their *Vorsteher*. Then once again, in early 1732, just as his congregation was on the point of consolidation, Beissel resigned his leadership and withdrew to the seclusion of a cabin on the banks of the Cocalico Creek, a wild, forbidding place far from other European settlements. There as in his earlier withdrawals, he indulged in mystic reveries that unleashed his creative powers. The result was dozens of new hymn-poems published, with contributions from others, as the *Vorspiel der Neuen Welt* (*Prelude to the New World*, 1732).

But this most dramatic of Beissel's withdrawals, was, like the others, short-lived. By the fall of 1732 he was active in the world once again, and the flow of devotees had once again followed him, now into the once-remote Cocalico area. As their numbers grew, they found them-selves to be a coherent congregation that they called *das Lager der Einsamen* (the Camp of the Solitaries), which in a short time would become known to the world as the Ephrata Cloister.[9]

At the core of the Camp were the "solitaries": celibate monks and nuns entirely devoted to Beissel's basic principles of mystical Pietism, celibacy, Sabbatarianism, Dunkerism, and a severely ascetic way of life. Surrounding them was a scattering of Householders, farmers who respected private property and the rule of secular law, worked their farms, raised families, and otherwise lived in the ordinary world yet were devoted to Beissel personally and followed his teaching, if not his style of life, as far as they could.

With population growth came the physical transformation of the original *Lager*. The small, makeshift cabins could no longer accommo-date the multiplying devotees or the meetings for worship and cere-monies. So Beissel began a building program that would continue for a decade and end in the creation of a cluster of buildings that, while satisfying the Cloister's physical needs, expressed Beissel's spatial imag-ination, impelled by his "awareness of God's presence."

First came the *Berghaus* built of wood and stone; it housed four sol-itaries and had space for guests and ceremonial events. Then came the first of the dormitories, a three-storied structure called *Kedar* (1735), with cells for about thirty sisters on the upper floor and brothers below, separated by a floor of spacious meeting rooms. Other buildings followed: the *Bäthaus* (1740), a house of worship and a meetinghouse two stories in height that included a balcony for the women and the elderly, chairs for the worshippers "decorated with Fraktur writings," and, in the middle of the room, a special seat for Beissel, behind whom sat the choir. While the *Bäthaus* was under construction, Beissel ordered the erection of a special building to be called *Zion* (1738), some distance from the contaminating influence of the sisters. It would be the habitation of the most zealous of the solitaries, a group to be known as the "Zionitic Brotherhood." The building, of three stories, was one of the largest structures in the compound and was said by some to have special chambers for secret rites.

In the same burst of construction in the late 1730s and early '40s was a second habitation for women of which little is known, and a four-and-a-half-story meetinghouse for the Householders, which he called *Peniel* (1741). Two years later yet another dormitory was built adjacent to *Peniel* that Beissel called *Hebron*, or *Saron*. But Beissel's spatial ambitions were still not fulfilled. In 1746 he brought together the celibates into a Brotherhood of Bethania and had a three-and-a-half-story meetinghouse built for them that he called *Bethania*.

Such were the main buildings. To architectural historians, they were simply German structures of traditional design. But to Beissel, none were merely traditional human habitations and architecture. They were for him expressions of God's teachings and humanity's search for salvation. So the passageways were narrow, illustrating the "straight and narrow path"; the doorways were low "to force the worshippers to obey the command that 'every head shall bow . . . on entering the house of prayer.'" All the names—*Kedar, Zion, Hebron (Saron), Paniel, Bethania*—were chosen by Beissel as references to beliefs and points of doctrine often buried within tangles of esoteric meanings, some of which have proved to be beyond the comprehension of modern scholars.

Two buildings in the Ephrata Cloister, Saron, *the sisters' dormitory (1743) and* Sall, *the meetinghouse (1741), and a cell for the solitaries.*

Especially elusive but to Beissel profoundly important were the measurements, the numbers, involved in these constructions. The exact measurements, based on calculations from various biblical and mystical sources, mattered greatly, not so much for their practical use as for their expression of heavenly truths. The expression "40 x 40" as the lineal measurement of a holy house could refer to Adam's days in paradise or Israel's days of testing on Mount Sinai, or Jesus' days in the desert. The number 10 was sacred as the years before Jesus entered his public ministry; "3 x 10" was the completion of the Trinity. The six points of the Star of David united Boehmist, biblical, cabalistic, and alchemical signs and referred also to the days of the work week which, when juxtaposed, constituted 666, the well-known sign of the beast in Revelation. But of more immediate significance were the dimensions of the rooms of his buildings and the individual floor plans, all of which reflected significant spiritual meanings.

Like all of the life at the Cloister, these measurements were in some way modes of worship, in which outward appearances were signs and symbols of truths revealed to Beissel and his followers, just as they had been to Kelpius. So too were personal names, which were transformed "as a sign that they have come into a rare condition, different from that of the great and wicked world." Beissel adopted the name Friedsam Gottrecht (Peaceable, God-righteous), though he was commonly called Father. His faithful colleague Michael Wohlfahrt became Brother Agonius, while the beautiful and gifted Swiss-born Anna Thomann—singer, choir leader, and painter—became sister Anastasia.

By the late 1740s Ephrata, its physical structures complete and its rituals and way of life fully evolved, had reached its classic state. By the early '50s erosion in membership if not in zeal had begun to set in, and it was at that stage, a time when the surviving devotes were still confident of their purpose and steeped in what seemed immemorial traditions, that the community was visited by a clear-eyed, knowledgeable outsider who recorded in great detail the life of the Cloister over a day-long cycle.[10]

The Swedish Reverend Israel Acrelius, pastor of the Lutheran church in nearby New Sweden, had been a student at Uppsala University and maintained a strong interest in theology as well as natural history. He had heard of Ephrata, and what he heard intrigued him. On August 20, 1753, he arrived for a visit. He was met warmly by the Cloister's most

Peter Miller and Israel Acrelius. The limner of this contemporary image of Miller is unknown, but the sketch seems to conform to what is known about this major figure of the Cloister.

learned scholar, Peter Miller (Brother Agrippa), a graduate of Heidelberg University, who "understands the oriental languages," Acrelius wrote, "speaks Latin, discusses theological controversies as well as other sciences," is friendly, open-hearted, and prudent. Acrelius could not have had a better guide than this eighteen-year veteran of Beissel's holy community, especially since he considered that most of the other brethren he met were "very stupid."

With Miller as his guide, he began by inspecting the buildings, noting in detail the small doors and windows, the dark, narrow passageways, the spare, stark cells, "about four paces long and two broad" furnished only with narrow benches on which the brothers and sisters slept with "either a stone or a piece of wood under their head." Particularly interesting to Acrelius was the complicated arrangement of the brethren's church, with its latticed gallery for women that hid them from view while allowing them to see the brothers and sisters of the congregation below—"an old and becoming custom," Miller explained when Acrelius asked, rather critically, about the logic of the arrangement.

Two aspects of Ephrata's life were of particular interest to Acrelius, and he dwelt on both at length: the brothers' and sisters' clothing, and their diet and routines in evening meals. They wore no shirts next to their skin, he reported, only a "long, close coat," fastened down to the feet, with narrow sleeves and collars fitted close to the neck, made of wool in the winter and linen or cotton in the summer, with a girdle around the waist. On certain events they added a habit thrown over the head like a chasuble in front and a cape in the back, some with hoods attached. The effect, to Acrelius, was to make the long, raggedly bearded men look even thinner than they were as a result of their exceedingly lean diet.

Of that Acrelius learned much by joining the brethren for the evening meal. The food consisted of barley boiled in milk and pumpkin mush, with slices of bread on which, though butter was available, they spread "a kind of cheese-curds." The meal began with the reading of a passage from the Bible and proceeded in silence. There were no plates. Each brought with him or her a small bag holding a wooden spoon and a knife. At the close, the worshippers licked their knife and spoon, dried them with a cloth they had brought with them, and restored the knife and spoon to the same bag. Later Acrelius asked about the healthiness of the diet, and Miller explained why they avoided, but did not prohibit, meat, and how their vegetarian diet, of cabbages, roots, greens, and dairy products, gave them spirit, vivacity, good cheer, and good health.

Miller made clear that in addition to the brethren's belief in diet as critical to the Cloister's way of life, work, too, strenuous and productive work, was essential. Work occupied most of the members' time when they were not in prayer or meditation. Most of the men, in the allotted time periods, worked in the fields, meadows, and woods and at the several mills that the Cloister operated. Also, living alone, they did their

An Ephrata sister, one of several such formalized sketches that appear in the Cloister's writings.

own cooking, house cleaning, and clothes washing. The sisters, who lived under a strict regime of scheduled activities, engaged in spinning, sewing, gardening, nursing, writing, singing, and above all copying musical scores which they decorated with colorful, free-flowing, imaginative designs that elevated their uninhibited work, supported by Beissel, to the level of an art form.

All of this Acrelius recorded, but he was not an impartial observer. An orthodox preacher and an academically trained theologian, he pressed again and again on sensitive points of doctrine in his running conversations with Miller. He tried to remain calm and respectful as the exchanges became heated, only occasionally allowing himself a hint of disdain, a whisper of mockery, a barely audible tone of hauteur. And indeed at one point Miller was clearly exasperated by Acrelius's questions about the timing of Ephrata's celebration of the eucharist, and declared that the brethren "do not place high value upon disputations." Acrelius immediately dropped the subject "that I might not have made myself a disagreeable guest."

But later the debate continued. Acrelius pressed Miller on the question of baptism. Why the full immersion? Why not a partial dipping or a symbolic sprinkling? Miller replied simply that like Christ's apostles, "the person must be submerged." There was, he said, a limit to what was explicable. When once, he recalled, a stranger had asked him to explain certain "mystic words," he had told him that "I could not, and that I did not busy myself with such things." But as the two grew friendlier Miller felt increasingly free to discuss a range of sensitive subjects: from marriage (a vital concern for this celibate community) to war, oaths, faith and nonbelief, and the uses and forms of Christ's sacraments.

The most sensitive subject was introduced by Miller. Do you believe, he asked the learned visitor, "that the pains of hell [are] eternal?" Certainly, Acrelius replied, "as certainly as the joy of heaven is eternal." "Nay," replied Miller, "I do not believe that the soul, which is a part of God's being, can perish eternally." "Dear Mr. Miller," Acrelius responded, "you are a benevolent man, but let not your charity extend so far as to wish to extinguish the fires of hell." "Yea," Miller said, "as long as you are evil and I good, then we shall never agree, but if we are both good, then we shall well agree." Acrelius could see that the discussion would end in distinguishing *æternitas* (eternity) from *æviternitas* (a long period), and the debate ended there.

Once again Acrelius was struck by the oddities and strangeness in the Cloister's life: the brothers' effort "to look pale, thin, and wretched," allowing their beards to grow "up to their ears," and their Quaker-like conviction that each person possesses an "inward light . . . and an impulse of the spirit." They had no written laws, only oral understandings of the "perpetual natural law . . . written upon the hearts of all men" and that are the same as the ten commandments. Nor were there set prayers "unless they come extemporere into the head." But what seemed strangest of all was their adherence to Jewish customs. Most of their Bible reading came from the Old Testament (especially the Prophets and the Psalms), not from the New. They were seventh-day Sabbatarians, worshipping on Saturdays not Sundays, to the anger of the surrounding secular authorities, and they "count their hours after the Jewish fashion, from the beginning of the day, so that our six o'clock is their one, and our twelve their seven."

So the discourse with Miller proceeded, with increasing clarity on the life of the Cloister and its people. Though Miller was a learned spokesman and a genial guide, it was clear throughout the day that it was Beissel who was the force behind all of the Cloister's activities, the dominant will determining the group's organization, procedures, goals, and achievements. It was he who explored and refined the intellectual content of the Cloister's worship and clarified and amplified the intellectual foundation of the entire undertaking.

Now, in the Cloister's maturity, Beissel lived alone in the house that had been built for him and from which he ruled, at times despotically. He alone could decide who might or might not be invited to the "love feasts" and could call all members of the Cloister to attend church services beyond those routinely scheduled. For this Beissel had at hand, Acrelius noted, a rope that stretched between the men's and women's separate cloisters, with a bell at each end, and

> when it comes into his head, and he pulls thereon, and the bell rings, and even if it were in the middle of the night, all must get up and assemble their church to hold service.

It was by chance that Acrelius was able to witness the regular monthly service in which all the men and women participated.

He joined Miller in walking up through the footpaths on the long hill to arrive at the church. The brothers were already seated on benches on both sides, and the women had gone to their places in the gallery. At the center, facing the brethren, with the choir to his rear, sat Beissel. He began what to Acrelius was an astonishing performance.

Beissel seemed to be preparing himself by holding his hands on his sides, then throwing his head up and down, casting his eyes "hither and thither," pulling at his mouth, his nose, his neck, until he began to sing "in a low and fine tone." The sisters took up the melody, the brothers followed, and finally "the high choir" joined in. The result was "a delightful hymn, which lasted for about a quarter of an hour."

At that point Beissel rose and began his sermon, which to Acrelius seemed "rather ridiculous than devotional." With his hands clasped together and his eyes turned upward, he spoke of the natural darkness of man's understanding, and prayed for enlightenment. Then he resumed his seat and preached about holiness and the need for watchfulness. At the end he spoke of the relations between faith, love, and charity but got so tangled up in the details that he "did not know where he was at home (what he believed)." All of this was delivered at feverish speed, "in hasty language, with rapid gestures."

> Now he struck out his hands, now he pressed them to his breast, now he placed them upon one side, now upon another, and now upon both. Again, he scratched his head, then patted himself on the nose, and then wiped his nose on the back of his hand. Meanwhile, in the congregation, which he frequently called Jerusalem, some were moved and shook their heads, others wept, others slept, and so on. The sermon was concluded with an Amen.

When Beissel finally subsided, a period of common conversation began "wherein each one relates what he has upon his conscience," on all of which Beissel gave his judgment. Miller proposed that a psalm should be sung. Beissel instructed a brother to begin, but he himself "raised the tune," and the singing began. "Each one holds a note-book as well as a psalm-book . . . looking into both alternately." "Different brothers, as well as sisters, understand vocal music," he added, "as also does Father Friedsam."

Beissel did indeed, in his own way, know music, but he also knew more of theosophy and of God's many meanings in symbols and mystical languages. Beissel's principles, his beliefs, and the rituals he developed for Ephrata, the visitor correctly noted, "were derived from other sects and in part the product of his own brain." And they were voluminous, prolix, and frequently obscure, many of them beyond the understanding of even his most devoted acolytes. Thus Beissel's view of baptism by threefold immersion owed much to the Philadelphians and the Inspirationists but particularly to the Neu-Täubers, or Dunkers, who baptized him in 1724. To Beissel personally—inwardly—baptism was a cluster of symbols and meanings, some related to Boehme's and others' concept of the divine virgin Sophia, the female attribute of God's wisdom shared by androgynous mankind until the fall and thereafter the object of aspiring men's passionate desire for reunion and spiritual rebirth.[11] While the rituals of the love feast, foot washing, and laying on of hands in consecration were derived from the Dunkers, strains of Catholicism could also be found in Ephrata's beliefs but faded in the welter of other doctrines and practices drawn from the radical Pietists, the Labadists, and the Mennonites.

Beissel's views, derived from so many sources, were never codified, as Acrelius noted, never set into a firm creed, for fear, Beissel's faithful collaborator Michael Wohlfahrt explained, "that if we should once print our confession of faith we should feel ourselves as if bound and confined by it, and perhaps be unwilling to receive further improvement." The result of such conceptual fluidity may not have been what one of Beissel's most scholarly and sympathetic modern biographers feared, "a psychosexual hodgepodge," but it was at times something close to it: a blur of theosophical and biblical references, portentous prophecies, esoteric apothegms, divine revelations, apocalyptic visions, and eschatological forebodings—all suffused with elements of commonplace magic and references to Beissel's sexual concerns and his fascination with androgyny as basic to the secrets of divinity.[12] Much of what he wrote appeared in collections of proverbs, aphorisms, epigrams, poems, hymns, prophecies, revelations, and simply "sayings" (*Sprueche*). Thus his *MYSTISCHE* Und sehr geheyme SPRUECHE ... und dan folgens einige *POETISCHE GEDICHTE* (*Mystical and very secret sayings ... followed by several poetical verses*)—a volume printed and published by Franklin in German, and later in English as *Ninety Nine Mystical Sentences*, followed by sixty-two poems and several instructions for teachers of Christian lessons.

The *Sprueche*, said to be mystical and very secret, at least at first glance appear to be neither, but rather homilies and moral teachings familiar then and now. But for Beissel, immersed in a Boehmist world view, they had deep implications for human salvation. Thus:

> Whosoever loveth his life shall loose it, and whosoever loseth the same shall find it.

> If thou hast sowed thy seed, bring the same in due time under ground, lest the birds of heaven will eat it up, and thou shalt suffer famine in harvest-time.

> Whosoever lovest God is from God, and hath the unigenite son remaining in himself, for the same did proceed from God.

> All actions of a man bring him to the same end, for whose sake they are done, either for life or death; therefore let no works be found on thee whose possessor is death.

The *Poetische Gedichte* attached to the *Mystische und sehr geheyme Sprueche* were more carefully composed expressions, a sampling, in effect, of the very large body of poetry that Beissel wrote. He was not, his critics, then and now, agree, an accomplished poet. He wrote too much, Oswald Seidensticker later wrote, and too clumsily. The former baker, he said, piled strophe on strophe as if kneading loaves of bread. And indeed his meters are often forced and rigid, his rhyming is occasionally obvious and clichéd, and the longer poetic compositions at times lose shape and coherence. But despite these and other weaknesses, he used poetry effectively to stress his principal theosophical themes, at times "with bursts of true poetic inspiration."

> His verse [a modern literary scholar writes] ranges from terse, clipped iambic dimeter to *Langzeilen* of up to seven accented syllables; from the elevated Alexandrine quatrain to the simple folksong strophe; from the short, pregnant epigrammatic couplet to the long lyric stanza.

And he could match sound with meaning in lilting wordplay (lost in translation):

> *Wir loben in Freuden, und lieben in Leiden /*
> *und leben auf Erden in himmlischer Freud.*

> (We praise in joy, and love in sorrow /
> and live on earth in heavenly joy.)[13]

What is particularly striking about all of these expressions, prosaic and poetic, is their extraordinary number.[14] Miller's two-part collection of Beissel's more extended prose writings, entitled *Deliciae Ephratenses* (1773) numbers 630 pages, but there is no count of his *Sprueche* in their many forms or of the "poetic verses" he composed. One can, however, at least guess at the number of hymns he wrote, co-wrote, or adapted from German sources. The faithful Miller reported that Beissel "composed not less than one thousand tunes for four voices . . . his printed hymns number 441."

But while producing the myriad *Sprueche*—the maxims, the spiritual sermons, the epistles, and the proverbs—Beissel did publish one book, of thirty-seven pages, which his critics then and now agree is the closest to a composed treatise he wrote and might be treated as such. Its original title was rather grand: *Göttliche Wunderschrift . . .* , but translated by Miller it became simply *A Dissertation on Man's Fall* (1765).

It is a work, Miller explained in a note to the reader, that can justly be termed "the wonderful discovery of the celestial *Weiblichkeit* (femality: female force) whereby are unsealed those sublime mysteries which lay hid in eternity." Beissel began to "unseal the wonderful arcana, . . . the amazing secrets," of his *Wunderschrift* autobiographically. He recalled "the days of my godly youth" lived in "superlative purity" but always probing, searching, against all resistance, "into the original being and life of all things," to find "how evil could proceed from that which was good from all eternity." He had struggled against his own male rebelliousness ("Good God! What tribulations had I to pass through") to find the lost virginity, the female aspect of God, Sophia, that existed before the time of evil. But his own self-will, "the firey will of man" continued to defeat him in his search for "the Sophianic and celestial femality or virginity." This led him to pry into the "mistery of the separation of both tinctures [*tincturen*, i.e., genders] which radiated out into the opposites of all creation (male and female, rough and smooth, etc.). In time his struggle was resolved when he understood the fall of the first created man.

At that point the narrative flow of the *Wunderschrift* begins, and what follows is a story, interrupted from time to time by asides, repetitions, interjections, obscure wording, admonitions, and exclamations, but a narrative nonetheless. It is the story of the essential struggle of humanity to recover the initial state of perfection when Adam, like God, was identified with the eternal spirit of Sophia, wisdom, and was an androgynous being. Once that state of androgynous perfection had been destroyed, all of life became a struggle for dominance between the male fiery force (*männliche Feuerleben*) of violence and power and heavenly femininity (*himmlische Weiblichkeit*). Man's fierce fire had dominated until Christ, the second Adam,

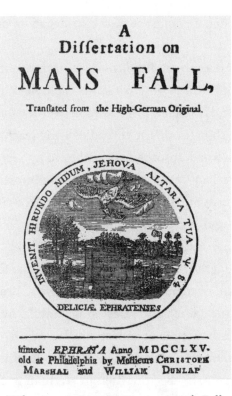

A
Diſſertation on

MANS FALL,

Tranſlated from the High-German Original.

Printed: *EPHRATA* Anno MDCCLXV. old at Philadelphia by Meſſieurs CHRISTOPH MARSHAL and WILLIAM DUNLAP

Title page, A Dissertation on Man's Fall.

who was both female and male, the one virginal man (*Jungfräulicher Mann*), was crucified. His flesh was sacrificed, but the wound in his side was an open entrance for the everlasting virgin Sophia, from whom mercy flows out for the salvation of mankind. In Christ the androgynous balance had been recovered. And it therefore became incumbent on mankind to search for the embrace with Christ, to whom only virgins can be betrothed.[15]

The bridal imagery is persistent here as it is in Beissel's other writings. The love of Christ, one modern commentator writes, was "so consuming [for Beissel] that one would forsake human marriage in exchange for total surrender to God." And indeed for Beissel mundane marriage was, as he entitled one of his earliest publications, *Das Zuchthaus fleischlicher Menschen* (1729) (*The Prison of Sensuous Men*). The devotees at Ephrata, like the followers of Kelpius years before, awaited the passionate embrace of the Bridegroom and prepared for the heavenly feast.

Such is the bare outline of the complex narrative in Beissel's *Wunderschrift.** But it is full of obscurities and complexities of language—at times, to a secular reader, impenetrable. Yet for those aware of the many strains of thought that it embodies—the teachings and experiences that Beissel had absorbed from the many sectarian traditions and practices he had encountered—it is a palimpsest that only the most learned and sympathetic can properly understand. So the most recent scholarly and sympathetic interpreter finds in the *Dissertation* no less than seven separate topics buried in Beissel's complex prose: the fall of man and the doctrine of God; creation and sin; ministry and authority; rebirth, overcoming "secret and mystic death" by baptism; the trinity; the true church and priesthood; and the final restoration of all creation to the holy state of androgyny.[16]

The *Dissertation* first appeared in Miller's English translation in 1765, but it had probably been written in German in the 1740s, a time when Beissel's talents had been fully released and his writings were emerging in profusion. In addition to all his major concerns with the search for knowledge of the divine and maintaining the integrity of Ephrata as the ultimate expression of his beliefs, Beissel encouraged, to an astonishing degree, the development and refinement of the arts.

Within the rigid structure of Ephrata's daily life, from dawn to the

---

* The above is based on a close reading of the *Dissertation* and Jeff Bach, *Voices of the Turtledoves* (University Park, PA., 2003), pp. 37–43. For a different interpretation, by Jan Stryz, based on the belief that Beissel's thought was "his own idiosyncratic version of alchemy" — that esoteric science not having been limited to physical objects but pertained, as well, at least by analogy, to spiritual and literary matters. Beissel had in fact been exposed to the alchemical thinking of the Rosicrucians, and his persistent references to bride and groom echo imagery derived not so much from Boehme and Gichtel as from the Rosicrucians' famous text *The Chemical Wedding of Christian Rosenkreutz.* "The connection between an allegorical wedding and the alchemical process had been explicitly mapped by the time [Beissel] was writing." Jan Styrz, "The Alchemy of the Voice at Ephrata Cloister," *Studies in American Esoterism* (2003); 134, 136–40.

small hours of the night, time was allowed not only for labor of various kinds but also for engagement in two schools for the development of the arts: a writing school and a singing school. The former concentrated on training in and production of elaborate forms of *fraktur* calligraphy and the copying of musical scores.

Ephrata did not invent the elaborate decorative art of *fraktur*, nor was it practiced only by them among the Pennsylvania Germans. It originated ages earlier as a folk art in Switzerland and the Rhineland, where the young Beissel may first have seen it. But the products of the Cloister were unique in their inventiveness, intricacy, lavish coloration, and symbolic content.

Fraktur was Gothic lettering "broken" (fractured) into its constituent parts and reconstructed with elaborate imagery of nature (tulips and other flowers, vines, fruits, trees) all intricately interwoven with swinging curves and intricate scrolls, and replete with religious symbols, especially that of the matching pair of turtledoves. The paired doves were the key image in all of Beissel's works, in part representing the soul's quest for direct contact with Christ, in part contrasting, in the doves' mournful cooing, with the brutality of carnal life, and in part recalling the legend that a turtledove, flying to a tree near the cross on which Christ hung, sang the soft prayerful "Kyrie, Kyrie, Kyrie," which became the first word of the Christian prayer *Kyrie Eleison* (Lord have mercy).[17]

But not all the symbols buried in the immense elaboration of *fraktur* lettering and border decorations were familiar, and many had esoteric meanings. Thus one finds in Ephrata's handbook of calligraphy, *Der Christen ABC* (1750), the masterwork of the gifted Sisters Anastasia and Efigenia, examples of wildly imaginative lettering alive with swirling curves and scrolls of floral designs. So crowded are the intricate configurations, so complex and obscure the symbols within the floral elaborations, that at times it is difficult to see what letter it is that is being decorated.

But for Beissel and his devotees such literalism was not the point.

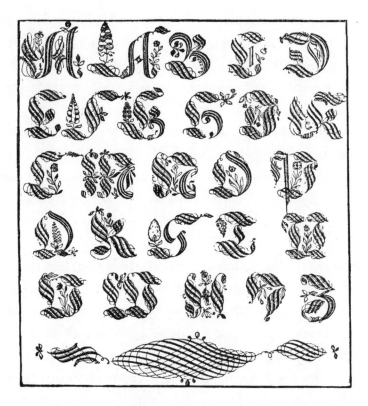

The fraktur *alphabet used in Ephrata's hymnbooks.*

For each scribe, an imaginative and beautiful letter was an expression of the search for God. No design was borrowed from another. Each had been born within the artist, who could spend years at work "as a means," the *Chronicon* said, "of sanctification to crucify their flesh." Bringing a design to completion was a form of spiritual rebirth. The results were evident for all to see. "The walls of all the rooms," a late visitor wrote, "including the meeting room, the chapels, the saals, and even the Kammers or dormitories, are hung and nearly covered with large sheets of elegant penmanship of ink-paintings . . . called in German *Fracktur-schrifften* [*sic*]."[18]

All of the brilliantly elaborated art of *fraktur* was brought to bear on the production of illuminated hymnals, which Beissel inspired and to which he devoted much of his own efforts. The hymnals, voluminous collections of hymns, were adapted—in part, but only in part—from European, mainly German, sources. They were prayerful supplications suffused with mystical Boehmist themes, emotional and erotic, searching for redemption from Jesus, Sophia, and divinity itself, and celebrating the blessings they enjoyed.

The hymnists profess their love of Christ, their renunciation of all earthly things, their blending of joy and suffering, and their passionate anticipation of the coming of the Lord. Images, symbols, and allegories abound, some ancient in origins, some devised within the Cloister, some transmitted to Ephrata by the local influences of Kelpius, Pastorius, and other Pietist groups. At their best the hymns, though not designed as poetry, are carefully constructed in meter and rhyme. Thus the stanza of Beissel's *Auf du meine Seele*, selected for its technical poetic qualities, especially its rhyme scheme (ab, ab, cc, dd), by a discerning modern scholar.

Loben will ich alle Tage,
loben will ich auch bey Nacht,
loben in der Niederlage,
loben, wann ich bin veracht:
loben, wann ich traurig geh,
loben, wann ich schier vergeh,
loben, wann ich nichts kann machen,
und nicht rahten meinen Sachen.

(I will praise [God] all the day,
I will praise him also by night,
Praise him in defeat,
Praise him when I am despised:
Praise him when I am depressed,
Praise him when I nearly expire,
Praise him, when I can do no more,
And make no more choices.)

Though mournful and full of cries of suffering, despair, and grief, the hymns are also often joyful and radiant with the blessing of song and singing itself. Thus:

> *Halleluja, Gloria! Singt zusamen, ruft! Ja! Ja!*
> (Hallelujah, Gloria! Sing together, shout, Yes! Yes!)
> *Drum singt mit Freuden die Psalmen und lieblichen Lieder*
> (Therefore sing with joy the psalms and lovely songs)[19]

The hymnals are multidimensional, combining hymns with the musical scores to which the words relate, interwoven with blocks or borders of *fraktur* designs and lettering. The result are pages, whole hymnals, of brilliant designs, visually and musically, in effect a kind of provincial *Gesamtkunstwerk* that became famous then and later for the complex beauty it achieved. Perhaps the greatest of the hymnals, known as the Ephrata Codex, or the Franklin Codex (1747), was a two-part gift of the cloister to Beissel.* One part of the work was produced by the brethren, another by the sisters. "Both put their most skillful members to the task," the *Chronicon* recorded. Three of the brothers worked at it for three-quarters of a year. Their part contained "about 500 tunes for five voices; everything was artistically ornamented with the pen, and every

---

* The fortunes of this extraordinary product of Ephrata proved to be remarkable in themselves. Miller sent it together with some papers, in a box, as a gift to Benjamin Franklin, who saw it when he returned to London after a trip to Ireland. He admired it and for some reason lent it to John Wilkes, who apparently returned it. It then disappeared from view until it turned up a century and a half later in an auction in New York in 1927, "the property of a London consignor." It was bought by Gabriel Wells, a well-known antiquarian, through whom eventually it was deposited at the Library of Congress, where it has remained. It was one of the "actual manuscripts" of Ephrata that the Librarian of Congress showed Thomas Mann. "There they were," Mann later wrote, "spread out on a table before me, and I saw with my own almost incredulous eyes the actual productions of this naïve and dogmatic innovator in music." Thomas Mann, *Story of a Novel: The Genesis of* Doctor Faustus (New York, 1961), 121–22; Patrick Erben, *A Harmony of the Spirits: Translation and the Language of Community in Early Pennsylvania* (Chapel Hill, N.C., 2012), 195–96; Martin, *Ephrata Cloister*, 128–135.

A page from the Ephrata Codex, now in the Library of Congress.

leaf had its own head-piece." Beissel's name was in the front, "skillfully designed in Gothic text; around it was a text of blessing added by each Brother." The sisters' contribution, which is apparently lost, was simpler "but something wonderful shone forth from it." In all, the manuscript work of 935 pages contained 1,018 hymn texts. It is, a modern scholar writes, "the most magnificent manuscript to come from the Cloister. . . . [Its] beauty no description or facsimile can adequately portray."[20]

Pomegranate design from the Zionitischer Weyrauchs Hügel *hymnbook of 1739. Pomegranates are prominent in the Cloister's elaborate floral designs, as are other symbols in the print, especially the painted doves.*

But there were other major hymnals, fourteen in all, not as aesthetically grand as the Ephrata Codex but more available to the public. They circulated widely and were of peculiar importance to the intellectual life of the community. Two were most notable: the *Zionitischer Weyrauchs Hügel oder Myrrhen Berg . . . (The Zionitic Hill of Insence or Mountain of Myrrh . . .)* (1639), was the first book printed in Gothic type in America and was unique in including "hymns, which the awakened in Germany brought to light." No less than 692 hymns are included, 372 European, to be sung to the tunes indicated on the lines above the texts. The *Weyrauchs Hügel* was popular when it first appeared from Christopher Sauer's press in Germantown and remained popular for decades thereafter. For as the extended title explained, it included "many kinds of actions of love of God-sanctified souls, which are set forth in many and various spiritual and lovely songs [*geistlichen und lieblichen Liedern*]."

Das
Gesäng
Der einsamen und verlassenen
Turtel-Taube
Nemlich   der   Christlichen
Kirche,
Oder geistliche u. Erfahrungs-volle Leidens u. Liebes-Gethöne,
Als darinnen beydes die Vorkost der neuen Welt als
auch die darzwischen vorkommende Creutzes = und Leidens =
Wege nach ihrer Würde dargestellt, und in
geistliche Reimen gebracht
Von einem Friedsamen und nach der
stillen Ewigkeit wallenden
Pilger.
Und nun
Zum Gebrauch der Einsamen und Verlassenen zu Zion
gesammlet und ans Licht gegeben

E P H R A T A.
Drucks der Brüderschafft im Jahr 1 7 4 7.

Title page of the Turtel-Taube *hymnal, one of the major publications of the
Cloister.*

Even more popular among the hymnals and far more frequently
reprinted, excerpted, and referred to was *Das Gesäng der einsamen
und verlassenen Turtel-Taube, nemlich der Christlichen Kirche* (1747)
(*Songs of the Lonely and Forsaken Turtle-dove, namely the Christian
Church*). All of the 276 hymns and the 3 choral works included were
original compositions of the Cloister members; 212 of the hymns were
written by Beissel himself. The work was printed by the Cloister's

newly created press, on paper manufactured at Ephrata and bearing its emblematic watermark. The hymnal's local character is identified in the title by the symbol of the turtledove. The book was divided into six titled sections, which reappear in different forms in later editions. But the first edition of the *Turtel-Taube* is unique, for its first nineteen pages of introductory material—a *Vorbericht* and a *Vorrede* (foreword and preface)—together with the epilogue constitute the introduction to Beissel's theory of music, his process of composition, and especially his principles of harmony.

It is in music that Beissel—untrained in musical theory, in composition, in harmonization, in polyphony—found his greatest spiritual satisfaction. It is for his music and for the singers he so assiduously trained that he was most renowned in his own time; and it would be for his music that he would be memorialized, two centuries later.

For a modern secular reader it takes a great leap of imagination to grasp the meaning of music to Beissel. It was for him not simply an aesthetic pleasure or a graceful accompaniment to the hymns he wrote. Song, he had learned from Boehme, from Kelpius, and from the Philadelphians and other radical Pietists, was a language in itself, a divine, sacral language that transcended the many mundane languages of humanity, all of which inexorably distorted God's word. Even the Bible, though holy scripture, was—and as a creation of men's words could only be—a deficient rendering of the divine discourse. That could be found only in the deity's angelic world, which was suffused with songs of absolute purity to which mankind, when in a state of immaculate sanctity, might aspire. Like Kelpius before him, he thought of music as an escape from the multitude of clangorous languages of the mortal world, from bitter interdenominational struggles, and from the everyday turmoils of gross humanity. Music—elevated voices: songs and singing—was a language that led one to divinity itself. It was a way of recovering the single *Natursprache* that all of mankind had enjoyed until, at Babel, God had reproved men's unholy ambitions by scattering them across the face of the earth to live forever in a confusion of tongues.

But more than that: Beissel's passion for vocal music derived from the deepest sources of his mystical theosophy. For eternal ages, he explained in the foreword of the *Turtel-Taube*, the holy church has remained concealed in God, but ultimately, in these last days, it had "shown forth herself anew with vigor and strength as in the early ages." The holy church, through Christ, at whose baptism had descended "the heavenly Dove," had from time to time "drawn souls unto herself" who remained steadfast to enjoy the church's "renewing, revising, and sanctifying power" and who had discovered there concealed "all the wonders and powers of future glory.

> After the same manner in which God, reveals, forward into eter-
> nity through the Church, all his mysteries, it also remains for
> him to receive from the Church, praise, and the glorifying of
> his name, unto everlasting ages. In accordance with this, it was
> ordained by the spirit of the Church, or heavenly dove, that the
> talent of singing should be added unto spiritual services, and be
> employed in outspreading the praise of God unto endless ages.

God, Beissel wrote, "having ordained that through the Church his name should be glorified, there were required, voices, hymns and music written for the use of the singers." But hymns and music devoted to the worship of God could not be sought in the unsanctified mind but only in the abilities that God bestows. All one could do was renew one's "diligence in practicing self denial." "So much then as we make it our object to gain a knowledge of Church music and to improve the talent of singing, so much was the toil and labor to be overcome. In this way we were brought to see the loftiness of heavenly things." One can think, Beissel concluded, of this vocal spiritual work as a "field of flowers grown forth of many different colors and of various fragrance, as they were produced by the spirit of the Church, out of the *Mysterio* of God."

160   Illuminating History

These views persisted. Twenty years after Beissel's death Miller, still vigorous and well informed at age seventy-six, explained the cloister's music to his correspondent Franklin. Vocal music, he informed Ephrata's early printer, by then a celebrated icon of the Enlightenment, is a study and science inferior to none in all the world, and its rules are as universal and absolute as those of mathematics. It had been abused by such composers as Handel, he wrote, with their instrumental and other "theatrical diversions," which have "greatly hurted [song's] heavenly sweetness by their curl'd [*sic*] compositions when they . . . sometimes dwell two minutes on one syllable which is a great nousance in music. Further it is a grand mistake in a concert when all sorts of instruments are joined with vocal music . . . for thereby the dignity of the human voice is eclipsed." The only instrument consistent with vocal music, he added, was Franklin's own "new invented glass-organ." The main point, he wrote his esteemed friend (who had recently made him a member of the Philosophical Society), was that

> the human voice is a most noble instrument by which a man may reveal his most intimate recesses, even as God Himself made known by his eternal word. Many ways have been contriv'd to refine the voice for singing, and for this purpose castrates were introduced, for it was supposed that human cohabitation hurts the voice. . . . I should think the convents would afford the best voices without violating nature.

Thus Miller to Franklin in 1786. In the same year, in the *Chronicon*, he made the point more forcefully:

> Above all, must it be remembered that the spirit of this exalted art, because it is a pure, chaste, and virtuous spirit, suffers no unclean, polluted and sinful love for woman which so inflames and agitates the blood of the young as completely to undo them

in mind, heart, and soul; whilst in the more mature it awakens excessive desire after the dark things of the world.

It was entirely reasonable to say this, the *Chronicon* insisted, "for who does not know that carnal intercourse stains not only the soul but also weakens the body and renders the voice coarse and rough, so that the senses of him must be very blunt who cannot distinguish a virgin from a married woman by her voice. Much concerning the fall of man can be explained from the voice."[21]

All the Germans who had come to Pennsylvania had brought with them some version of their colloquial music, though not commonly associated with a passion for celibacy. As early as 1727, well before the founding of Ephrata, Beissel had conducted antiphonal choral singing at a general meeting of the Pietists in Pennsylvania. In the years thereafter he led his cloister to elevate their musical inheritance to a form of worship bound by rules he devised to enable singers to reach a suitable state of perfection. For this there were special conditions which, under the *Vorsteher*'s guidance, had to be met. The spirit of song, he insisted, needs to be "served in cleanliness." The singers must be pure themselves to approach the purity of angelic singers, and they must appear to be pure by performing in gowns of white. And as they reached for "angelic and heavenly" sounds, he taught them to restrain "the wants of the body" by reducing its requirements to a minimum, "so that the voice may become angelic, heavenly, pure, and clear and not rough and harsh, [producing] . . . grunting and gasping." Diet was crucial. *Meat* and other products of animals were to be avoided; also *milk*, which causes heaviness; *cheese*, which produces heat and the desire for forbidden things; *butter*, which makes one indolent and dull and discourages the need to sing; *eggs*, which arouse "capricious cravings"; *honey*, which makes one cheerful but does not make for clear voices. On the other hand, *bread* made of wheat or buckwheat is excellent, as are *potatoes*, *beets*, and other *tubers*, though *beans* are too heavy and arouse impure desires. And as for *drink*, only pure well water would do, perhaps made into a soup when a little bread is added. But any cooking of water that changed it "by unseeming art into a sort of delicacy is to be considered as sinful, vain, and an abuse." Important as diet was, however, it had nothing to do with the strength needed to achieve godly virtue. If it did, one "would wish to be completely liberated from [the need for food] and live a completely Enochian, supernatural and spiritual life."*

It was with these aspirations, conditions, and admonitions that Beissel began his direction of the singing school, a school chiefly for the sisters. It started around 1740, initially under the direction of a householder named Ludwig Blum, "a master-singer . . . versed in composition." But it was quickly taken over by Beissel, with the encouragement of the sisters, who promised to "steal the whole secret of the schoolmaster [Blum] and hand it over to him." Beissel's engagement with the singing school became passionate. It fulfilled his deepest urge to share in celestial harmonies. His fierce devotion to it seems to have had no limits. Sessions of the school, the *Chronicon* reported, "lasted four hours, and ended at midnight," when the usual worship service began. In these exhausting rehearsals, the *Chronicon* recorded, "both master and students appeared in white habits." The *Vorsteher*, "animated by the spirit of eternity, kept the School in great strictness and every fault was sharply censured. . . . At times he scolded for one or two hours in succession . . . and at such times he looked really majestic, so that even his countenance glistened." But the result was commonly tears on the part of the women and wrath from the participating brethren. The sisters believed the quarreling and tension were due to the differences of sex, and they threatened to leave the school. But the egregious Anastasia, always close to Beissel, convinced the sisters to relent, and the school continued as before. To mark the occa-

---

* "Enochian" refers to a magic cult largely developed by John Dee, the famed Elizabethan mathematician, natural philosopher, cartographer, and student of the occult. The casual reference here is one of many indications of the occult in Beissel's thinking.

sion, a choir of sisters sang a five-part hymn, *Gott wir kommen Dir entgegen* (God, we come to meet Thee).

To organize the school, Beissel divided the participants into five balanced choirs, each with a soprano, who usually carried the melody, an alto, a tenor (female), and two basses. The sisters when alone were divided into three choirs—upper, middle, and lower. At love feasts the sisters sang antiphonally "up and down the table," each part entering on cue, allowing for solo interventions as designed. They sang of prophecies, of the restoration of the prelapsarian Adam, of "heavenly virginity"—all in accordance with the principles of harmony that Beissel himself had devised. Often, in the major performances, the antiphony was dramatized by the singers' locations: the men seated in the *Saal*, the women responding unseen in the gallery. The women's voices were crucial. In fact, most of Beissel's songs and chorals were sung by women. In his seven-part songs, five of the voices were women's. The higher their voices, the more lyrical in lofty tessitura, the closer they came to the sounds of the angels that swirled in Beissel's mystico-musical imaginings, the closer to the language of God.

It was to explain in detail the sacral beauties of song and singing in approaching the heavenly spheres that Beissel published, as a preface to the first edition of the *Turtel-Taube* hymnal, a Treatise on Music.* Written "in a German," one of his translators wrote, "so peculiar as to almost deserve to be called a distinct dialect," the treatise begins with a discourse on the "God-given art of song," the "sublime and divine art [which] contains the purest and noblest spirit of eternal heavenly virginity." It then turns to a technical explanation of Beissel's principles of composition, chiefly his rules for harmonizing melodies, which Miller, years later in the *Chronicon*, wrote—optimistically—were so simple

---

* Beissel's title: *A Short, Yet Very Thorough, Description of the Manner and Make-up of the Heaven-sent, Sublime and Divine—as well as Very Useful—Gift of the Art of Song, Greatly Ennobled and Highly Ranked by God, Which is Useful, as Well as Necessary, in God's Church.* "Johann Conrad Beissel and the Music of the Ephrata Cloister," trans. Lloyd G. Blakely, *Journal of Research in Music Education* 15, no. 2 (1967): 126.

"that even a child could understand them." In fact, Miller's summary of Beissel's treatise is a clearer guide to Beissel's principles of composition than the *Vorsteher*'s own words.

Beissel composed the music, Miller explained, according to rules of his own making. Each of the seven notes in the scale, Beissel believed, had special characteristics. And indeed that is the first thing any would-be singer would have to learn. Knowing this, Beissel would examine the hymn to be set to music and decide on the right, the "natural" key. The key note determined the two other notes that went with it most "consonantly"; then these, along with the octave, became the "master" notes of the composition. Each piece would start and end with this master chord, with specific rules about which master notes should be used by the tenor, alto, and bass voices to create the desired harmony, the sopranos always carrying the melody. The other four notes in the scale were the "servant" notes. There were rules about which of these subordinate notes were to be allocated to the other voices. All of these rules were said to be put into charts that any composer could quickly use to check for correct harmony.

How the pitch was established without an instrument is not clear; perhaps Beissel had perfect pitch. There were no time signatures. Beissel selected the meter "as the nature of the thing required." The scores were barred, but irregularly, so that the music was free flowing, with musical emphasis on significant words. The main words of the texts in fact dominated the structure of the music. The initial theme was commonly repeated, fragmented, or expanded, then recovered at the end. The number of voices could vary within a single composition, and for all his austerity, Beissel introduced ornamentation: dotted rhythms, syncopation, rests in the melodic line, key changes, and shifting contrasts between full choirs, solos, duets, and trios. Beissel's own compositions were most often written for four-part harmonies, though often the melodies themselves became lost to the listener in the dominance of long extended notes and rich harmony, much of which might have sounded as if being sung falsetto.

All this, and Beissel's outpouring of musical compositions, did not happen at once. Ephrata's music developed over a period of years. Much of the early music, before the arrival of Ludwig Blum, appears to have been simply melodic tunes, much of it probably sung in unison. Thereafter the music was divided into parts, and complexity became common. With the devising of his system of harmonization, Beissel as a composer grew in confidence, and his works became longer, more ingenious and distinctive, and more satisfying as an approach to "the sweet consonances of the angelic choirs."

How original was his music—his hymns and extended chorales? How limited, how effective? Many of the original melodies were derivative, drawn from old German chorales and songs, from the once popular Protestant psalter of Ambrosius Lobwasser (1573), the pious hymnody of Johann Freylinghausen, and the vernacular *geistliche Lieder* and *Volkslieder*. In time, under the influence of Pietism and mystical lore of the early seventeenth century, Ephrata's music became more subjective, more vividly erotic, conveying more of the passions that dominated Beissel's celibate life. So the "Song of Songs" (*Das Lied der Liederen welches ist Salomons*), with its passionate celebration of sexual love, was set to music at least twice.* But not everything was derivative or traditional: some of Ephrata's music, ingenious blends of tradition and contemporary Pietism, were worked into original themes. And almost everything Beissel composed, from his earliest tunes of childlike simplicity to the most extended multivocal chorales, was erratic in meter as he matched notes to emphatic words of his text. Further, his harmonic scoring, while efficient, was rigid (the same master note would always form the same chord) and could only have been a constraint on his musical imagination.

---

* The opening verses of the "Song of Songs" appear in the hymnal *Paradisches Wunderspiel* ("Mochte er mich nur küssen mit einigen von den küssen seines mundes dann seine liebe ist lieblicher dann wein" [Let him kiss me with the kisses of his mouth for thy love is better than wine]) decorated with a floral depiction of the paired turtledoves. The illustration dominates the page and secures the association of the biblical text with the music of Ephrata. Erben, *Harmony of the Spirits*, 227.

Yet his music, an early biographer wrote, "the outpourings of religious enthusiasts whose nervous systems had been wrought up to a high pitch by incessant vigils, fastings, and an abstemious mode of life," was effective—startlingly effective, especially as Charles Brewer noted, when sung in the middle of the night, when outside sounds were at a minimum.[22] Everyone who heard Ephrata's choral singing—and it attracted listeners from everywhere in the surrounding area—was gripped by what they heard. Some were ecstatic, some felt uplifted. The sophisticated Anglican preacher Jacob Duché visited the cloister in 1771 and reported that the music of the women's choir

> had little or no air or melody; but consisted of simple, long notes, combined in the richest harmony. . . . The performers sat with their heads reclined, their countenances solemn and dejected, their faces pale and emaciated from their manner of living, their clothing exceeding white and . . . their music such as thrilled to the very soul. I almost began to think myself in the world of spirits, and that the objects before me were ethereal. In short, the impression this scene made upon my mind continued strong for many days, and I believe, will never be wholly obliterated.

A later writer, William Fahnestock, steeped in the lore of Ephrata, recalled that the choir's tones "imitate very soft instrumental music, conveying a softness and devotion almost superhuman to the auditor." The singers, he wrote, scarcely opened their mouths or moved their lips, "which throws the voice up to the ceiling, which is not high, and the tones, which seem to be more than human, . . . appear to be entering from above, and hovering over the heads of the assembly."

One can only imagine what Beissel felt as he listened to the high, hushed soprano notes sung by the emaciated celibates he had trained, to tunes he had written, in harmonies of his own devising. Had he thrilled to the possibility that for a few moments he had heard the voices of angels and thereby touched the heavenly spheres? If so, those moments must have been the climactic passage of his tumultuous life which could never be renewed or re-created by a younger generation. For he well knew, as Miller would so sadly say to Franklin after Beissel's death, that they of the Cloister "shall not propagate the monastic life upon the posterity since we have no successors, and the genius of the Americans is bound another way."

Ephrata was the great and unique achievement of a sensitive, imaginative, ambitious, and charismatic young tradesman tossed up by the upheavals of a desolated Germany to create a small heaven on earth where spiritual perfection might be reached by the zeal and passion of those in love with God. Beissel was a genius of sorts—indeed a provincial progenitor of Mann's Leverkühn—whose talents and soaring aspirations emerged in an open, unencumbered land. So Miller, looking hopefully beyond the mortality of Beissel and his celibate community, concluded the *Chronicon Ephratense* with these words of gratitude, which would have parallels through generations of American life:

> because this country at last, after much opposition, received [Beissel] who had been driven out of his fatherland, and granted him and his whole family complete liberty of conscience, therefore it will always be blessed and be a nursery of God, which shall bear him much fruit, for the promise given to Abraham must be fulfilled: "In thy seed shall all generations of the earth be blessed."

V

The Hutchinsons' Network and Beyond

THE CONTOURS OF ATLANTIC HISTORY

The idea of Atlantic history—the concept of a distinct Atlantic world, with its own life, involving the peoples of four continents—has been with me as long as I have been studying history. I first wrote about it in an article, "Communications and Trade: The Atlantic in the Seventeenth Century," published in 1953 in the *Journal of Economic History*. By the end of the seventeenth century, I wrote, the Atlantic region had become "a single great trading area [whose] economic enterprise created not only a crisscrossing web of transoceanic traffic but also a cultural community that came to form the western periphery of European civilization." What had provoked this view was a small finding in the research for the work then in progress on the New England merchants in the seventeenth century. "In the middle years of the seventeenth century and forward, a number of European trading families spread out over the Atlantic world," and I cited examples that had come to hand: the Povey family's trading network, with kin in London, Jamaica, and Barbados; the Winthrops, based in England but trading through kin in Massachusetts, Rhode

Island, Connecticut, Tenerife in the Canaries, and Antigua in the West Indies. Of one Anglo-American family network I knew a great deal, and I described it in some detail.

> The Hutchinson family trading unit was based upon the continuous flow of manufactures exported from London by the affluent Richard Hutchinson to his brothers Samuel and Edward and his nephews Elisha and Eliakim in Boston, Massachusetts. They, together with Thomas Savage, who had married Richard's sister, retailed the goods in the Bay area and, through middlemen, sold also to the inland settlers. They conducted a large trade with the West Indies, sending provisions and cattle in exchange for cotton and sugar which they sold for credit on London. This West Indian trade of the Hutchinsons was largely handled for them by Peleg Sanford of Portsmouth, Rhode Island, whose mother was another sister of Richard and who was, hence, cousin and nephew of the Boston merchants of the family. Peleg, who had started his career as a commercial agent in the West Indies, exported their horses and provisions to Barbados where they were sold by his brothers, the Barbadian merchants William and Elisha Sanford.

And thereafter I explored such relationships as far as I could in this small publication.

I was well aware that I was dealing with obscure documents, however suggestive, and local stories mainly of the North Atlantic trading circuits. But a sense of the full dimensions of Atlantic history had been stimulated by my reactions to reading Fernand Braudel's famous book *The Mediterranean and the Mediterranean World in the Age of Philip II* (1949). Like so many others, I was overwhelmed by Braudel's erudition, his control of a vast polylingual literature, apparently covering all major aspects of human existence in the Mediterranean world in the sixteenth century, and his effort to conceive what his colleague Lucien Febvre called "a revolution in the mode of conceiving history." In fact, it had been Febvre's rather feverish review of *The Mediterranean* that had drawn me into the excitement that greeted the book. It was, Febvre wrote, "une autre histoire." (The French seem to be adept in producing "autres histoires"; Pierre Nora's is the latest.) In 1950, in the *Revue historique*, Febvre was more specific. Braudel's book, he declared, was not merely a "professional masterpiece." "It marks," he said, "the dawn of a new time, of that I am certain." And he concluded with this charge to youth:

> Read, re-read, and meditate on this excellent book. . . . Make it your companion. What you will learn of things, new to you, about the world of the sixteenth century is incalculable. But what you will learn simply about man, about his history and about history itself, its true nature, its methods and purposes—you cannot imagine in advance.[1]

With this Braudel clearly agreed, and he expanded on his apparent transformation of the study of history first in an article in the *Revue économique*, and then in several commentaries that followed. But when I read the book I discovered that Braudel's great transformation was to have described the Mediterranean world of the sixteenth century in three separate dimensions of time, in separate sections: first, events that move slowly, glacially, geological in time; then structures and groups that move in shorter periods of time (i.e., social and economic structures); and finally the short, quick nervous oscillations in time (i.e., politics, wars, and everything else). This way of organizing a total historical world was certainly new, but to me it seemed schematic, essentially static. The separation of events by speed of movements in a given time and place seemed to me to destroy any sense of actuality. Did the "short, quick, nervous oscillations" of men in action have no organic connections to "structural" events or to geological movements? The book was panoramic and wonderfully descriptive, but I could see no comprehensive, regional development, no essential change, or transformation. I thought the core of history was missing, and I said this, and more, in a review of the book, "Braudel's Geo-history—A Reconsideration," published in the *Journal of Economic History* in 1951. The review was noticed in France and was twice reprinted there, but mainly to show that the "Anglos" didn't get the message.

But if I failed to appreciate Braudel's schematization of history, I did deeply respond to his grasp of the Mediterranean region as a historical entity in itself, and to the breadth of his vision. I could imagine a future history of that region's movements in time, its evolution, and its evanescence from what it had been in the time of Philip II. The history of the Atlantic world, in the three centuries from the time of the discoveries, could similarly be seen as a great event in motion that laid the basis, as it evolved, for the advent of the Western world as we now know it.

I did not write about this further until many years later, but I was aware of the emerging geopolitics of the Atlantic concept, from Roosevelt and Churchill's Atlantic Charter, to the Marshall Plan, the North American Treaty Organization, and a plethora of nongovernmental organizations throughout the Western world in support of the Atlantic Alliance. There was even a journal, I discovered, *The Atlantic Community Quarterly* (founded 1963) devoted to monitoring the entire Atlantic community as it evolved.

All of this geopolitics was reflected in the awareness of historians. By the 1960s the term *Atlantic*, with implications it had not had before, was beginning to be commonly used by historians, and its meaning explored. In 1960 Frederick Tolles made the connections explicit.

> We first became familiar with the idea of the Atlantic Community as a strategic concept during the Second World War, but the Atlantic Community as a cultural fact was a matter of almost everyday experience to English-speaking people in the seventeenth and eighteenth centuries. [But] historians ... have only recently begun to treat the Atlantic civilization as a single unit.

"I don't know," he wrote,

> whether the term "Atlantic culture" . . . is yet an expression in
> common use or not. But if it is not, it should be. For it seems to
> me as useful and necessary a term as the indispensable phrase
> "Mediterranean culture," which we use to denominate the civili-
> zation of the ancient world.[2]

Tolles's interests centered in British North America, but the same
awareness had been developing in Europe.

In 1947 Jacques Godechot, at the University of Toulouse, made his
first tentative foray into Atlantic history in his *Histoire de l'Atlantique*.
"The history of the Atlantic is not . . . an absurdity," he wrote somewhat defensively; in fact, it illuminates the history of everything to the
east of it and particularly the history of modern France. He concluded
with thoughts "toward an Atlantic civilization," a theme developed
further by the Belgian historian Jacques Pirenne, whose *Grands cou-
rants de l'histoire universelle* included a section entitled "The Atlantic Ocean Forms an Interior Sea Around Which Western Civilization
Developed." By 1950 such references by European historians multiplied rapidly, in publications by V. M. Godinho in Portugal; by Max
Silberschmidt in Zurich, by Pierre and Huguette Chaunu in Paris; and
then decisively and elaborately by the influential Belgian medievalist
Charles Verlinden in his essay "Les origines coloniales de la civilisa-
tion atlantique" in the first volume (1953) of the trilingual *Journal of
World History*.

It was shortly thereafter, in 1954–55, that a landmark was reached
in the development of this emerging literature. It happened that
Jacques Godechot was a visiting research fellow that year at Princeton University, where he collaborated with his host, Robert Palmer.
Both were engaged in large-scale projects spanning the nations
of the Western world, Palmer on the first volume of his *Age of the
Democratic Revolution: A Political History of Europe and America*,

1760–1800 (1959–64), Godechot on his *La grande nation: l'expansion révolutionnaire de la France dans le monde, 1789–1799* (two volumes, 1956). Both projects involved the Atlantic world as a historical entity. Their interests converging, they collaborated in preparing a joint paper entitled "Le probléme de l'Atlantique" for presentation at the Tenth International History Congress in Rome. In it, the two historians raised the question of how best to conceive of the Atlantic phenomenon, whether there was *one* Atlantic civilization or more, whether it had at its foundation the "idées maitresses" of Judeo-Christianity, Roman law, and Greek reason, and whether after the pan-Atlantic affinities of the eighteenth century and despite their common culture, America and Europe had grown apart.

Though the paper had broad political and ideological implications, it was mainly didactic and academic, and was suffused with an air of discovery. The authors were therefore shocked by the acerb, even angry reception the paper received at the congress. Some commentators said it was too philosophical to be history, others that it was a mere response to Soviet policy and would fade away, still others that it was "a step towards one world." A young Marxist denounced it top to bottom for obscuring economic developments and for asserting that America and Western Europe had developed toward freedom while the East had not. He hoped that no such subject would ever be heard of at any future congress. The authors responded in different ways: Godechot rather defensively, Palmer more aggressively. Thirty-five years later Palmer was still explaining the responses at the congress. The underlying source of the animosity to the paper, he wrote, had been that "a certain French national self-image was offended. We were thought to downgrade the importance and uniqueness of the French Revolution."

I had read Palmer and Godechot's paper shortly after it was published in 1957 and the objections at the congress as well. For me the identity and conceptual usefulness of the history of the Atlantic region had been strongly reinforced and some of the vital questions related to it had been posed. In the years that followed I could only dabble at the edges of the paper's themes and work them silently into current writing, until in the 1990s I found my way back to it as the core of a major project that would occupy me for at least fifteen years. It was well under way when in 1996 my paper, "The Idea of Atlantic History" appeared in the Dutch journal *Itinerario*.

I had no delusions of being an Atlanticist Braudel. Quite aside from lacking the requisite languages and control of related disciplines, from anthropology to zoology, I disagreed with Braudel's time-dimensional, static approach to history. And I was amused to think of what my fate might have been as a would-be Braudelian if I fell under the master's disapproval, as had Pierre Chaunu. Braudel denounced Chaunu's eleven-volume *Séville et l'Atlantique* because it was not only un-Braudelian but *deliberately* un-Braudelian. Its purpose, Braudel wrote, was "not at all the same as mine." Chaunu's monumental research had been too narrow, Braudel declared, and his multivolume book had been too hastily written. "If he had submitted his text to me, what nice arguments [*belles disputes*] we would have had."

I didn't need any arguments, *belles* or otherwise. I knew my own limitations and the likely disinterest of my own generation, even those at work on discrete monographic studies such as those included in the John Hopkins University's program of the 1960s on Atlantic history and culture. Their books were valuable, but they lay apart, unique in their local contexts, unrelated to any overriding common concept. I knew that I could not develop the large-scale, integrated regional subject alone, nor could any individual historian, even working with a team of researchers. It would be the work of a generation to describe the multicultural, economic, and political networks that bound the peoples of the Atlantic world together. At this point what could best be done would be to bring the concept of an Atlantic world into common historical discourse—to create an awareness of its dimensions and thus to elevate the vision of specialist historians to the larger world of which their work was a part. I needed a way of bringing together young historians working on related Atlantic themes in such a way that, as Lara

Putnam put it, they would recognize "events we ... explained in terms of local dynamics are revealed to be above-water fragments of ... submarine unities."[3] I knew how deeply absorbed one becomes digging deep in archival research, and how relieved one feels when local subjects are suddenly seen in broader contexts and acquire new meaning at a higher plane of generality. I knew I could at least do something myself to help bring together some of the events of the evolving Atlantic world and at least suggest its historical contours—and did, in *Atlantic History: Concepts and Contours* (2005) and in the introduction to *Soundings in Atlantic History: Latent Structures and Intellectual Currents, 1500–1830* (2009).

But it was something broader and intergenerational that I was after, something to bring the subject into general prominence, to engage the imaginations of the rising generation—something that would ultimately render the concept of an Atlantic world a commonplace, a silent assumption, of historians in any of the four continents, and something quite different from the wildly burgeoning field of global history. As I later wrote, global history and Atlantic history are very different. Global history, the lead writer of the new, innovative *Journal of Global History* (2006) explained, is the study of connections and comparisons "across continents, ocean and countries over very long spans of time ... for moral purposes, connected to the needs of a globalizing world" and leading to the creation of "meta-narratives that might ... deepen our understanding of diversity and scale up our consciousness of [the] human condition." The studies that have appeared in the journal, scattered across many areas of the globe and time periods, do follow that description in one way or another. But they are related to each other only abstractly by degrees of similarity in scope and scale. This is very different from the conception, structure, goals, and purposes of Atlantic history, which is the history of the multitudes of networks that bound the four Atlantic continents together into a historical entity, the stages of whose growth and evanescence can be traced.

The Atlantic region was never isolated, never wholly autonomous, without contacts with the greater world. Spanish commerce reached, tentatively, west into the Philippines and China, and Spain's rule in the western hemisphere was part of an empire that was centered deep in eastern Europe. But the dynamics of the Atlantic region were not driven by global forces. Like the earlier Mediterranean world, of which so much has been written, the Atlantic region had its own histori-cal identity, its unique contours, and its own interior propulsions. In time—with the end of imperialism in the Americas, the demise of the slave trade, and the transformation of the European economy—the region's integrity would be transformed and would become part of a greater system, a global system, which it had helped define.

The result was "The International Seminar on the History of the Atlantic World, 1500–1825," founded at Harvard in 1995 and active until 2013.*

Funded by the Mellon Foundation, with the specific support of the sociologist Harriet Zuckerman, then serving as the foundation's project officer for research in the humanities, the Seminar began cau-tiously as a one-year experiment, then advanced in stages, scrutinized annually. It had been carefully planned. Young historians at the start of their careers who gave evidence of interest in an Atlantic subject were invited to apply for admission. The meetings would convene at Harvard annually for ten days or two weeks each summer to dis-cuss a broad aspect of Atlantic history announced in advance. Each member would contribute a paper containing original research on the announced theme. The meetings were in session morning and after-noon on weekdays and chaired by senior scholars, specialists in the seminar's topic, drawn ultimately from seventy-six universities spread widely across the United States. The fortunate accidents of personal

---

* The term *seminar* is used throughout in two senses: when capitalized, it refers to the project as a whole; when not, it refers to individual seminar meetings.

travel plans made it possible for senior scholars from twelve European universities to participate as session chairs. The discussions were expected to be, and were, intense. One member wrote that the Seminar proved to be a "history boot camp." Another wrote that "the rigor of the Seminar meant the time in Boston could never be mistaken for a New England vacation."

In all, over the years 366 young historians participated in the seminar meetings and submitted papers. They were a very mixed group. Forty-three percent of the participants were female. They outnumbered men in three seminars; in seven they made up 45 percent or more of the groups' memberships, and they constituted 65 percent of the seminar of 2009, devoted to the history of science and medicine, and their backgrounds were equally diverse. Of the 168 women whose nationality can be established, only 43 percent were natives of the United States. The rest were citizens of eighteen nations from Latin America, Western Europe, and Africa.

The American members had done or were doing their doctoral studies at 162 American universities (61 in the East, 26 in the Midwest, 48 in the South, and 27 in the West); six had or would have doctorates from British or Canadian universities. The foreign scholars had done their advanced studies at 16 universities in Europe, Latin America, and Africa and at 43 American universities. Ten of the Seminar members were African American, and there were five Black scholars from Canada, Brazil, Jamaica, and Bermuda, as well as three from Africa. In the course of the 15 seminar meetings, 37 papers were presented on Black history (slavery, the Atlantic slave trade, the "Black Atlantic," comparative slavery, miscegenation, and emancipation). Of the Hispanics in the seminar meetings, 40 were native to 10 Latin American countries and Puerto Rico, of whom 21 were studying in U.S. universities; 3 were doctoral candidates in England and France; 6 were Hispanics native to the United States, and there were 6 from the Iberian Peninsula.

The diversity of the members' personal backgrounds and academic training proved to be of fundamental importance for the success of the program. Though the members in each seminar were working on some aspect of the same broad subject, there was almost no uniformity in the views they brought with them. A few of the participants had known each other from previous conferences, but rarely did any two members in a single seminar meeting come from the same university or bring with them common educational backgrounds or similar projects. Even the few who came from the same institutions were working in different areas, under different supervision, had no overlap in their projects, and did not cluster in any one seminar meeting. The same was true of the foreign members, though drawn from far fewer institutions. Of the British, 10 came from Cambridge, 5 from Oxford, 3 from the London School of Economics, and 2 each from Bristol and Warwick; but no two of them had had similar academic backgrounds, interests, or projects, and rarely appeared together with others of their institutions in the same seminar group. All, upon arrival, were absorbed in their own monographic research, with only incidental concern for larger contexts, of which in fact their technical studies were a part.

The diversity had a creative effect. Each year at the opening session, the members were warned of the variety of their colleagues' research, the likelihood that many of the presentations would involve unfamiliar material drawn from unfamiliar sources. They were urged not to be intimidated by their ignorance of the technical material in the papers but to consider the assumptions, logic, and consistency involved and above all their relation to Atlantic history as a whole. Since each member entered the discussion from the perspective of his or her personal research and was then confronted with research and ideas developed from quite different approaches, an adjustment of some kind had to be made, and thought was required to relate their work to others' that was different but relevant to what they were doing. Often members remained silent at the start, wary and reserved as they adjusted to the larger dimensions of the topic, but within a day or two of the discussions they began to loosen and became quite informal.

Over the ten days or two weeks the members (who were housed in the same inn) got to know each other and avoided confrontation in favor of queries and exploration of what was new to them. The result was not consensus but appreciation of the larger dimensions of what the members had been working on and a clearer sense of the broad regional framework within which their personal work might best be understood.

The members' enthusiasm was evident from the first session (1996). To the emerging regional Atlantic concept, the members, as the discussions proceeded, responded strongly. Advanced graduate students and particularly newly appointed junior faculty, firmly grounded in their initial research but unsure of the larger meaning and relevance of their work, were at precisely the point in their careers when they were most open to new ideas, interested in examples of broad structures within which to locate their monographic studies, and eager for the stimulation of sympathetic outsiders at work on parallel and contrasting aspects of a common project. The Seminar, a former Princeton graduate student recalled, "convened at a propitious time for me. I was in graduate school, suffering one of those existential crises that graduate students experience with some regularity. . . . The seminar helped me frame my work . . . Interacting with established scholars and other graduate students in these diverse fields provided me with a sense that I was creating scholarship that was linked to the ideas and work of others in a meaningful joint enterprise." Another, a newly appointed assistant professor at the University of Wisconsin, put it more simply: "my experience at the Atlantic seminar . . . came at a crucial time in my life. Even now [eight years later] . . . the underlying assumption of a broad Atlantic framework undergirds my understanding of the nineteenth century and remains key for understanding the nature and import of post-colonial nation-making in the region." And this from an independent researcher in Maryland's archives: "It is not every day, after all, that I find myself following without difficulty a lively discussion of *cualidad* so engrossed I hardly remember I do not speak Spanish."

But the members' enthusiasm was not confined to the Seminar itself.

With astonishing speed, the members began to express their interest in publications: first, in essays on aspects of Atlantic history, then in fully developed monographs, and throughout the years that followed, in articles in the scholarly journals.

Essay collections on Atlantic history first appeared in 2002 with the publication of a notable volume of papers on the British Atlantic world, edited by two members of the 1997 seminar. Other collections edited by members of the Seminar, alone or in collaboration, followed. Three more such edited volumes were published in 2003, four in 2005, three in 2006, and an astonishing eight in 2007. In all, twenty-nine such volumes of essays on Atlantic history, by Seminar members, together with others, appeared between 2002 and 2010, covering everything from the slave trade to warfare, science, social structure, and race relations, and concentrating on groups as varied as Africans, Jews, Germans, Huguenots, Ulster Presbyterians, and the indigenous peoples of the Americas.

At an understandably slower pace but still with remarkable speed, fully developed monographic studies of aspects of Atlantic history by seminar members and others appeared in quick succession. In all, thirty book-length studies on Atlantic history were published between 1998 and 2013—six such volumes in the single year 2008. No doubt accidents of timing in research, writing, and publishing account for much of the chronological clustering of such publications, but it is clear that the concept and formulation of the Atlantic region as a coherent historical entity struck a responsive chord that drew on dynamics deep within the currents of historical thought, and that the Seminar had a propulsive effect on this historiographical development.

An effort was made to list out all the members' publications, articles as well as books, before and after their seminar meeting. The publication records of the members of the earlier years of the program were most useful since they were fuller than those of more recent years. While many of the publications show little or no identifiable influence of the Seminar experience, a surprising number do. These subsequent publications are the products of the research the members had taken with them into the Seminar, but the frame, the pitch, of the ultimate publications often shows an effort to cast the subject broadly, regionally.

Perhaps more revealing than books, because they are more flexible and more sensitive to newly developing ideas, are the many articles published by the Seminar members in the course of the program's fifteen years.

A few titles may be listed. They are instructive.

"Rules, Rights and Redemption: The Negotiation of Jewish Status in British Atlantic Port Towns, 1740–1831"
"America and the Atlantic World"
"'The Music Is Nothing if the Audience Is Deaf': Moving Historical Thinking into the Wider World"
"A Plea for a New Atlantic History"
"Centering Families in Atlantic Worlds, 1500–1800"
"Native Americans and the Atlantic World"
"El distrito de Londoninense de la calle Coleman y el mundo atlantico del republicanism radical, 1624–1661"
"Weird Science: Identity in the Atlantic World"
"Procurators and the Making of the Jesuit Atlantic Network"
"The Algonquian Word and the Spirit of Divine Truth: John Eliot's Indian Library and the Atlantic Quest for a Universal Language"

Among the most interesting articles were those of a French historian who brought to the seminar an intensely researched study of the French settlers in the Illinois territory in the eighteenth century. The seminar, she later wrote, "was essential to my intellectual development." It opened up a world of networks in which French interests, hitherto neglected, were vital. After 2003, when she and a colleague published *Histoire de l'Amérique française*, she began to produce what would become a flood of publications, among which were three articles that were unique in their challenge and advocacy: "The Reluctance of

French Historians to Address Atlantic History" (2006); "Making New France New Again: French Historians Rediscover Their American Past" (2007); and "La nouvelle histoire atlantique en France: ignorance, réticence et reconnaissance tardive" (2008).

Atlantic history, in various ways, was clearly entering the awareness and vocabulary of historians of the early modern world. In 2002 the subject received the resounding endorsement of Germany's leading Latin American historian, Horst Pietschmann, of Hamburg University, in his *Atlantic History: History of the Atlantic System, 1580–1830*, a collection of twenty-nine papers by various historians presented at a conference in Hamburg in 1999. "The existence of . . . 'Atlantic History,'" Pietschmann, who twice visited and participated in the Harvard Seminar, wrote in his introductory essay, "as a historical sub-discipline between European and global history can no longer be denied." Despite the fact that "numerous open question[s] of fundamental importance remain," he wrote, "'Atlantic history' is nowadays widely accepted in Western Europe and different parts of America." It was a view endorsed elaborately three years later in a *Festschrift* to Pietschmann containing twenty-six papers in English and Spanish.[4]

Evidence of how widely accepted the Atlantic region had become as a historical entity in itself and as a framework for specific transnational and intercontinental studies has appeared in many forms. Atlantic history was the subject of a major session at the American Historical Association convention, part of a three-year project of the National Endowment for the Humanities designed to help community college professors incorporate the wider dimensions of American history into their survey courses. Commonly, here and abroad, conferences have been held like that sponsored by three collaborating scholarly centers in Pennsylvania, on "Networks of Atlantic Culture and Politics, 1699–1751" (2014). Some efforts have taken more permanent form. The University of North Carolina at Greensboro has created an Atlantic world research network, an elaborate program to study the ways "the peoples and civilizations of Europe, Africa, and the Americas have encountered, collided, and combined. . . . This new network brings the Atlantic world to the University of North Carolina and *around the world.*"[5] And the University of Pittsburgh has created a professorial chair in Atlantic history, as has the Ecole des Hautes Etudes en Sciences Sociales in Paris.

One partial replica of the Harvard Seminar has developed abroad. Historians in Germany and elsewhere in Europe have organized a summer academy on Atlantic history that meets for three or four days annually in different locations in Europe—to date, Bayreuth, Galway, Hamburg, Lancaster, and Seville. As in the Harvard Seminar, the participating members are students from many countries whose works-in-progress form the basis for the discussions. Their most recent meeting, in Seville, was organized by historians at the Université Versailles-Saint Quentin in France, the University of Bayreuth in Germany, and the Universidad Pablo de Olavide in Spain, and it included participating members from Spain, Colombia, France, the United States, England, and Ireland. Its general theme was "Globalizing the Atlantic," a challenging concept that marks a new and important dimension in Atlantic studies.

It is perhaps fitting that in 2011, six years after the first meeting of the Atlantic History Seminar, two former chairmen of seminar meetings— one a Briton who teaches in the United States, the other an Irishman who had directed his university's humanities center and who had at first written critically of the concept of Atlantic history—gathered together a phalanx of Atlanticist scholars to summarize, in *The Oxford Handbook of the Atlantic World, 1450–1850,* what they considered to be the present state of the art, its limitations, and its likely future. And that was followed, four years later, by the *Princeton Companion to Atlantic History,* edited by historians at the University of Virginia, Columbia, the University of Texas, Duke, and New York University.[6]

Such were the basic characteristics of the Seminar, but its work was not confined to the annual summer meetings of young historians working on their first major research study. The Seminar sponsored workshops—eighteen in all—on critical issues for discussion by senior scholars, as well as conferences—seven in all—in which both younger and senior historians participated and a program for small travel grants for research. The conference of 2005 was unique. It was organized as a tenth anniversary summary of the work to date. Almost one hundred historians from all over the Americas and western Europe and a few from Africa submitted papers for this anniversary conference. The summaries of most of the papers (eighty-two) were privately printed as a 329-page volume entitled *Atlantic History Soundings: Proceedings of the Tenth Anniversary Conference of the Atlantic History Seminar* (Harvard University, August 10–13, 2005). A copy is available in the Harvard College Library.

By 2005 the Seminar had become, in its annual summer seminars and many conferences, workshops, and grants, a significant center for Atlantic historical studies. But though the Seminar grew and became more complex, the heart of the project lay in the work-in-progress papers and in the discussions that developed from them. Though much of what was said in the seminars is lost to the formal record, notes were occasionally taken, and abstracts of all of the papers are available online.*

As was mentioned above, each year's seminar explored a single broad aspect of the history of the Atlantic world. The members brought to their groups the results of their unique research based on sources unused by the others. In the course of a week's or fortnight's discussion some of the monographic papers coalesced in ways that illuminated some part of the greater Atlantic whole. None of the seminars dealt exclusively with generalities, but each, within its limits, cast light on some aspect of the whole.

What follows is not a summary of the papers presented but something of the light they shone on the region's complex life and evolution.

The first seminar was devoted to the movement of people within and among the four continents—the patterns of their migrations and

---

* The Seminar's website is located at https://atlantic.fas.harvard.edu.

resettlement—and the profound consequences that resulted. The single most important transit was the forced displacement of 6.7 million Africans to the western hemisphere before 1776 (5.8 million would follow by 1866). It was the greatest of all the transoceanic movements of people to the Americas. Two full days of the seminar were devoted entirely to the demographics of the slave trade with strong emphasis on the differing ethnicities among the West African peoples and the resulting ethnically distinct slave regions throughout the Americas.

But while the forced exodus of Africans to the Americas and the conditions of their resettlements were dominant themes, other population displacements smaller than that of the Africans were significant in other ways. A series of papers made clear that migrants to the West—some seeking refuge from religious establishments, some hoping for land and economic opportunities otherwise unavailable—came from all over Europe to form, with the Africans, what would later be called a "mixed multitude." The Atlantic region was a world in motion, its populations shifting, large groups reorganizing their communal life in new and strange circumstances. Some would move gradually into the American interior and thereby disrupt, transform, and debase the traditional lives of indigenous peoples.

There were many approaches to the subject of the second seminar, "Ideas of Empire, Imperial Politics, and the Governance of Colonies: The European Powers in America," but the dominant emphasis fell not on the Europeans' governing power in the western hemisphere but on the agency of American natives in the creation and maintenance of the European empires. The imperial powers governed the native populations not simply by sheer power, fiat, or administrative management but to a remarkable extent by negotiation with the subject peoples. One of the most original and illuminating papers explained the vital role of interpreters as cultural brokers between the races, establishing cross-cultural links that made communication and intercultural exchanges possible.

∼

AT THAT POINT, *at the end of the second seminar in September 1997, the program turned unexpectedly to the first of what would be eighteen workshops devoted to highly specified issues relevant to the major Atlantic themes. It met in mid-November. Its purpose was to discuss the Franckesche Stiftungen (Francke Foundations) associated with the remarkable university at Halle, near Leipzig. I had read much about that unique establishment—or cluster of establishments—which included, in the early eighteenth century, besides the university, a unique orphanage, a reformed system of education, a printing and publishing business, and a center for the production and worldwide distribution of pharmaceutical products—all of which had been the direct or indirect creation of August Hermann Francke, a dynamic polymath and evangelical Pietist whose vast learning matched his inventive ambition and religious zeal.*

A globalist in the range of his vision, he maintained a voluminous correspondence that included several exchanges with Boston's Cotton Mather. For Mather, desperate to transcend the confining provincial world of Puritan New England ("We Americans here live beyond ultima Thule") and seeking access to the European discourse on advanced Protestant thought, found in Francke not only someone whose ideas on religion and whose piety were similar to his own but a charismatic figure on the European stage who might give him access to that greater world. So he wrote to Francke repeatedly (in Latin), flattering him as "the wonder of Europe," "incomparable," and "marvelous." He proposed that together they might unify the splintered Protestant communion and reform its errant excesses. Carefully but emphatically he reminded the great man that the Americas had been the world of the Anti-christ until the Christian missionaries [i.e., Puritans] had brought the Word to the pagan natives still in thrall to Satan's influence. To Mather's ingratiating letters, Francke replied occasionally, mainly to describe his own achieve-

ments in Halle. In time the correspondence dwindled away, but I knew enough to want to know more. I was determined to see the foundations, or what remained of them, and get a realistic view of Francke's whole compound of projects.[7]

Despite the difficulties of freeing time to travel, I managed to get to Halle in 1993 and to see something of the major enterprises. What interested me most was the extensive archive. Among much else it contained all the reports of the Pietist missionaries throughout Europe and parts of the Americas in the eighteenth century. But my visit to Halle was short. I had time only to take some notes on the various categories of information in the archives. I decided then that at the first opportunity I would organize a conference of some kind to explore not only the Halle archives but also the Pietist diaspora in general. That opportunity arose in November 1997, after the second summer seminar.

The workshop was led by the Thomas Müller, head archivist of the Francke Foundations, who came from Halle to Cambridge for the occasion. It included four American specialists on the German overseas migration and the outreach of Pietism.[8] One of the group, Renate Wilson of Johns Hopkins University, was an expert—the nation's sole expert—on the history of the lucrative pharmaceutical trade in the eighteenth century, which involved the history of chemistry and medicine and also the sophisticated management of this commerce. Her account of the religious foundations' involvement in this profitable trade was startling. Müller explained the foundations' orphanage and classroom teaching, its medical training, its library and bookstore, its communication network, and its search for contacts in Asia as well as Europe's western colonies, each with its published reports and letters. The other participants in the workshop contributed their own perspectives on the foundations' activities and noted how the archive's holdings could enrich studies now under way. Several members noted the anti-Catholic zeal that dominated the foundations' enterprises, and the Pietists' rivalry with the Moravians. All agreed that though the foundations' activities in North America were a sideshow to its major fields of endeavor in Asia and northern and eastern

Europe, it was a basic source for understanding the networks that bound together the far reaches of the Atlantic world.

∾

THE SEMINAR THAT year, on "Cultural Encounters in Atlantic Socie-ties," resumed the theme of the negotiated roles of indigenous peoples and went beyond that to fresh studies on cultural relations in which the members who had worked independently in universities across this country and in Europe and Latin America found remarkable agreement. One of the central issues was language and other forms of communication among peoples of different cultures. One especially impressive paper led the group in discussing the great seventeenth and eighteenth centuries' search for the universal language that humanity had enjoyed before its sins had brought on the diversity of Babel. In New Spain, given the failure of linguistic communication, the Fran-ciscan missionaries staged one-act Christian morality plays in the Nahuatl language in which all the actors were indigenous. Further, in lieu of the general failure of writing as a form of communication, oral discourses, often as storytelling, were commonly used.

Intercultural trade, barter, and exchange in the highly commer-cialized Atlantic system were the subject of the next seminar, on "The Economy of the Atlantic World." The topic was not, of course, new. There was a well-established literature on the Atlantic economy, works like Horst Pietschmann's studies of Spanish America's commercial complex. But some members found, in the interstices and in subtle passages, a wealth of enlightening discoveries. From the papers and discussions the members got a sense of a huge, vibrant, increasingly integrated commercial system that brought together into organic rela-tionships business activities that stretched over the Atlantic world. The details mattered. So the pan-Atlantic gun and powder trade was shown to have had a distinctive effect on the traditional system of tribal kingship in the Volta and Niger area of West Africa. So the wine trade centered in the Canary Islands and Azores reached consumers in ports, inland towns, villages, and plantations throughout the western hemisphere as well as in Europe. And so American sugar, tobacco, rice, farm products, and fish fed markets an ocean away.

For two centuries the Atlantic economic system grew, became more complex, shifted in its basic contours, and reached a climactic point in the mid-eighteenth century. A simple listing of some of the papers in this seminar shows the magnitudes and complexity of the Atlantic economy in action.

- Women's role in fostering the slave trade in Igboland of Nigeria
- How the Iroquois Indians became entangled in the Atlantic economy
- The role of the Dutch state in fostering Atlantic trading operations
- The centralization of rice marketing in South Carolina, which allowed for creative strategies under local control
- The emergence of North American flour merchants as dominant figures in the all-important Atlantic grain trade (a complex and delicate system "like a cobweb")
- How tobacco production and marketing became not only a powerful force in the Atlantic economy but helped shape Spain's, France's, and to some extent Britain's domestic economies

Two papers generated especially extended discussion and shed brilliant light on the Atlantic economy. One was on the circulation of the silver produced by Spain's mines in Potosí. For decades thousands of tons of silver were carried by muleback a thousand miles across the Andes to Buenos Aires, ending in the Habsburg treasury, with effects that reached deep into central Europe. But mules, as one writer noted, needed by the thousands, are hybrids, offsprings of female horses and male donkeys, hence their production in large numbers must have been a major enterprise on which the silver economy rested. The seminar was intrigued by this and set about calculating the estimated number of mules that must have been bred, the number of specialist mule-breeding haciendas there must have been, and where they must have been located for the stages of the trek.

Less dramatic but of great interest was a particularly original paper on how seamen and ship masters, waiting in American port towns during trade negotiations, lading periods, and bad weather, became involved in local societies, formed ties to resident colonists, became conduits of the news and life of the greater world, and thereby created vital and enduring personal contacts among the peoples of the Atlantic world culturally, socially, and mentally, as well as economically.

The mental world came into sharp focus in the 2000 seminar, on "The Circulation of Ideas," a topic that would later be explored further in two more specialized seminars, "The Transit of Christianity" (2006) and "The Americas in the Advancement of European Science and Medicine" (2009). The circulation of ideas was detailed in part by papers that traced the reception in the Americas of European writers of the Enlightenment, some famous (Priestley, Paine, Grégoire, Voltaire, and especially Hume), some less well known or obscure (Elisha Perkins and his quack medicines, John Weemes and his philosemitism, John Jebb and his extreme political radicalism, Moses Mendelssohn and the expansion of Jewish rights). Equally important were general ideas that radiated through areas of the Atlantic world: the *translatio* tradition (civilization ever moving west), the variant concepts of enslavement (chattel, political), *limpieza de sangre* (purity of blood lines), concepts of aberrant behavior, and the circulation of Scottish "sensibility."

Discussions in the 2001 seminar, on "The Atlantic Revolutions," shifted the time period to the late eighteenth and early nineteenth centuries. A common and powerful theme quickly emerged in the discussions of the revolutionary upheavals on three continents: the struggle of newly emerging nations to design the structure and character of their statehood, and the legitimate principles of membership or citizenship. This was true of the recently created United States; the chaotic new nations of Central America; Haiti and its entanglements with France; the failing state of "Gran Colombia"; the slow and chaotic emergence of Argentina from its viceroyalty origins; Mexico and its complex problem of race-based citizenship; Ireland in the aftermath of its failed rebellion; and the reconstituted Portuguese empire after its transfer to Rio de Janiero. Membership, citizenship in the new revolutionary states was a profound problem that could not be solved at once. It persisted and persists today. The papers exploring it were subtle and imaginative.

Clearly focused as the previous seminars had been, they were followed in 2002 by a sprawling seminar on "The Structure of Atlantic Societies." The subject meant different things to different participants. To some it meant exploring the family life of African Americans, north as well as south. For others it meant the creation and fortunes of Euro-American "elites": in Rio de la Plata, in the Lower Cape Fear region of North Carolina, in New York, and in Philadelphia. But the elites among the native Americans were no less important, as shown in several papers, especially in a striking essay on the loyalty to Spain of the Indian nobility of Cusco, Peru, which reflects the "mature colonial society in the Andes." The papers on elites were matched with others on the lower orders and their statuses in the local social structures.

"Networks," the next theme of the seminar (2003), went to the heart of the Atlantic region's basic organization, which was a progressively elaborating system of contacts that spanned the Atlantic but linked local, domestic systems within the four continents. So the British Caribbean entrepreneurs spun webs of associations with creditors, consumers, and suppliers in Britain and beyond. So the Moravians established religious missions throughout the Atlantic world that became focal points of contact for the networks of their communions. So Amsterdam's women maintained a system of family ties within the broad Dutch trading empire. Especially intriguing was the network of radical Puritan republicans based in London's Coleman Street Ward, some of whom settled in Massachusetts before being banished to Rhode Island, where they quickly established their utopian democracies while their homeland brethren met their fate at the hands of Cromwell's guards. And there were other transatlantic networks of radical passions. The Acadians, expelled from Nova Scotia, spun their own web: they settled first in experimental communities in France and only then fled via Nantes to Spanish Louisiana, where they kept something of their distinctive culture. The seminar debated at length a presentation describing Andean society in the sixteenth century as a scattered network of cultural enclaves, implying a theory of cultural pluralism clearly at odds with Spain's official rejection of minority rights.

The theme of networks carried over to a special seminar of 2004 held at the University of Cambridge, in collaboration with Cambridge's Centre for Research in the Arts, Social Sciences, and Humanities. The membership was especially varied. Ten of the twenty-three participants were from universities in England, Ireland, the Netherlands, France, Canada, and Spain, and they brought with them research findings and perspectives different from what the Americans were able to contribute. The stated theme of that special seminar was "The Atlantic World in Motion" which was partly reminiscent of the initial seminar of 1996. There were several papers on the physical movement and resettlement of people: the repeated movements of slave labor among the various sites of mahogany exploitation in Central America; the back-country north-south movements of the Tuscarora Indians in response, ultimately, to transatlantic economic and political pressures; and the secondary migrations of the slave population in Louisiana. And there were studies of the remarkable power of maroon settlements (bands of escaped slaves and indigenous fugitives, especially in Jamaica and northwest Ecuador).

But the subject that proved to be dominant in the Cambridge discussions was, once again, citizenship and other forms of membership in revolutionary and postrevolutionary states. Surprisingly, one paper explained how the British courts developed a flexible theory of legal identity that would keep pace with people's transnational movements. Equally surprising were the solutions by the North American courts of the baffling problem of expatriation, which in legal form might destroy the notion of "a national community." Outsider and insider statuses were everywhere difficult to define, whether the question was how citizenship could be construed in multiethnic, multinational Central America, or how Argentina might best define the legal status of enterprising north European entrepreneurs who flocked to Rio de la Plata in search of lucrative deals, or how to define the status of abandoned military engineers sent from Spain to Mexico and who failed to assimilate with the local populations. The discussions probed all of these problems of membership in the national states that emerged from the upheavals in the late eighteenth century.

The Cambridge seminar in March did not preclude the annual Harvard seminar of 2004. The topic was "Indigenous Cultures," and it was methodologically one of the most far-ranging and original series of papers and discussions that the Seminar had yet sponsored. Numerous papers went beyond demography and normal historical discourse into anthropology, and beyond that, to the prehistory of native peoples. The geographical range of the papers reached from Canada to Patagonia and from the Antilles to the Illinois country and the Pacific coast of Peru.

But despite the geographical diversity, common themes emerged as the discussions proceeded. The pattern of Jesuit relations with native peoples was the same throughout the western hemisphere, whether in New France or New York or the Brazilian Amazon. The indigenous peoples struggled everywhere with the imperial authorities to retain something of their customary beliefs and practices. For this they could pay a bitter price. In Mexico City the Indian leader Don Carlos of Texoco was burned at the stake for defying Christian beliefs. In South Carolina the Indians themselves were active in Indian enslavement in response to pressure from the British after the devastating Yamasee War. In western Mexico villagers gated their communities against the conquering forces and immersed themselves in myths of a primordial past. In El Salvador and Guatemala a sense of "defining moments" in the deep past was the basis for cultural adaptation and negotiation. Study of the prehistoric archaeological record in the Illinois country revealed people long experienced with navigating cross-cultural frontiers and able, as a result, to integrate more easily into the early modern Atlantic world.

Other topics were discussed with similar ingenuity: the meaning and misunderstanding of gift exchanges; the complex development of Lingua Geral Amazonica as a distinct contact language in the Brazilian Amazon. Differences, obscure in themselves, reflected deeply held and persistent cultural assumptions, as did the remarkable collaboration in Mexico City between the Nahua elite and the municipal officials in the construction and arrangement of the triumphal arches for the Catholic festival of Corpus Christi. That collaboration, under ethnohistorical analysis, revealed the native peoples' own deeply buried and powerful conceptions of political order that flourished despite all of Spain's ideology, political power, and economic strength.

The series continued in 2006 with a meeting on "The Transit of Christianity." A vast topic, it may have appeared to be familiar, covered by a well-established literature. It was assumed that the propulsion to bring Christianity to the western hemisphere derived from at least three sources: the passion to evangelize the hemisphere's pagans; the search for secure refuges for prosecuted European dissidents; and the hope of finding utopias abroad or to construct them free from the domination of the Christian establishments. But there was nothing commonplace in the twenty-six papers that were presented in that seminar of 2006. The participants brought to the meetings the results of fresh, original, sometimes startling research. Thus, the Christian burial rites carried over from Europe contrasted with those of enslaved Africans, whose ancient burial practices were a form of resistance to the dehumanizing program of slavery. The specific subjects differed, from Tenochtitlan confraternities in Mexico to the radical Protestants in the Carolina backcountry whose leaders were implicated in ritual murders. But different as the individual topics were, they all added points of penetration into the massive, irreversible transformation of Atlantic life by the transit of Christianity.

The diversity of the individual papers in the seminar on Christianity's impact on the indigenous peoples of America was followed by the sharply focused papers in the following seminar, on "The Struggle for the Americas." The struggle for control of the western hemisphere involved all the imperial powers of Europe. The configuration of the Atlantic imperial structures was flexible, changing repeatedly throughout most of the three centuries of the colonial period. In the scramble for possession, certain of the Caribbean islands were at first Spanish, then French, then English. The paper on Cromwell's disastrous Western Design ended in the transfer of Jamaica from Spain to England. After decades of conflict, the island of Hispaniola was divided between France (Haiti) and Spain (Santo Domingo). The borderlands throughout the Americas were always centers of conflict and fragile in their loyalties. They were, one participant wrote, "lawless and precarious spaces" in which the imperial powers struggled to maintain order. It was not until the mid-eighteenth century that borderland struggles abated and geopolitical structures stabilized—but even then, conflicts of imperial ambitions smoldered and could burst into flame in a crisis.

The seminar uncovered unexpected aspects of the imperial struggles. Two papers explored the reasons for France's failure to establish itself as an imperial power in the Americas. Five of the papers presented ways in which the imperial powers were dependent for success on engaging the support of, or alliances with, the native peoples. Two papers explored the debate of the imperial powers on whether or how to use enslaved Blacks in their armed forces. One (Dutch) member plunged into the formidable intricacy of Hugo Grotius's thinking in justifying Dutch expeditions to the Spanish Caribbean, elaborating and applying his famous doctrine of the freedom of trade and navigation to justify a Dutch ship captain's raids.

But the main contest through the entire colonial era was between Spain and England for imperial hegemony in the Americas. Seven of the papers were devoted to probing that centuries-long conflict, which was impelled by England's discovery by the late sixteenth century of Spain's brutal conquest of the Aztecs, which fostered anti-Spanish sentiments that helped justify England's intervention in the New World. All of these papers were, in one way or another, as one member wrote, assessments of "the Anglo-Spanish struggle for territories and riches in the New World, which in turn was ultimately associated with the competition for power and reputation in Europe."

That competition again and again erupted into actual combat, in small raids, in borderland skirmishes, and in planned, large-scale engagements. War between the major imperial powers was inevitable and became a dominant feature of Atlantic life in the seventeenth and eighteenth centuries. The seminar of 2008 was therefore devoted to "The Atlantic as a Theater of War."

Among the twenty-nine papers presented in that seminar were studies that identified and analyzed peculiar modes of military combat that had been extemporized to suit the peculiar conditions of the time and place. Lord Dunmore became famous for freeing slaves who would join his royal naval force off Virginia's coast, but more striking was his assemblage of two hundred ships and over two thousand souls—many slaves and servants, loyalists, prisoners of war, and others—to form a polyglot "floating town" that survived under barbarous conditions for fourteen months, ostensibly as a threat to Washington's forces in eastern Virginia. Two papers traced the military role of pirates and privateers: at first a useful force to supplement regular naval powers, but then a rogue element that had to be constrained, and in the end deliberately eliminated. Martial law, imposed by the British in Manhattan in 1775, failed as a military tactic, created savage conditions in the city, and alienated precisely the loyalists it was intended to protect. The struggles within Rio de la Plata to devise a stable republic persisted for fifty years, turning a peaceful commercial center into a "warrior society" in which war was a "normal" component of social life. In 1768 Spain promulgated a set of rules for military conduct that in effect elevated the military to the status of an autonomous corps, above civilian institutions. The rules survived into the nineteenth century and were, at least indirectly, the source of political turmoil in the Latin American states.

But the peculiarities of war in the Atlantic setting went beyond established institutional boundaries. The practice developed in the North American south of using bounties of slaves as inducements in army recruitment. Further, European raids and battles in the western hemisphere, both with and against indigenous warriors, became savage to new extremes. The barbarism of the French and Indian raid on the Ohio town of Pickawillany (1752), which included cannibalization, shocked the French officers and sparked a transatlantic debate on the limits of violence that were compatible with proper notions of honor, civility, and virtue. And the great British navy, one paper explained, failed in its mission in the American war not for lack of personnel or supplies but for the inability of its senior officers, used to fighting on the high seas, to recast their strategic thinking and provide security for their loyalist American supporters while establishing a permanent land base for their operations.

The final two seminars turned to different categories of Atlantic history. Both reached deeply into the intellectual and cultural substrata of Atlantic life and into the creative intermingling of minds an ocean apart. The first of these was on "The Americas in the Advancement of European Science & Technology, 1500–1830."[9] The exceptional quality of the twenty-three papers presented is indicated by their publication as a group within a year of the seminar's meetings, together with the authors' "collective reflections." Edited by Neil Safier, one of the seminar's chairs and himself a major contributor to the subject (he is now director of the John Carter Brown Library), the papers were preceded by a "conversation" between Safier and myself on "Atlantic Soundings" (*Atlantic Studies* 7, no. 4 [special issue], 2010). Many of the papers probed separate, unique issues. One explored the beliefs in and the attempted documentation of differential body types, to the disadvantage of Native Americans—beliefs edging toward a theory of heredity. Another explained the use of mathematics and optical instruments by a creole scientist in New Spain as an illustration of the work of the international Catholic scientific community that could integrate different scientific methodologies. Still others traced the increasingly sophisticated science of cartography, advances in the intercontinental technology of ship design and sugar mills, and the motivation for and accomplishments of French and Spanish scientific expeditions to unknown parts of the Americas, with their discoveries that expanded the information available for scientific study: strange creatures and plants—sloths, and the hummingbird's "torpor."

Medicine appeared in many papers, with stress on the contested reception of indigenous medical practices by European theorists and experts and on the treatment of diseases—yellow fever, scurvy, smallpox, and mysterious unexplained epidemics. Various cures were examined— medicinal bark (*quina*), "Seneka snakeroot," ginseng—as was the geography of disease locations and theories of medical topography.

But beyond the specific issues, a major theme dominated the seminar's papers and the discussions that followed. Again and again the subject involved questions about the nature of scientific knowledge— what knowledge could be accepted as valid, by what criteria could that be judged, and by whom? Most commonly the epistemological problem arose from questions of what status should be accorded to the native peoples' customary practices—cures and drugs—that had no scientific or other theoretical basis but whose efficacy could not be doubted. And further, should creoles educated in the colonies be accorded the status of European scientists and established medical practitioners?

To these questions several papers were devoted. One traced the strange fortunes of an inoculation enthusiast who found in South Carolina's slave population a laboratory for the study of smallpox. He failed

to convince the locals in Charleston of his findings and theories but suc-
ceeded with the cognoscenti of London. Another described the contentious and inconclusive debate circulating in the Anglo-Atlantic world on
the validity of a Marylander's cure for croup—"a model for making new
medical knowledge." The paper on *quina* was presented as an example of
"knowledge production" based on the empirical findings of an Ecuador-
ian official that challenged the authority of the European experts. And
a third showed the problems faced by white naturalists in British plan-
tation societies attempting to navigate between two competing traditions, one that praised the Indians' and slaves' vernacular knowledge of
the natural world and the other that assumed that such knowledge was
simply "vulgar errors," superstitious and false. The Indians' and slaves'
"rude experience," some said, could not be true knowledge until it was
transformed into matters of fact by established authorities.

The final seminar (2010) was devoted to "Justice: Europe in America, 1500–1830." The topic had been chosen as a way of touching on
some of the deeper areas of the merging of cultures that would
define the Atlantic world in the early modern period. Fourteen of the
twenty-one papers presented at the seminar turned on the relation of
indigenous customs and rules to the formal structures of European
law imposed by the imperial powers. Each, in various ways, sought
to dominate or accommodate the other to form some kind of justice
acceptable by all. The process was so complex, the voices so numerous,
that one member called the result "legal polyphony." In one example,
the Andean caciques, seeking justice, engaged in a "legal dialogue" by
incorporating their "customary law" into the Castilian legal tradition,
grafting in as well some elements of natural law, popular notions of
justice and fairness, a recreated *jus commune*, and Roman law. It was
on the basis of such diversity of sources that the litigants learned to
base their claims. Another paper traced the development in Yucatán of
the *fuero* (exemption for Indians from prosecution in ordinary royal
courts) together with limited judicial autonomy. Treated as protected

legal minors, the natives proclaimed the sophistication of preconquest native law and the advantages of limited self-rule, which led to a separate judiciary for natives that survived until independence.

A study of law and justice in Córdoba del Tacumán found that the common views that law and justice were simply imposed by an "absolute state" distorted the truth. Commonly, the law was localized: "the King's justice remained under local control and fed a home rule tradition." "Local autonomy" was achieved by a Basque *audiencia* judge in late colonial Mexico through his transatlantic network of Basque merchants who opposed the Bourbon reforms aimed at fortifying central authority in Spanish America. The clamor for freedom and equal justice by Black loyalists in the Bahamas and Jamaica rested on a unique form of republicanism inspired by both enlightenment ideals and the egalitarianism of revival meetings. But though their petitions to the courts failed before the influence of the slave-owning whites who declared their arguments unconstitutional, the search for justice persisted, most often in the form of intercultural localism.

∾

WITH THIS THE summer seminar program came to an end. There is no sure way of assessing the intellectual success of the seminar meetings, but the results may be estimated by the responses to two questionnaires that were sent to all members, one in 2005, the second in 2010. In all, 121 of the 366 members (33 percent) responded—92 in 2010, 45 in 2005—sixteen people commented on both occasions. Thirty-three percent is perhaps a small return, and the 245 who did not respond may have had quite different views from those of the respondents. But since the respondents included critics of the program, in general and in detail, and since the distribution of the respondents by gender and nationality mirrors almost exactly that of the membership as a whole, it would not seem unreasonable to see the returns to the questionnaires as roughly representative of the membership at large. And in any case,

137 responses—some written at length—are in themselves a database worthy of study, whether or not they represented statistically the views of the total membership.[10]

That most of the 121 respondents wrote favorably of their experiences in the Atlantic History Seminar is perhaps not surprising since they were a self-selected group under no obligation to respond yet interested enough to want to record their views. What is surprising is the number of those who recalled the Seminar—some shortly after the event, some long after—not merely as an interesting experience but as a significant influence on the development of their ideas and careers. Thus a historian of French imperialism at the University of North Carolina, nine years after the seminar he attended, wrote that "most of my most rewarding professional contacts, inspiration for my work, and belief in the powers of history to enlighten, dates from my participation way back in 1997." Such comments recurred, as much from representatives of major research universities as from those from community colleges. A member from St. Johns University wrote: "it is hard for me to contemplate what my career would look like without my involvement in the seminar and in Atlantic History more broadly." So too from the University of Central Florida: "the seminar was, for me, a pivotal moment . . . a turning point both in my academic career and overall in my historiographical approach," and the same from UC Davis; from Dartmouth College; and from Central Connecticut State University. From Northwestern University: the seminar "was seminal in my development as an historian. . . . I would not be the historian I have become without the seminar." And from Harvard: "The Atlantic seminars and workshops at Harvard gave shape to my inchoate longing not to be confined to a single national historiography. They gave a name, status, and extraordinarily generous institutional backing to this new and exciting arena of endeavor . . . it molded the book I ultimately produced."

But if a significant number of young American historians reported that the Atlantic History Seminar had been an important event in their professional development, several of the Europeans wrote in even more enthusiastic terms. Thus a junior professor at the Royal Netherlands Naval College wrote that he "had never encountered such a challenging event in my whole academic career . . . after a week, I was completely exhausted." The seminar, a graduate from the Universidad Autónoma de Madrid wrote, "was a turning point both in my academic career, and, over all, in my historiographical approach." It was "an amazing intellectual experience," a historian from the Universidade de Évora, Portugal, wrote, "a turning point in . . . my process of becoming a historian."

Not all the respondents were so enthusiastic, and a few, echoing criticisms that were emerging in the scholarly literature on the subject, raised questions, some sharply, about the concept of Atlantic history. One respondent found "conceptual fuzziness" and an undue emphasis on Britain and British North America. Another found little distinction between Atlantic history and traditional "top-down" imperial history. Some believed a western hemispheric concept was more useful; and others were concerned that inland localities had too few Atlantic contacts to be part of the region's identity. One respondent, enthusiastic about Atlantic history as a useful "perspective and style of approach," believed that the concept, which had had little traction before 1995, had developed so swiftly that by 2010 some had become "Atlantic world weary" and that the basic idea was in danger of becoming passé. And one of the most thoughtful of the respondents confessed that the Seminar had "helped me to become confused about several ideas at the heart of my research that I thought I had understood. Will you believe me," he wrote, "when I say that I am deeply grateful for that?"

I did indeed believe him. For me too, the seminars had a great effect not only in broadening my knowledge of the fifteen major topics of the seminars but in bringing new light, again and again, to ideas I thought I knew well but that I could now see were superficial and incomplete— "above-water fragments of . . . submarine unities." I too had become "confused about several ideas . . . that I thought I had understood." And I was, and am, grateful for that.

Epilogue

THE ELUSIVE PAST

I have never kept a diary or any other personal record, if for no other reason than that I could not imagine whom I would be addressing—how intimate the comments should be, how formal the tone. But when occasions arose when it seemed reasonable to comment on my sense of history, its character as an elusive form of knowledge, its possibilities and limitations, I took advantage of them and wrote out what I thought. There is nothing systematic in what I wrote from time to time. These remarks, mostly extracted from various essays and books, were not designed as parts of a whole; nor are they all at the same level of generality. But they do serve as memos of my understanding of the nature of history and of some of the problems of studying and writing about it. The quotations have been lightly edited for clarity.

Thus my introduction to an essay on context in history:

I am not concerned with anything abstract, with anything that might be called the philosophy of history, nor with such fashionable topics as history as fiction or any of the postmodern theories. I am concerned with one of the central problems in the everyday practice of history that contemporary historians actually face, none of whom, as far as I know, believe naïvely that historians can attain perfect objectivity; none of whom dream that a historian can contemplate the past from some immaculate cosmic perch, free from the prejudices, assumptions, and biases of one's own time, place, and personality; none of whom deny that facts are inert and meaningless until mobilized by an inquiring mind, and hence that all knowledge of the past is interpretative knowledge, yet all of whom assume that the reality of the past can be subjected to useful inquiries, that among the responses to those inquiries some views can be shown to be more accurate depictions of what actually happened than others, and that the establishment, in some significant degree, of a realistic understanding of the past, free of myths, wish fulfillments, and partisan delusions, is essential for social sanity. They know that history, never a science, sometimes an art, is essentially a craft, and they try to improve their craftsmanship, knowing that they will never achieve anything like perfection, that in fact the inescapable limitations in what they can do will confine their work to crude approximations of what they seek, but that to despair for want of realizing the ideal would be to forfeit the mission that they are equipped to fulfill.

◆ ◆ ◆

The past is a different world, and we seek to understand it as it actually was. In a very loose sense, of course, one can say that all historical study is the search for past contexts since historians always try to reach deeply into the circumstances of the past. But the present effort to penetrate into the substructures of thought and behavior, the perceptual maps, the interior experiences that shape overt expressions and events goes beyond the boundaries of traditional historical study—and it is full of problems.

At the simplest level, the difficulties of reaching back and locat-

ing events in their contexts are obvious. We cannot divest ourselves of our own assumptions, attitudes, beliefs, and experiences—strip away everything that intervened between then and now—in order to appreciate fully, identify with, that other, distant way of thinking, feeling, and behaving. We cannot experience what they experienced in the way they experienced it. We cannot contract our expanded sense of possibilities into their more limited sphere, nor project our skepticism into their sense of wonder and belief. And we can have little notion of what were commonplaces to them, underlying but shaping circumstances so ordinary and unremarkable as to have been subliminal—everyday discomforts (of clothing that itched, of shoes that tore the feet, of lice, fleas, and vermin); the ubiquity of filth in public places; the automatic, unthinking management of personal hygiene; the constant expectation of incomprehensible illnesses and sudden death; the reality and urgency of animist forces; the absence or scarcity of print; the slow pace of communication and travel; the sense of utterly unbridgeable social distances, distances so great as to stimulate awe, not envy. All of those ordinary circumstances of life are almost completely unrecoverable precisely because they were so ordinary, so unremarkable hence unremarked.

And beyond that there is another obvious and overwhelming difficulty in recovering the contexts of the past. The fact—the inescapable fact—is that we know how it all came out, and they did not. No more by them then than by us now could the future be imagined. The natural orientation of their experience was to their past. Our perspective, in studying their lives, is formed by what proved to be their future, which is our past, the ignorance of which was the most profound circumstance of their lives. We will never fully recapture their uncertainty and recreate it in the fabric of the history we write.

The logic of what we do leads us in the opposite direction. Knowing the outcome, we feel it to be our obligation to show the process by which the known eventuality came about. So we try to describe the path from then to now, and in doing so select for our accounts the elements in a once indeterminate situation that appear to have led to the future outcome. Our histories will therefore attempt to make clear, if not the inevitability of what happened, at least the logic of why it happened as it did, and so it seems that we have no reason to dwell on initial uncertainties, or to attempt to recover the original ambiguities and make them real.

◆ ◆ ◆

There is no better example of the vital element of uncertainty in the lives of people in the past than what is happening to us at this very moment, this evening, January 16, 1991 [an interview and public discussion at Dartmouth College].[1] *As we all know, one hour ago (the morning of January seventeenth in the Middle East) American planes began bombing Iraq. But as we speak here tonight, no one on earth knows what the outcome will be. Just before we began this conversation, someone asked me what a historian in the year 2050 will say about the origins of the war with Iraq. I said that it is an impossible question to answer, because the historian of 2050 will know, as we do not know, how it all came out and what the long-term consequences proved to be. The eventual interpretation will be based on that outcome.*

The deepest consequence of our present situation, which later historians will hope to understand, is precisely the uncertainty we feel tonight. Will the air war succeed? Will a ground war be necessary? Will Saddam Hussein's army live up to its reputation and exact a terrible toll in American lives? Or will they fail, and will Americans and their allies simply sweep through to Baghdad? Or will something completely different happen, something we cannot now imagine? Future historians will know the answers before they write a word about this war, and they will read that knowledge back to give an account of how the result emerged through clear stages of development, reducing the alternative outcomes to triviality.

The great uncertainty that we are all experiencing this evening,
at this moment, is an unrecoverable reality for future historians.

◆ ◆ ◆

To the extent that one succeeds, at least in part, in recovering contexts of historical events or circumstances, one runs into two other
kinds of problems.

First, you can find yourself facing what is essentially a moral prob-
lem, because to explain is, implicitly at least, to excuse. One could,
for example, spend quite some time explaining the reasons why
Jefferson did not free his slaves and why the Constitution did not
eliminate slavery. But it seems to be moral obtuseness to say that
Jefferson and the framers of the Constitution had their reasons
for this. However sensible those reasons may have been, to try to
explain them seems to be an attempt to excuse them, while what
historians should be doing is condemning them and focusing on
the obvious immorality of slavery. . . . The second problem is that,
in explaining the full context of how things were and functioned,
one tends to lose the dynamics. The disturbing elements, the dis-
equilibrating forces, the motives for change, are by definition sub-
ordinated in any situation one describes, since it is the stable—that
is, the dominant—elements you must describe. If you give a fully
contextual picture of what was going on at a particular time, by
definition the disturbing elements that will lead to change are sub-
ordinated to the stable elements. Therefore, how can you show why
things changed?

There are vivid illustrations of this. Australia's historians cel-
ebrated their nation's bicentennial in 1988 by publishing a mul-
tivolume history of Australia, and they did this in an unusual
way. Australia was colonized by the British in January 1788. So
the bicentennial historians devoted an entire volume to Australia
as it existed in that year. Then, subsequent volumes were devoted
to similar cross-sections, or deep probes, at fifty-year intervals

after 1788. These are remarkable volumes that cover all aspects
of Australian life in those years—everything that was going on
in the politics, culture, economy, society, et cetera, in the selected
years, and all the connections among these aspects of life. But
there is no indication of why or how Australia changed between
1788 and 1838 or between 1888 and 1938. What were the dynam-
ics? You understand what Australian life was like in 1838, but
it's accidental if you can see why 1888 was so different. . . . One
Australian historian, Graeme Davison, has described the theory
behind this work, but I think the problem of explaining change
remains. One finds suggestions [of dynamics] only in the inter-
stices of what they wrote.

◆ ◆ ◆

Thus my response to the question of the relation between history
and fiction. The basic distinction, I wrote, is obvious and profound:

The literary imagination is boundless—and should be boundless.
History is an imaginative construction, too; but the historical
imagination must be closely bounded by the documentation—
limited by the evidence that has survived, and limited too by the
historian's obligation to be consistent with what has previously
been established.

As I wrote on another occasion:

If it's history, it can be disproved. You can't disprove a novel, but
you can disprove history; and that seems to me all the difference
in the world. Creativity in science, the physicist Richard Feynman
said, is imagination in a straitjacket. So, too, is creativity in history.

◆ ◆ ◆

Yet when I searched for the essential qualities of exceptionally creative historians, I wrote:

It is the wholeness of their visions, the capacity to conceive of an entire world and not merely one problem or one issue or one theme, that is the crucial element. In this capacity these historians are comparable, I believe, less to other scholarly historians than to the novelists who have created entire worlds, populated them, furnished them, traced their traumas and triumphs, their growth and decline. Faulkner, for example, conceiving a "mythical kingdom" in a county in northern Mississippi complete with an identifiable population of shopkeepers and mechanics, farmers and tenants and gentry—a county, Malcolm Cowley wrote, with "a population of 15,600 persons scattered over 2400 square miles. It sometimes seems to me that every house or hovel has been described in one of Faulkner's novels; and that all the people of the imaginary county, black and white, townsmen, farmers, and housewives, have played their parts in one connected story."

The central instinct, the crucial, necessary "genius," if I may use that word, that lay behind the creative historiography of the most energetic and creative historians seems to me to have been the capacity to project, like a novelist, a nonexistent, an impalpable world in all its living comprehension, and yet to do this within the constraints of verifiable facts.

◆ ◆ ◆

The impossibility of writing history with perfect objectivity and the fact that historical writing is, in the end, an act of imagination are no new discoveries, but they do not mean that history is inevitably a form of free-floating self-expression and that any version that comes up is as good as any other. As the economist Robert Solow remarked, the fact that there is no such thing as perfect antisepsis does not mean that one might as well do brain surgery in a sewer. The correspondence to actuality in history, the struggle to describe what actually happened, however dimly we may perceive it, is the essence of history. And that is so for everyone who writes a single page or paragraph or sentence of history, no matter what the technical epistemological problems are said to be—including those who write books with admirable objectivity on historians' failing efforts to attain objectivity.

◆ ◆ ◆

Nothing is more certain to distort history by anachronism than making up direct discourse, fictional conversation as if spoken by historical figures. And that is true no matter how skilled the historian is.

Samuel Eliot Morison, for example, slipped into fictional discourse repeatedly in his biography of Columbus, especially in describing the tense days and hours before the great discovery. He puts in the mouths of Columbus's sailors words like "Keep her off, damn your eyes—must I go below and take the stick myself?" Or again: "Hear anything? Sounds like breakers to me—nothing but the bow wave you fool—I tell you we won't sight land till Saturday. . . . Here's a hundred maravedis says we raise it by daylight." I don't know how fifteenth-century Spanish and Portuguese sailors actually talked to each other, what their slang was, how they used ordinary street language, but these yo-heave-ho pseudo-quotations sound to me like conversations one would have found in boys' adventure stories that students in St. Paul's School would have read early in the twentieth century—crossed, perhaps, with phrases that "Old Salts" in Northeast Harbor, Maine, were supposed to have used. To me, it's not sailors of the fifteenth century that are made vivid in these fictional phrases, but a romantic twentieth-century historian straining for effect.

◆ ◆ ◆

In certain areas in recent years historians have made progress in reaching into subjective experience. While technical psychohistory is still more a matter of theoretical discussion by social scientists than of practice by historians, ways have been found to explore public opinion in the past, to identify attitudes of various kinds, and to judge the pervasiveness and circulation of certain key notions. The range of such studies has been broad. Political thought has provided an important entrée. Working out from ideas as such to the broader aspects of political thought where ideas connect with social assumptions and attitudes, historians have been able to enter private worlds otherwise closed to them. . . .

And other, even more original and imaginative ways have been found to enter the realm of interior experience. Some of the most interesting have reached into nonverbal expressions of private experience and established subtle connections between nonverbal and verbal communication. Carl Schorske's Fin-de-Siècle Vienna: Politics and Culture *(1979), in which aspects of interior worlds are uncovered through examination of the connections among a variety of expressions of art forms, has set an attractive new style in scholarship. Schorske's fusings of urban architecture and political attitudes, of painting and "the liberal ego," and of the descriptive and metaphoric meanings of the garden—these connections among art forms and public life, constructed into a general picture of a community's "psyche," are being emulated and seem destined to shape the work of many historians of culture seeking a deeper understanding of human experience than traditional historical analysis provides.*

Schorske's style was, in fact, influential even before his book appeared. Six years earlier his student William McGrath published Dionysian Art and Populist Politics in Austria. *It not only demonstrated the common pan-Germanistic roots of Viktor Adler's socialism and Gustav Mahler's "meta-musical cosmos" (passages from the score of Mahler's Third Symphony precede a chapter on the Liberals' Linz Program) but located the origins of all of these diverging lines of history in the shared outlook of a particular circle of students in a single secondary school, Vienna's Schottengymnasium, and then in a political club at the University of Vienna. These writings on the German-speaking world of the late nine-*

teenth and early twentieth centuries may one day be brought into useful comparisons with accounts of similar circles in other cultures: Bloomsbury, Yeats's Dublin, or Herzen's world of Russian exiles in London, for example. And it may be possible to depict the cultural history of an entire era in terms of key "circles" of shared feelings and outlooks.

◆ ◆ ◆

There are areas in which biography and history are intermingled intimately. A good biography is a piece of history, but there are distinctions to be made—distinctions, I should say, suggested by Paul Lazarsfeld, a sociologist, when he was urged to write a memoir of his own career. He asked himself what possible justification there could be for doing this. He said in "An Episode in the History of Social Research"[2] that he could find only three reasons:

The first justification is if one is a person of great consequence in human affairs—Churchill or de Gaulle or Roosevelt; or a great figure in intellectual history, like Kant or Einstein. Any circumstance in such a person's biography is important, because we need to know every possible detail in order to understand what he or she did and why. If Napoleon hadn't had the temperament he had, if the details of his early life had been different, the world would be very different. Consequently, almost anything one can find out about the details and circumstances of Napoleon's life is important.

Second, Lazarsfeld said, an individual can be a representative of a group of some importance. He himself or she herself might not be important, but as a representative of some group of people, he or she might be very much worth studying in detail. In this sense, a relatively obscure person can very well justify an extensive biography that would be a contribution to history.

And, third, he concluded, some people are excellent witnesses. Although they may not have been representative of anything in particular and certainly did not shape history, they were present at the right place and the right time. Harold Nicolson, for example.

He was a diplomat, a prolific author, near the center of Britain's political and high society world from the 1930s to the 1960s, and he recorded what he saw, heard, and said. His diary and letters, published in abridged form in three volumes, is a fascinating witness to important events, especially as it captures the contingencies, the uncertainties, the false starts of the public events in his time and also the intersection of private and public events.[3]

It seems to me that these are very good categories of biographies as history. For the rest, biographies are studies in human character, studies in human nature and in the fascination of people as such. Some people are strange, profound, amusing, evil, benevolent, intriguing, revealing—in all sorts of combinations. And one's understanding of and interest in human nature are expanded by knowing about them—even such strange figures as Sir Edmund Backhouse.

Backhouse was an aesthete and accomplished sinologist, who was also a pornographer and literary forger, who lived in an almost completely imaginary world. Somehow he managed to convince hard-headed men of affairs of his realism and practicality, passed himself off as the lover of China's Empress Dowager, and fooled almost everybody with an apparently invaluable diary of the late Manchu years, which he faked. Trevor-Roper devoted a large book to him, and I read it with great interest, simply because Backhouse was so outrageous and interesting. However, that doesn't necessarily make good history, except as the historical background is drawn—in Backhouse's case, the story of late Victorian aestheticism and the decay of the Manchu Empire.

◆ ◆ ◆

I learned much about biography and history in writing an account of the most despised loyalist of the American Revolution, Thomas Hutchinson, the last royal governor of Massachusetts. Despite the patriots' vilification of him as the worst would-be despot who threatened their liberties, I found myself sympathetic to that rather stiff, intelligent, highly literate, uncorrupted, honest, upright provincial merchant-turned-judge-and-politician. And as I wrote, I discovered myself involved in a small technical maneuver entering into the pages I was writing. I found that

> *quite unconsciously I was dropping the attributions. In writing biography, one is always saying, "he said," "she felt," "he believed"— by way of separating the author from his or her subject, denying the identification—and one seeks phrases that would avoid the repetition. It's one of the tiresome things about biography—and so one becomes ingenious, with phrases like "it occurred to him"; or "for her it was a matter of. . . ." But at that point, a slippage can take place. The attribution can become vague and only implied— and then I discovered a complete slippage that crept into what I was writing. I had dropped the attribution altogether, in sentences like, "The mob was out of hand," rather than "Hutchinson said or thought the mob was out of hand." The movement of the prose was such that the attribution became at best only vaguely implied, and as I continued in this way, the whole texture began to change. The voice was no longer Hutchinson's, it was mine.*
>
> *The point is, in biography more than in any other form of history, the authorial stance can get confused. The voices tend to merge, with the positive effect of strengthening the author's and hence the reader's identification with the subject and the negative effect of lessening the author's capacity to have enough distance from the subject to exert critical control, to assess the subject's perceptions, and in the end to judge his or her behavior. It also robs the author of any ironic capacity—of the kind of irony that permeates the biography of another putative villain, Archbishop Laud. Trevor-Roper's biography of that obsessed man is as ironic as any novel written by that great ironist, Thomas Mann. Mann—to digress—is superbly ironic in the fictional narrators he invents to tell his tales, like the naïve, gullible humanist Irish monk Clemens in* The Holy Sinner, *who credulously*

retails as truth the mythical and miraculous tales of Pope Gregory's oedipal sins, his bitter penance, and final redemption, all of which Mann concocted, with ironic amusement, from the twelfth-century narrative poem by the middle-high German knight and poet Hartmann von Aue. Similarly but more serious is his narrator of the life of the doomed musical genius Adrian Leverkühn in Doctor Faustus. *The story is told not by Mann but, ostensibly, by Leverkühn's lifelong companion, Serenus Zeitblom, whose biographical views Mann is free to treat ironically. And then there are his straight ironies, as in that early story "The Prodigy" (the title itself is ironic: "Das Wunderkind"). In that small piece, Mann tells, with exquisite irony and a comically pseudo-pedantic voice, the story of a boy pianist in a velvet suit giving a recital to the fatuous pride of his bourgeois relatives. These are brilliant works of rich irony, precisely the kind of irony denied to historical biographers.*[4]

No historian writing biography could distance himself or herself from the story by inventing or discovering a putative narrator through whom he or she might comment ironically. One might have treated Hutchinson ironically, and I thought of trying to do that. But he was too vulnerable a target for that, too slight for anything but a light touch here and there if one were to avoid mockery. And mockery was not what I was after. And in any case I found him so thin-skinned and put-upon that I found myself identifying more and more with him, as I puzzled over his basic problem, namely, what had he done wrong? What should he do? I wrote, dropping the attribution. He had no choice (ditto). He must enforce the law (ditto again). And so, faithfully and fatally, he did.

◆ ◆ ◆

The first and in some ways the most important transformation that has overtaken education in America was completed before the end of the colonial period and underlay the entire subsequent history of American education. But that becomes apparent only when *one thinks of education not only as formal pedagogy but as the entire process by which a culture transmits itself across the generations; and when one assumes the past was not incidentally but essentially different from the present; when one seeks as the points of greatest relevance those critical passages of history where elements of our familiar present, still part of an unfamiliar past, begin to disentangle themselves, begin to emerge amid confusion and uncertainty. For these soft, ambiguous moments where the words we use and the institutions we know are notably present but are still enmeshed in older meanings and different purposes—these are the moments of true origination. They reveal in purest form essential features which subsequent events complicate and modify but never completely transform.*

◆ ◆ ◆

I do not think history has collapsed into sociology or anthropology or some kind of ethnosocial science. We will always need to know, in some sequential—that is, narrative—form, what has happened in the past, what the struggles were all about, where we have come from; and we will always need to extend the poor reach of our own immediate experience into other lives, accurately portrayed, that have gone before. But we will do so in more complicated and sophisticated ways than we have in the past. History in the richest sense must be, I believe, both a study and a story—that is, structural studies woven into narratives that explain the long-term process of change and short term accidents, decisions, and encounters which together changed the world from what it had been. But we must still be storytellers, narrators—though of events lodged deep in their natural contexts.

Appendix

MORISON AND HANDLIN

I t is the practice in the faculty of arts and sciences at Harvard (and I assume elsewhere) to present to the faculty a memorial Minute on the life and services of departed members. In the years after World War II, when the Harvard faculty was relatively small, these essays could be extensive, and collections of them have been published in book form. But recently they have been restricted in length. What follows are two Minutes I wrote devoted to two of my teachers. The contrast between them could not have been more vivid; nor could their devotion to the university they served have been more intense. The first is the Minute verbatim, the second is an extension of what was submitted to the faculty.

Morison

Samuel Eliot Morison, the greatest American narrative historian since Francis Parkman, died on May 15, 1976, in Boston, in his eighty-ninth year. He was then still living in the house at 44 Brimmer Street in which he had been born and which he had inherited from his

Samuel Eliot Morison.

grandfather, Samuel Eliot, who had built it in 1870. Such continu-
ities lay at the heart of Morison's career, shaped his achievement as
a scholar and writer, and help explain his extraordinary service to
Harvard College and University.

His contribution to the life of his alma mater fits no ordinary pattern. Except for one term at the University of California and three
years at Oxford as the first Harmsworth Professor, he taught at Harvard all his professional life. But while his classes were always well

regarded, they were never particularly popular, and he had very few graduate students. There is no "Morison School" of American historians, though many historians were influenced by him. His respect for the history department and for his contemporaries in it was great; but while he fulfilled his teaching obligations with his usual efficiency and style, he assumed no administrative duties of any kind and did not shape the development of historical studies in the university. Yet his contribution to the life of Harvard, like his contribution to the literature of history, was enormous and altogether unique. Peculiarly positioned to experience personally, as it were, the whole course of Harvard's history, he revealed it to the world and to itself as no one had ever done before and as no one will probably ever do again, and this was in miniature what he sought to do for his native state, for the life of those who sailed the seas, and for the American nation.

Morison's family had been prominent in the history of Massachusetts and of Harvard almost from their founding. His father's people were Anglo-Irish, his mother's English; both lines were established in Massachusetts by the end of the seventeenth century and quickly became associated with the college. One eighteenth-century great-great-grandfather, Samuel Eliot, endowed the professorship of Greek literature that still bears his name but did not attend the college; he was the last in the family to suffer from such a disability. Two generations later—the generation of Morison's grandparents—the Eliot cousinage seems to have *become* Harvard: one cousin of that generation, Samuel Eliot, the historian's beloved grandfather, served as overseer; a second was Pres. Charles William Eliot, whose father had been treasurer of the college; a third was Prof. Charles Eliot Norton, whose father, Andrews Norton, had been Dexter Professor. To this maternal line of Eliots, "frugal and ascetic, dedicated to literature and other good works," was joined the very different strain of the Otis family, "genial, worldly, and luxurious in their tastes," Morison's grandmother Emily Marshall Otis being the granddaughter of the Federalist grandee Harrison Gray Otis. The Morison family had strayed away from Boston at one point—to

Baltimore, where they directed the Peabody Institute—but only tempo-
rarily; Morison's father returned in due course, having acquired "more
courtly manners than the general run of Boston young men," which
may have helped him in his courtship of Samuel Eliot's daughter.

Morison's parents settled in with the Eliot household on Brimmer
Street, and the historian grew up at the very heart of proper Boston society. He recalled it in later years as an affluent but not extravagant community, provincial in some ways but wide in culture, tolerant, liberal,
and devoted to reform causes. "When a family had accumulated a certain fortune," Morison wrote of the Boston of his childhood, "instead
of trying to build it up still further to become a Rockefeller or Car-
negie or Huntington, and then perhaps discharge its debt to society by
some great foundation, it would step out of business or finance and try
to accomplish something in literature, education, medical research, the
arts, or public service." Morison followed this pattern perfectly. "It was
never suggested," he wrote, "that 'Sammy' should go into business, or
make money, or do anything but what his tastes and talents impelled
him to do, no matter how unrenumerative." As expected, he attended
private schools in Boston, where he was taught a strictly classical curriculum, and then went off to St. Paul's School in New Hampshire, where
the same kind of education was continued. By then he had long since
become expert in the two sports that most interested him and that he
continued to enjoy almost all his life: riding and sailing. He was as familiar with the many stables that then flourished in the Charles Street and
Beacon Hill area as he was with the North Shore waters and the coast of
Maine, which he came to love above all other places on earth.

None of this was exceptional for a boy of his social position and
physical vigor; nor was his entrance into Harvard with the class of 1908.
For him the college represented no break with the culture of his origins.
His immediate family was constantly involved in the management of
the college, the faculty was closely integrated into the Boston society
Morison knew, and undergraduates were always in evidence. On Sun-
day afternoons, he recalled, upperclassmen came calling on families

like his: "one could see them, resplendent in frock coat, fancy waistcoat, and high hat, carrying a cane, walking up and down Commonwealth Avenue to call on the mammas who had invited them to dine or dance."

He fitted into this college life easily, a handsome, vigorous, and affluent young man, and proceeded with no great distinction through a course of studies that emphasized mathematics, until in his junior year his academic interests took fire. It was then that he found in historical study the perfect field for his lifework. He had been brought up in a city that "fairly reeks with history, in a family which had taken part in historical events since the founding of the colonies, and . . . [had] been given an old-fashioned classical education with a foundation in ancient languages." But more important than all that was the discovery, through his teacher, Edward Channing, of the writings of his grandfather's friend Francis Parkman. In Parkman's narrative volumes on the century of conflict between England and France in the New World, Morison found an inspiration that never faded. For Parkman was not only a captivating narrator whose stories read like novels but also "a man of the outdoors, an accomplished horseman, fisherman, and hunter, a lover of the great northern forest"; he wrote not as a library scholar but as a participant, following Polybius's dictum that a historian should be a man of action. He visited the scenes he described, lived as did his subjects on the fish and game he could catch, shot the rapids, joined a band of Sioux Indians at one point and a monastery at another in order to know personally the experiences and sensibilities of those whose lives he proposed to describe. And yet Parkman had the self-discipline and thoroughness of the most devoted research scholar, and the literary skill of a novelist.

It was that remarkable combination of scholarship, literature, and action all fused into the service of historical self-awareness that inspired the twenty-four-year-old Morison and set the goals of his prodigiously productive life. A romantic? "No tags, please," Morison replied to this reiterated charge: "Read me first!" But he *was* a romantic. From the moment his interest in history dawned. he cast everything he wrote into a dramatic structure of human struggle, and conveyed in every way he could the passion that he knew underlies human events. From the very beginning, he thought of himself as a storyteller (history, he never tired of repeating, *had* to be a story: "Who will read Sir Lewis Namier tomorrow?") and the stories had to be involving and in some way heroic. The mere recital of facts was as meaningless as "scientific" analysis, all trends and factors, devoid of people, conflict, passion, values, and accomplishment; and he had no interest in compiling social data.

The fit of Morison's choice of career with his temperament and natural gifts was remarkable. Inspired by the romance of history, he nevertheless had extraordinary technical abilities. He was exceptionally self-disciplined, a good linguist, and capable of the most exacting and concentrated study of documents and the most prolonged efforts of composition. He had an instinct for accuracy on details, unstrained common sense in interpretation, and an almost flawless ear for natural and effective prose rhythms. Above all, he had the urge, indeed the passion, to express his personality in writing. Sometimes, he wrote, "some incident, view, or scrap of poetry strikes a bell that reverberates through the deep and brings to the surface impressions and memories extending over many years. When that happens I feel impelled to write something immediately." He was incapable of writing history that was wholly external to him. He did not pick subjects defined by the objective progress of historical knowledge; he did not define problems systematically or attempt to resolve the strategic blockages in historical understanding. He proceeded as a poet, taking as subjects his personal interests, things he loved and knew personally. It was this need for personal self-expression, filtered through the demanding objectivity of historical narration, that carried him through six decades of continuous creativity as a historian and that defined the subjects he wrote about.

He began his professional career, after a year of study in Paris, with a doctoral dissertation on the life of his great-great-grandfather, Harrison Gray Otis, using family papers conveniently stored on Brimmer Street. Published in 1913, this solid two-volume "life and times" biography—rather charmless by Morison's standards but a distinguished piece of historical writing by normal criteria—established his professional reputation. But though the politics of his Federalist forebears was a personal subject of great interest to him, it did not touch the deepest springs of his personality, which were then, and always remained, a passionate love of the sea—a love, he said, so great "that writing about it is almost as embarrassing as making a confession of religious faith." In his second book, *The Maritime History of Massachusetts* (1921), he found direct expression for his love of the sea and was able to pour into it all the knowledge he had picked up from the old sailors whose memories went back to the days of the great clipper ships. It was his first work of art, and it remains a wonderfully readable and informative book, yet a very personal document. He must have known as he wrote it—"in one swoop, on a wave of euphoria; only eleven months . . . elaps[ing] between the beginning of research and the finished copy"—he must have known that he had found his perfect subject in the stories of those who had sailed the seas, and with it a unique and idiomatic manner of writing history.

By the time it appeared, he was a lecturer in history at Harvard, having taught for a term at the University of California and having served briefly in the army and with the research team of the American delegation to the Versailles peace conference. In 1922 he was appointed the Harmsworth Professor of American History at Oxford University, where he remained until 1925. While there, with his usual diligence, he completed an edition of documents of the American Revolution and the two-volume *Oxford History of the United States*, the forerunner of the immensely popular survey he published with Henry Steele Commager in 1930, *The Growth of the American Republic*. But the great events of the Oxford years took place not in England but in Spain, which he visited in 1925. In the Columbian Library in Seville he was shown Ferdinand Columbus's copy of the works of the tragedian Seneca, with the strange prophecy of the discovery of America, next to which Morison saw inscribed in Ferdinand's hand "this simple but glorious annotation . . . 'This prophecy was fulfilled by my father . . . the Admiral in the year 1492.'" At that moment, Morison later recalled, he determined to get on with the work on Columbus he had been contemplating, to follow his voyages personally by sail and so to get to the truth of the question of Columbus's own contribution to the epochal discovery.

On the same trip Morison was taken to the Chapter House of the Cathedral of Toledo, and there he saw the great series of portraits of the cardinal archbishops from the beginning of the Christian church to the present. "And when I looked at that, I said, how short our annals are in the United States. What would be the longest series of people I could find? Ah, I have it . . . the Presidents of Harvard College, from 1636 on." With the Harvard Tercentenary only eleven years away, plans should be made to write the whole history of America's oldest institution, and Morison decided to do it.

Upon his return to Harvard, now as full professor, he proposed to President Lowell that he be appointed Harvard's official historian on its three-hundredth anniversary and be given full access to the archives and subsidies for the eventual publications. Lowell agreed, and Morison's first major project was launched. The books that resulted, published on schedule in 1936, were *The Founding of Harvard College*; the two-volume *Harvard College in the Seventeenth Century*; the extraordinarily readable survey, *Three Centuries of Harvard*; and the edition of essays, *The Development of Harvard University, 1869–1929*. Of these five volumes, which together comprise the *Tercentennial History of Harvard College and University*, the first three, on the early years, form a masterpiece of historical writing; along with the later Columbus biography, they are probably the finest products of Morison's pen. They not only elevated Harvard's history to a new plane of sophistication and completeness and celebrated the Puritans' commitment to learning in an unforgettable way, but revealed aspects of American cultural history until then unknown, and made a major contribution to intellectual history generally. The college and university could now be seen as national rather than regional institutions, consistent with President Conant's effort to broaden their constituencies to the nation at large. Again, the personal identification, the personal expression, the muted emotion, rigorously disciplined and objectified, generated the motive force; again, the story was of people, not of stylized or quantified creatures—passionate beings, wayward souls, natural, striving, ambitious, frustrated, and familiarly human people. Again, Morison fascinated his readers by conveying his own fascination with the human subjects, the personalities, he was writing about.

Offshoots of this major effort appeared in characteristic profusion: *Builders of the Bay Colony* (1930), a volume of biographical studies of the Puritan leaders; *The Puritan Pronaos* (1936), an intellectual history of Puritan New England; and a string of monographic essays on the technical problems he encountered in writing the Harvard histories. In addition, during the same years Morison founded and largely edited the *New England Quarterly*, a journal that still flourishes, now in its ninety-second year of publication.

When the Harvard volumes were through the press, Morison turned back to his other resolve of 1925, to write an exhaustive biography of Columbus based on a personal retracing of the discoverer's ocean voyages. Harvard friends and the college itself produced the funds and equipment he needed, and Morison launched the famous Harvard Columbus expedition. His two vessels roamed the ocean seas in 1939–40, following Columbus from Spain to the Canaries, then through the Caribbean islands and along the Spanish main, verifying every reported landfall, checking every observation and journal entry. The resulting biography, *Admiral of the Ocean Sea* (1942), vindicated Columbus's claims and established him for the first time as a skilled navigator. The book, which proved to be extremely popular, also magnified Morison's and Harvard's fame, brought the historian the first of two Pulitzer Prizes, and paved the way for the easy acceptance by President Roosevelt and the U.S. Navy of Morison's next major project, his monumental *History of the United States Naval Operations in World War II*.

Like the Harvard history, the naval history was Morison's idea. Roosevelt, a navy man whom Morison had known slightly, admired the Columbus book and welcomed Morison's proposal that he be appointed the nation's official historian of naval operations in World War II. The Columbus book helped too in securing the navy's acceptance of Morison's terms: that he be free from all but security censorship; that he be allowed to withhold publication until he could consult enemy documents; and that he have free access to all U.S. naval vessels on active duty as well as working space at appropriate naval bases. Here was the ultimate opportunity for all Morison's ambitions, the perfect fusion of all his interests. He would participate personally aboard any vessel he chose in the greatest naval war in history; he would have the complete support of the U.S. government; and he would have access to all the evidence, printed and oral, public and secret, that could be produced. Only Thucydides, among historians, had seen so great a struggle at such close hand and enjoyed the freedom afterward to write the story out in full.

Morison was fifty-five, recently appointed Jonathan Trumbull Professor of American History, when, as official historian with the rank of lieutenant commander, he joined his first naval operation; he was seventy-five, retired from Harvard and from the navy with the rank of rear admiral, when in 1962 he published the fifteenth and final volume of his naval history. It is a fabulous achievement. A participant's history, based on a veritable mountain of documentation (six-foot-high stacks of reports for each major engagement of the war), it attempts to portray the entire panoramic scene of battle on all the oceans of the globe while depicting in finest detail exactly what happened in every engagement and why. The apparent ease with which Morison assembled this immense story, with the help of a very small staff of assistants and his faithful secretary, Antha Card, is almost miraculous. Even more remarkable is the unflagging drama of the narrative and its integrity as a single story. No one could write these thousands of pages of narrative without some repetitions in episodic structure, some artificiality of staging, some self-conscious dramatics. The miracle is that there is so little of this in such a well-ordered mass of narrative detail.

The honors that fell to him when the dimensions of this accomplishment became clear surpass those accorded any modern historian. He was treated like royalty when he traveled abroad, and in his own country he had become an institution long before the U.S. Information Service recognized him in 1975 and filmed for the record and for foreign audiences an hour-long interview with him at his home in Northeast Harbor, Maine.

By then, the year before he died, he had long since put the naval history behind him and had completed the last of his major projects, which he had conceived in vague form while working out the Columbus book decades before. It was a comprehensive narrative of all the coastal explorations of North and South America, based on personal retracings, by sailing vessel and airplane, of the voyages of discovery that had revealed the boundaries of the New World. With the assistance of his friends James Nields and Mauricio Obregón, of Bogotá, Colombia, Morison sailed and flew in the track of all the discoverers, from the Norsemen to Walter Raleigh—most elaborately Magellan, whose circumnavigation he retraced—verified their journals, mapped their expeditions, recorded their adventures, photographed their landfalls and the ruins of their settlements, and boiled the whole massive story of their accomplishments into two big volumes crowded with maps, photographs, portraits, and charts, which he called *The European Discovery of America*. The first volume appeared in 1971, when Morison was eighty-four; the second in 1974, two years before he died. When this final work was finished, he called on the Rev. G. Harris Collingwood, rector of the Church of the Advent, where Morison regularly worshipped, and asked Collingwood if it would be possible for him "to make a public statement of my thankfulness for God's mercy. Today I finished the volume of the Southern Voyages; it was a plan of writing I began fifty years ago."

Morison's energy at every stage of this lifelong career of historical writing was prodigious, and he worked with apparent ease. Down to

World War II he never wrote in the summers but spent those months sailing, traveling, and reading, and he advised young historians to do likewise. But as he grew older, time became more precious to him, and as he wrote at the age of seventy-six, "knowing that death will break my pen, I now work almost the year round, praying to be spared to write what is in me to write." In his last thirty years he turned out one small book almost every summer, while moving ahead on his major projects. The many works of those years are not all of uniformly high quality. The discipline that had controlled the personal expression in the Harvard series and the naval history began to slip. The writing became somewhat self-indulgent, the author's personality increasingly intrusive. But the books continued to charm, and Morison's protean creativity remained unimpeded. A preliminary bibliography lists a total of well over fifty volumes, and no one knows how many journal articles, edited documents, scholarly notes, speeches, and private publications he wrote.

And yet, for all of this, he remained an amateur rather than a professional historian, much like his master, Parkman, though he had skills and knowledge that Parkman never dreamed of. He had no interest in keeping up with the latest developments in historical interpretation or technique, dismissing applied psychology and analytical, not to say quantitative, history as a betrayal of the historian's obligation to tell the human story of what has happened. He was in due course elected to the presidency of the American Historical Association, but he did not attempt to shape the policies and played no role in the politics of that organization. Professional colleagues, even those who knew him well, found him an imposing but stiff, unbending, and rather taciturn personage. The story is told that once Morison attended the national historical convention, and to everyone's surprise, he appeared on the hotel mezzanine crowded with wheeling-dealing, gossiping academics. Into the melee he strode, tall, erect as always, his hands cocked in his jacket pockets, peering myopically ahead into the middle distance. The crowd fell silent and parted before him, and then, as he walked on, it closed behind him at a respectful distance. And so, with his characteristic half-smile directed at one and all, he paced back and forth through the crowd, passing immaculate on dry land. Finally an old friend of his from Boston came on the scene, went up to Morison, and said, "Sam, what are you doing?" "Doing?" said Morison with surprise. "*Doing!* Why what do you think I'm doing? *Mixing!*"

To the postwar generation of students at Harvard, he was a magisterial figure from a distant world. He insisted that the men in his classes wear coat and tie, and he himself lectured at times in naval uniform or in riding breeches. The latter was less surprising to those who recalled that when he started his teaching career as assistant to Albert Bushnell Hart, he used to gallop over to Massachusetts Hall from Brimmer Street and pack up his blue books in saddlebags before continuing his ride. He seldom made specific appointments, suggesting to people who wanted to talk with him that they "just stop around some time" at his study in Widener Library. But when they did, they often found him preoccupied with his own work and forgetful even of who the visitors were. He was an utterly private man, sensitive in a most complex way, uneasy with people who were not part of his own social sphere, and removed from the everyday broils of academic life.

His remoteness from the ordinary scene was at times amusing. He recorded laconically in one autobiographical account that he had won what he called "the usual prizes given to historians." But in fact these "usual" prizes in his case included two Pulitzer Prizes, two Bancroft Prizes, the Loubat Prize, the Jusserand Prize, the Christopher Award, the St. Thomas More Award, the Mahan Award, the Emerson-Thoreau Medal of the American Academy of Arts and Sciences, the gold medal of the American Academy of Arts and Letters, the Kennedy Award of the Massachusetts Historical Society, the Presidential Medal of Freedom, seven battle stars of the U.S. Navy, the Legion of Merit with Combat Clasp, the Order of Merit of the Italian government with the rank of Commendatore, twelve honorary degrees, and the unique Balzan Foundation Award, which he and three Europeans shared with the pope.

Morison cultivated his privacy. He gave instructions that no memorial service be held for him at Harvard, and he took steps to see to it that no one would write an intimate biography of him. In the end it was a vulnerable sensibility that he was protecting; but it was always exposed. He could no more suppress his feelings than he could stop writing. He was deeply attached to his first wife, Elizabeth Greene, writing for private circulation a book in her memory when she died in 1945. For his second wife, Priscilla Barton, nineteen years his junior, he displayed an affection bordering on adoration. To her he dedicated almost every book he wrote after their marriage in 1949, and when she died in 1973, he published privately a profoundly felt and moving memoir of her life and of their marriage. He had begun it in 1970 when he was eighty-three, in the fear, he wrote, that he would die without leaving behind for her to read a testimony of his love, appreciation, and respect. Such sensibility was the deepest part of Morison's nature. It was the sensibility of an artist, but an artist who lived by a special credo, which he requested be inscribed on his gravestone: *"Dream dreams, then write them—aye, but live them first!"*

He was, in the Latin meaning of the word, superb: proud, bold, egregious; and he cast some of the spell of his imposing personality and of his ceaseless creativity over his college and university, for which he had a lifelong affection and which he served, in his unique way, for over forty years.

Handlin

Oscar Handlin was the most influential and creative historian of American social life in the second half of the twentieth century. He was born in Brooklyn in 1915, the son of Russian Jewish immigrants who ran a small grocery store. Eighty years later, in a deeply reflective mood, he gave an account of his wayward but intellectually intense boyhood in a paper he called "Being Jewish: The Endless Quest." It probed what he recalled of his foundational experiences and his then-present thoughts of the world around him.

Oscar Handlin.

His native world, he wrote, was only nominally Brooklyn; in fact, it was a small district of the borough called Mapleton. Populated entirely by émigré Jews who called themselves "Litwaks" (Lithuanians) though they came from all over the Jewish Pale of Eastern Europe, it carried on the devout, theistic culture of Orthodox Judaism. Born into the inner life of that Yiddish-speaking, Hebrew-worshipping world, Handlin as a boy experienced it all, identified with it, felt comfortable in it ("the street provided boys a setting for their social life . . . 62nd street welcomed ball players"), and he felt the urge to participate as expected.

For him the love of learning lay at the heart of it all. He recalled his mother listening secretly at the door while her brothers fed on the learning denied her, and his father, who read when he could, simply, he told the young Handlin, for no other reason than to know. Though dutiful, with "misty visions of the rabbinate," Handlin, in his youthful search to understand God and His meanings, became restless in his comfortable native subculture and sought to explore and transcend it. Just before his thirteenth birthday his father presented him to a yeshiva in Manhattan, and he professed to the elders his desire to learn. "Come," they said, and he did. But enrolled in the yeshiva in his search for the grounds of the theistic culture he had inherited, he found not answers but puzzles that confounded him. "Talmud baffled me," he recalled; "the structure of the whole escaped me . . . my initial excitement faded and I learned little." Thereafter in his secular high-school years, he apparently broke free of the discipline of both home and school and devised a private schedule that came to settle on omnivorous reading ("manic browsing," he called it) in the Brooklyn and New York public libraries, which carried him into and quickly through the demands of Brooklyn College. But his early years had not been wasted. He had failed to achieve the knowledge of divinity he had sought, but he had learned vital truths. He knew that growing up in Mapleton was simply given ("Birth made me a Jew, that is a person who studied out of the desire to grasp the Tree of Life—that is, to learn"). "It was a fact, taken for granted. It was not good; it was not bad, and it was not a matter of choice." Above all, he learned the rule of life: to "recognize the world as it was and not as it should be. . . . A hard and abrasive world left no room for illusions. Problems such as discrimination . . . could be painful . . . but they were not surprising, and they set the terms within which people like us had to exist in the world as it was." And in addition, he had learned to aim high. "Nothing less would do than to strike at once for the very top, bypass high school, even college, proceed directly to study for the rabbinate. Never mind my spotty preparation, my imperfect Hebrew, my nonexistent Aramaic. Plunge in; nothing but the best—that is, the most difficult—would do."

And so in 1934, at the age of eighteen, with a degree from Brooklyn College, he felt led to Harvard, which he considered the national citadel of learning. His arrival at Harvard was extraordinary. He took a cheap excursion train trip to Boston, put up in the YMCA, and at eight-thirty in the morning (the train arrived at six a.m., and he was impatient), he knocked on the door of Michael Karpovich, to whom he had a letter of introduction, and said he wanted to enter the graduate school. Karpovich, a displaced Russian scholar new to the ways of American academia, startled and disheveled, pulled himself together, took Handlin on a quick tour of the campus, and phoned the young professor Crane Brinton for help. The result was that Handlin spent the next day in an extended and, in his view, quite satisfactory discussion with Brinton on the eighteenth-century Enlightenment. He was accepted.

After receiving his doctorate under the direction of Arthur Schlesinger, Sr., in 1940, except for two years of teaching in Brooklyn, he taught at Harvard until his retirement. It is an indication of the early recognition of the breadth of his talents that his first regular appointments at Harvard (1945) were as instructor, then assistant professor, in social science, approved jointly by three departments: history, psychology, and sociology. By then the publication in 1941 of his dissertation on Boston's immigrants, 1790–1865, had begun a stream of writings— at least forty books written or edited and innumerable articles and reviews. His *Commonwealth: A Study of the Role of Government in the American Economy: Massachusetts 1774–1816* (1947), written with his wife, Mary Flug Handlin, published six years after the dissertation, is a masterwork of technical scholarship. It revealed, at a time when democratic impulses had become widely accessible, the forceful role of government in the early development of the economy—a controversial conclusion relevant to the public debates of the postwar years. Four years later his lyric, evocative *The Uprooted* (1951)—with its famous opening, "Once I thought to write a history of the immigrants in

America. Then I discovered that the immigrants were American history"—won the Pulitzer Prize and carried readers, as no work of history
had done, into the interior, emotional world of immigrant experiences.
It stimulated a generation's interest in the passages of uprooted people
through the tortuous strains of resettlement and assimilation.

But, while he wrote extensively on immigration he was never confined to that subject or any other. He led the nation's historians in
shifting the emphasis away from Frederick Jackson Turner's rural and
western orientation to that of the nation's urban life and complex eth-
nicity. He wrote on the earliest period (the seventeenth-century origins of slavery, and the popular sources of revolutionary thought) as
well as on the latest (Al Smith, Watergate), and he wrote two comprehensive works on the nation's entire history.

He was unique in his understanding and explanation of history.
It was not for him an assemblage of information but a form of intellection, a cognitive process, which he expressed year after year in his
books and articles and in the classroom as well. His lectures contained
little descriptive information or narration. They were tightly woven
analyses of the structures of events and circumstances that explained
how things came to be the way they were. The lectures were dense, for
some difficult to grasp.

I experienced the full force of his intellect and personality and one
of his deepest held convictions about history when I first met him. As
a largely unsupervised graduate student, I was struggling with a dissertation on religion and economic development and had got myself
tangled up in the theories of Max Weber, Ernst Troeltsch, and others,
and was told that the person to see was young Professor Handlin,
who knew about such things. When he asked me what the problem
was, I explained it at length, exhaustively, with every twist and detail.
Then I waited for his response. I can still recall it. He said "ECH," and
waved his hand dismissively. I got the message, and it was liberating.
I never again got caught up in theoretical issues in approaching a
historical problem.

His services to the university were extraordinary. While lecturing to undergraduates, he directed the graduate work of eighty doctoral candidates, whom he encouraged, inspired, and protected. They all felt that he cared about their interests, and with his nation-wide network of contacts in the profession, he would do what he could for their emerging careers. An excellent administrator, he was a dominant force in the affairs of the history department, served as the Harvard University librarian (1979–84), and began the library's modernization. In a crisis he took over the directorship of the Harvard University Press (1972). He created and directed the Warren Center for Studies in American History as well as his own Center for the Study of the History of Liberty in America. And he was equally active outside the university. He was a co-founder of a new television station that emphasized local affairs, and he became for a time a television commentator. He served as Fulbright commissioner, as an overseer of Brandeis University, and as a trustee of the New York Public Library, and he testified in Congress for the reform of American immigration policy.

He was liberal in social controversies, especially those related to immigration, race, social justice, and equal opportunity. But then in the Vietnam era, shocked by what he took to be the naïve views of the left-leaning professoriat, he turned to the right and became deeply conservative in his politics. He could understand why students might try to turn the university into a political instrument. They were, after all, ignorant. And he could understand why political activists unaffiliated with Harvard might wish to do so. But he could never understand why some of his own Harvard colleagues, committed as he was to impartial scholarship and to the integrity of the university, would do so.

But if what he took to be the naïve political apostasy of some of his closest colleagues shocked and depressed him, the modernizing changes sweeping through fields of scholarship affected him even more profoundly. The traditional foundations of historical study were being challenged by fashionable ideas derived from philosophical sources. Where once there had been elemental certainties—that the people of the past had in fact existed, had acted and thought in their own terms, and that what they had done and thought could be discovered to some verifiable degree—there were now visions of past worlds that reflected not the objective facts—the truth of what in fact had happened—but the viewers' beliefs and purposes.

To this and other epistemological challenges Handlin replied again and again. History, he believed, was essentially a craft with rigorous demands and standards, but everywhere he saw signs of its corruption. For some, facts being inert until animated by the imagination, meant that history and fiction were indistinguishable. And indeed invented speech and imagined emotions were becoming popular even in serious works of scholarship. Where once historians had seen a large picture based on broad knowledge within which to locate their specific research there were now isolated monographs vaguely, if at all, associated with larger themes. History, he declared to the American Historical Society in 1971, was "a discipline in crisis," and in a series of essays and critical reviews he became a spokesman for the preservation of the craft's traditions and a scourge of theories misapplied to history, especially ideas borrowed from the social sciences.

In 1979 he gathered together seventeen of his polemical essays and published them in a volume called *Truth in History*. The title itself was provocative, and many of the essays were challenging, pugnacious, and unforgiving as he defended the heart of his beliefs. He began with a simple proposition:

> There is a real world out there, not one just imagined as in a dream or a nightmare, not just as a vision in the haze of a narcotic spell or a mystic ashram, but actual—not something conjured up by the observer. . . . How do we know truth from illusion? Now / then? Of the two common kinds of tests, I turn away from that of theory, the procedure known in philosophy as epistemology. I refuse to play that elaborate and high-flying game of abstractions. My line is that of the alternative test of experience, valid for 1896

and 1796 and 1696 as it is for 1996. . . . My dispute is not so much
with the abstractions of philosophers, fashionably facile though
some of them may be. My concern lies rather in the use clumsy
writers of history have made of those theories.

And he cited individual historians and the errors of their work.

Understandably, many of the reviews of the book were critical.
Some of Handlin's greatest admirers found the book "sad and angry,"
but they were the first to say that it was a book that should be read by
every historian.

The essential problem, Handlin believed, was not simply the naïveté
and misunderstandings of specific historians but the conditions in
which they worked. The context of academic life had changed in ways
that had helped undermine history's traditional rigor. The post–World
War II expansion—in numbers of universities, of departments, of students and faculties backed by escalating resources—had led to perfunc-
tory scrutiny of qualifications and a market mentality. For historians
that meant increased fragmentation and specialization "in erroneous
imitation of the hard sciences." It was a "swelling universe and a shrink-
ing community" that in effect limited student choices and weakened
"peer review" by faculty respectful of their colleagues' domains. The
university, he concluded, "had become a giant platform in which mil-
lions of individuals do their thinking while administrators stand to one
side hoping that these unrelated activities result in no conflict."

These concerns of the 1970s persisted in Handlin's mind, but they did
not impede the flow of his own scholarship. Years earlier—in 1961—he
and Mary Handlin had set out the terms of what would become Handlin's most ambitious project: to write a comprehensive history of liberty
in the United States in all its myriad forms. This was to be a history not
of the theories of freedom but of liberty as it was lived—the actual lives
of the American people over four centuries. To begin and to clear the
ground, they published a prologue and prospectus in the form of a short
volume they called *The Dimensions of Liberty*. Concise, tightly written,

it sketched the questions that the vast subject necessarily provoked—liberty and the exercise of power, the ends and uses of power, the effects of voluntary associations, wealth and power. But within these large categories they touched on a multitude of specific issues, sketching the halting way forward, narrating revealing episodes, and ferreting out unsuspected sites of liberty and the hidden reaches of excessive power. A monograph packed with ideas and relevant facts, intriguing questions, and esoteric findings, *The Dimensions of Liberty*, designed as a mere preface, is a brilliant work of scholarship and of the informed imagination.

But Handlin, then engaged in so many enterprises, academic and otherwise, put the *Dimensions* book aside in part to concentrate on the Center for the Study of Liberty in the United States that he had created and directed. Years passed before he could resume work on the studies that would fulfill his original ambition. It was in 1986 and with the collaboration of his devoted second wife, the historian Lilian Bombach, that he resumed the glittering promise of the liberty project. And once resumed, the work seemed simply to flow out from the collaborative authors. In 1986 the first volume appeared (*Liberty and Power, 1600–1760*); three years later the second volume (*Liberty in Expansion, 1760–1850*); three years after that the third appeared (*Liberty in Peril, 1850–1920*); and in 1994 the fourth (*Liberty and Equality, 1920–1994*) completed the series. In all, the four volumes, published over eight years, contain 1,268 pages of text and 194 pages of notes.

Liberty in America (the collective title) was not an academic monograph series written in crabbed prose but a series of extended discussions written clearly, at times colloquially, even casually, to make the point for a broad audience that liberty had never been a secure state in America's history but an unsteady, erratic progress as its citizens struggled, at times bitterly, against obstacles to live freely without the control of external restraints. "The nation [they wrote in the preface to Volume four] born in the chaotic disorder of seventeenth-century settlement had learned to curb power by consent and embarked on a never-ending process of assuring its citizens' capacity to act."

The plenitude of details—social, political, and cultural—and the sweep of the immense story woven through the four volumes are unique and uniquely impressive. If there is a problem for the reader it is likely to be the difficulty of keeping in mind the structure of the whole while immersed in specific episodes.

In 1994, when the fourth volume was published, Handlin was approaching the age of eighty and turned to considering the world as he knew it and aspects of his most intensely personal experiences. Within the single year that followed his eightieth birthday he published three papers in quick succession: "Being Jewish: The Endless Quest," in which he described his boyhood; an account of his later, professional life in "A Career at Harvard"; and "The Unmarked Way," a discourse on "the stream in which humans of 1996 fly." Citing a host of writers and thinkers in Europe and America, roaming through the whole history of Western civilization, he summarized in "The Unmarked Way" the basic character of modern life. "At some point, midway into the twentieth century," he wrote, "Europeans and Americans discovered that they had lost all sense of direction. Formerly, familiar markers along the way had guided their personal and social lives from birth to maturity to death. Now, disoriented, they no longer trusted the guideposts and groped in bewilderment toward an unimagined destination."

The transformation had come gradually. "Put it this way," he wrote. "People by 1945 could no longer be sure of the direction in which history took them," but at least they believed there was a direction and they could choose among theories to explain it. After 1945 they were less sure that there was any direction in human affairs. Something had profoundly altered their outlook. What was it? Not the atom bomb, global war, totalitarianism, dehumanizing machines, poverty. In the latter part of the paper he probed the various possibilities that he could see, with emphasis on the declining role of religion and faith.

But he could feel the tremors of an unsteady, increasingly disoriented world not only at a global level, in the sweeping cosmologies of Spengler, Nietzsche, Toynbee, H. G. Wells, Camus, and Kafka; nor in the "shrieking silence" of the urban landscapes of Edvard Munch and Edward Hopper. Handlin felt it most ominously in his own small world of Cambridge and Harvard.

He had done his best to maintain the highest level of teaching. He had shunned popularity. When attendance in his American social history class topped four hundred, he dropped it. "I did not believe," he wrote, "that an earnest desire for that kind of knowledge really moved that many undergraduates; and I feared that these lectures had become one of those experiences into which people drifted out of habit or reputation. Therefore I chose subjects which on the face of it were not likely to draw crowds . . . and I offered my courses at an hour that required students either to postpone or skip their lunch." Similarly, he had devised exams that aimed to stimulate students to integrate their information in response to the challenge of a statement in a remote source. He had never tied himself to a written text, never taught a "gut" course, never given the same lecture twice, nor had he taught any course "that was required or useful to some other end." Everyone in his classes was there "because he or she wished to." And he had never played the "rating game" with an eye fixed on course evaluations.

But his views and teaching style had not prevailed. Sadly, as the years passed, he had noted how his colleagues came to dread the effects of aging. "Accommodations in hair, dress, and language wish the calendar away . . . the distinguished scholar with an international reputation, who for years lectured to a class of two hundred, suddenly finds his audience dwindle to fifteen." Some gave up, surrendered to disgust as they served out the years to retirement. Or if they persisted, "feebly they interject little jokes to liven up the hour, inflate their grades, and lighten their reading assignments." They end up in their perorations "immured by a solid wall of despair."

In time, he concluded, "teaching had lost the meaning I had once imparted to it . . . I could teach but no longer learn." "The overall tone of Harvard had turned hostile or at best apathetic to scholarly values, now deemed less worthy than the pressing tasks of doing good for the world." The scientists, the medical school people, and the business and law professionals did their work in detachment. "But at the center, the power and the glory went to the new Kennedy School of Government, which provided a refuge for out-of-office politicians and for bureaucrats on leave." It was at that point that he turned with relief to a succession of noninstructional positions, in the university and without. But his concern for Harvard and its students persisted.

He sought ways of recovering the university's distinction, its ancient purpose and persistent values. In 1970–71 he led the senior Americanists in the history department in offering "a cooperative, non-credit voluntary course on Harvard's history." "The course does not attempt a comprehensive coverage." The lectures would seek only "to provide sample glimpses of a past still significant in the twentieth century" despite the changes that had occurred over the years. The course was offered, repeated, and revised, and in 1986—on the university's 350th anniversary—the lectures were published as *Glimpses of the Harvard Past*, with two essays and an epilogue by Handlin.

> Continuities persist [he wrote]. The worldwide recognition of Harvard's greatness already marked in Conant's years, indeed even in Eliot's years, has survived; and that recognition rests on the fruits of scholarship. For whatever concerns occupied the changing generations through the passing centuries, the concern with learning did not wither. Other interests waxed and waned; this sometimes blazed, sometimes flickered, but endured.

By the time *Glimpses* appeared Handlin was writing his final assessment of the university as he had known it over the seventy years since his brash arrival on campus. It took the form of a five-thousand-word essay published in *Harvard Magazine* in the fall of 1986. It is entitled "Peering Toward 2036: Does Harvard Have a Future?"

It evoked many of the themes he had recently written about, especially in the *Glimpses* book. But it went more deeply and intimately into transformations that had overtaken the university since the Depression years of 1933–34, when he had arrived in Cambridge. Then, he had found Harvard to be a small, compact community of scholars and scientists, most of whom lived within three-quarters of a mile from Harvard Square. Only a few had wandered to outposts near Fresh Pond or rural Belmont. It was a little world of its own, "held together by numerous subtle but powerful social and intellectual ties." It included the students who were "still free to drop in at faculty homes," and it included also certain alumni and members of the governing boards. Two values, sharply divergent from the world at large, bound them together: a guarantee of intellectual freedom and a rejection of the market mentality. All members felt that their freedom to search and speak was secure, and all had chosen a career in scholarship that rejected more remunerative alternatives. "Guided by a curious amalgam of monastic and gentlemanly ideals, [the teachers] took pride in their detachment from monetary values." They did not consider themselves employees of the university, doing a job for a salary. "They were members of a community which assisted them in doing the work they wished to do."

All this changed after 1936, Handlin wrote, and in a few deft pages he outlined the changes that had overtaken the university and the challenges those changes had created. Everything steadily grew in size—the faculty, the numbers of students, administrators, and service personnel. The cost of housing rose rapidly, scattering the faculty into the suburbs, to be replaced by better-paid research personnel and many associated with MIT, which too was expanding rapidly. At the same time, the homogeneity of the student body was lost in the growing desire to include Catholics, Jews, and occasionally blacks—to the point where "diversity became an end in itself." And new links to the greater world were suddenly created by easy air travel and the demands of the nation's welfare in the lingering years of the Depression and by the sudden burst of demands for critical support of the war.

The links to Washington and wartime industries strengthened the focus of loyalties from the Yard outward to the greater world and from immediate colleagues to other associates around the country and the world. One result was the monetization of values. Friends from the government and foundations encouraged the trend to setting monetary equivalents for the faculty's research, which resulted in the sense, subtle at first, that they had entered the marketplace "as sellers of their services." They began to negotiate conditions of employment.

There was a trend in all this to gigantism that was the result less of the explosion of knowledge than of an inability to weed out redundancies and "to distinguish between the weeds and the flowers." Growth was the prime source of change, but "a refusal to grow would freeze the existing allocation of resources and prevent exploration of new subjects important to students and the world of scholarship."

With competitiveness in salaries and working conditions elsewhere, and the frequency of two-career families, Harvard could no longer assume that it stood at the apex of the academic profession. Further, the university could no longer take for granted that what it did was valuable in itself. Its scholarship had to prove its value not on its own terms "but by service to the region, the nation, and the world." As such, it was vulnerable to the "stings of insensitive critics and demagogic politicians, . . . [and] it struggles to sustain scholarly standards."

After 1969 that struggle became more intense and more complicated, but in all the discord and controversies,

> the essential message remains unspoken—that Harvard is not a government agency, or a business corporation, or a foundation, or even a baseball major league, however important those may be. Harvard, a unique cultural treasure, serves a purpose valid in its own right. By virtue of its heritage and situation, it, even more than other universities, bears the responsibility for *veritas*, for advancing and transmitting learning.

And he concluded his account of Harvard over the years by repeating with emphasis his conclusion in *Glimpses*:

Here in the wilderness the first founders planted an institution that grew in ways they could not have anticipated. That poor [Puritan] people, their estates much wasted, in erecting a College sought to make the whole world understand that spiritual learning was the thing they chiefly desired. They would not have felt themselves total strangers in the University 350 years later.

In manner, some found Handlin strange. Naturally taciturn, he spoke in a low voice and often cryptically, but what he said could shift the entire tenor of a conversation. One had the sense that much unspoken lay behind what he did say, which, especially for his students, gave him a slight aura of mystery. Yet he was a master of amusing one-liners, perhaps the best known of which was his response when his younger daughter asked, what was the "magna" on her sister's diploma. Well, he said, it's not a "summa."

He once told me that he had begun a widely advertised evening lecture at a nearby university when the lights went out in the auditorium and stayed out. He was not much troubled by this since he did not use a written text or notes in any detail. So he continued on in the dark and finished in the regular time. After the lecture, talking with students and faculty, he had the sense that they were disappointed. In fact they seemed to feel they had been cheated, since he must simply have made the whole thing up. And in a sense, he had—as we all do in our various ways. But what Handlin "made up" in his long and immensely creative career was priceless in its scholarship, its imagination, and its humane sympathy.

Acknowledgments

It would be impossible for me to thank here all the colleagues, friends, institutions, and critics who have helped me over the years—to say nothing of the students who have challenged me and silently set high expectations. But there are some people whose help was critical. Elizabeth McCormack and Harriet Zuckerman and the foundations they represented—the Rockefeller Brothers Fund and the Mellon Foundation—made funds available without which little could have been done. And more recently Emma Rothschild helped indirectly as part of her Joint Center for History and Economics. And there have been extraordinary assistants, especially: Barbara DeWolfe, who worked with me for many years on the Peopling project, here and abroad, and whom I gladly recognized on the title page of *Voyagers to the West*; and Patricia Denault, who single-handedly managed all the arrangements for the hundreds of participants in the Atlantic History Seminar.

As to the present book, I owe a special debt to Jill Kneerim for guiding me to Norton and to Steve Forman, an imaginative publisher and a shrewd critic who, with his assistant, Lily Sivitz Gellman, helped turn a rough manuscript into book form. But my most immediate debt is to Jennifer Nickerson, whose knowledge of history, computer skills, efficiency, and saintly patience with my endless revisions have made the book possible. In the guise of an assistant she has been a collaborator from start to finish.

Notes

INTRODUCTION

1 I was not alone in this. I now discover that another teenager—my exact con-
temporary—John Huckans, then a student at nearby Loomis School, also found
Witkower's a source of excitement, and left a record of his impression. "Some
Bookstores from the Past," *Book Source Magazine* (July 2009).

2 For a full account of the governance of the deeply Anglophile Jefferson School,
which was controlled by the teachers in collaboration with the students, see
St. Louis Post-Dispatch, May 12, 1955.

I: KEAYNE'S WILL, "ALL OF IT WRITTEN WITH MY OWNE HANDS"

1 The handwritten original of Keayne's will is missing from the Suffolk County,
Massachusetts probate records, but there is clear evidence that the copy in the
Boston Record Commissioners Report X (City Document No. 150, pp. 1–53,
Boston 1886) is an exact transcription. The spelling, abbreviations, syntax, and
wording are perfectly authentic to the early seventeenth century and to what
we know of Keayne's voice. So meticulous is the transcription that the tran-
scriber must have had the original document in hand to refer to—a likelihood
supported by the appearance of Keayne's cursive signature, which somehow
must have been copied from the original to be placed at the end of the printed
will (page 53).

2 Helle M. Alpert, "Robert Keayne: Notes of Sermons by John Cotton and Proceedings of the First Church of Boston from 23 November 1639 to 1 June 1640" (Ph.D. diss., Tufts University, 1974). For Keayne's notes on Cotton's sermons on worldliness and business dealings, see pages 48, 63–67, 89–91. For a modern transcription of the passage reproduced on page 38 above, see Alpert, 287.

3 On Brereley and Grindletonianism, see David R. Como, *Blown by the Spirit: Puritanism and the Emergence of an Antinomian Underground in Pre-Civil-War England* (Stanford, Calif., 2004), chaps. 2, 8, app. D.

4 R. H. Tawney, *Religion and the Rise of Capitalism* (1926; reprint, London, 1937), 197, 210.

II: LASLETT'S CLAYWORTH: ANDOVER AND HEIDENREICHSTEIN

1 Milton Gaither, *American Educational History Revisited: A Critique of Progress* (New York, 2003), chap. 6.

2 Lutz Berkner, "The Stem Family and the Developmental Cycle of the Peasant Household: An Eighteenth Century Austrian Example," *American Historical Review* 77, no. 2 (April 1972): 405.

3 Berkner, "Stem Family," 398–418.

4 James A. Henretta, *Journal of Interdisciplinary History* 2 (1971): 379–98.

5 John Demos, *Past, Present, and Personal: The Family and Life Course in American History* (New York, 1986): ix.

6 Werner Jaeger, *Paideia: the Ideals of Greek Culture*, trans. Gilbert Highet, 3 vols. (New York, 1944), 3:119, 314.

III: HARBOTTLE'S INDEX, JOHNSON'S "CONNECTION," AND THE VILLAGERS' THEORIES OF GOVERNMENT

1 For slight differences in page counts, see the Massachusetts Historical Society's "Annotated Newspapers of Harbottle Dorr, Jr.," https://www.masshist.org/dorr.

2 Robert R. Palmer, *The Age of the Democratic Revolution: The Challenge* (Princeton, 1959), 21.

3 Oscar Handlin and Mary Handlin, eds., *The Popular Sources of Political Authority: Documents on the Massachusetts Constitution of 1780* (Cambridge, Mass., 1966). On the procedural history of the adoption of the Constitution of 1780 see: Samuel Eliot Morison, "The Struggle Over the Adoption of the Constitution of Massachusetts, 1780" (Massachusetts Historical Society, report of May 1917 meeting, pages 353–411) and on its fortunes up to 1915, Morison, "A History of the Constitution of Massachusetts" (Boston, 1917, reprinted from the Manual for the Constitutional Convention of 1917). On the theoretical basis of the constitution (social contract theory) and the political background of its

adoption, see: Ronald M. Peters, Jr., *The Massachusetts Constitution of 1780: A Social Compact* (Amherst, Mass., 1978).

IV: BEISSEL'S EPHRATA AND THE MUSIC OF THE SPHERES

1 Thomas Mann, *Story of a Novel: The Genesis of* Doctor Faustus, trans. Richard and Clara Winston (New York, 1961), 39–40, 121–22. For studies of Beissel's role in the *Faustus* book, see Theodore Karst, "Johann Conrad Beissel in Thomas Mann's Roman 'Doktor Faustus,'" *Jahrbuch der Deutschen Schillergesellschaft* 12 (1968): 543–85, and E. G. Alderfer, *The Ephrata Commune: An Early American Counterculture* (Pittsburgh, 1985), 192–205.

2 The voluminous bibliography on Beissel and Ephrata divides into two distinct phases. After a century of neglect after Beissel's death, the subject was revived at the end of the nineteenth century by devoted German-American antiquarian historians led by Julius Friedrich Sachse. A collector as well as an antiquarian scholar, he published a virtual torrent of studies, large and small, of the Pennsylvania Pietists, especially Beissel's people at Ephrata. Many of his sources he had himself discovered and brought into prominence. The ambiguity in the title of his major publication perfectly reflects his character as a historian: *The German Sectarians of Pennsylvania, 1708–1742, a Critical and Legendary History of the Ephrata Cloister and the Dunkers*, 2 vols. (Philadelphia, 1899–1900). His privately printed *Music of the Ephrata Cloister; also Conrad Beissel's Treatise on Music* . . . (Lancaster, Pa., 1903), though typically confused in organization and focus, opened that subject to general study. Other German-speaking antiquarians were equally enthusiastic in developing the subject. Their studies filled the pages of the various German-American societies' volumes—some with newly developed views of Ephrata's *fraktur* art, its architecture, and its symbols.

Most of these historico-antiquarian publications were written in the years of Sachse's lifetime (1842–1919), and then for a century the subject fell into obscurity. It was revived after World War II with much more sophistication and professionalism. Four of these scholarly books have been leads for me into my own views of Beissel and his utopia: Betty Jean Martin, "The Ephrata Cloister and its Music, 1732–1785" (Ph.D. diss., University of Maryland, 1974); E. G. Alderfer, *The Ephrata Commune: An Early American Counterculture* (Pittsburgh, 1985); Jeff Bach, *Voices of the Turtledoves* (University Park, Pa., 2003); and Patrick M. Erben, *A Harmony of the Spirits: Translation and the Language of Community in Early Pennsylvania* (Chapel Hill, N.C., 2012). The senior scholar of the cloister's music is Lucy Carroll, conductor and organist, who has done much to adopt the cloister's musical scores to modern forms. Her prominent publications—*Hymn Writers of Early Pennsylvania* (2008) and *The Music of the Ephrata Cloister* (n.d.)—as well as her collection of Ephrata's musical scores have brought out some of the inner qualities of the commune's music.

I have drawn from all these modern works, different as they are, in developing my own view of the Beissel phenomenon. While this book, not being a monograph, omits detailed annotation, I am happy to record my debt to all of these writers, from Sachse to Professor Erben.

3 Bailyn, "The Search for Perfection: Atlantic Dimensions," in *Sometimes an Art* (New York, 2015), chap. 9; Frank E. Manuel and Fritzie P. Manuel, *Utopian Thought in the Western World* (Cambridge, Mass., 1979).

4 Voltaire, "Église: Des primitifs appelés Quakers," in *Dictionnaire philosophique Vol. II* (1764), in *Œuvres Complètes de Voltaire* (Paris, 1878), 18: 501; Guillaume-Thomas-François Raynal. *Histoire philosophique et politique, des établissements & du commerce des Européens dans les deux Indes* (Amsterdam, 1770), 6:297–300.

5 *Chronicon Ephratense: A History of the Community of Seventh Day Baptists at Ephrata, Lancaster County, Penn'a*, by Lamech [Jacob Gaas] and Agrippa [Peter Miller], trans. J. Max Hark (Ephrata, Pa., 1786 [Lancaster, Pa., 1889]), 287; Miller to Benjamin Franklin, June 16, 1761, *Papers of Benjamin Franklin*, ed. Leonard W. Labaree, et al. (New Haven, Conn., 1966), 9:323–26.

6 Bailyn, *The Peopling of British North America: An Introduction* (New York, 1996): 123–25; Erben, *Harmony of the Spirits*, chap. 5, esp. 196–206; and Ernest L. Lashlee, "Johannes Kelpius and His Woman in the Wilderness," in Gerhard Müller and Winfred Zell, eds., *Glaube, Geist, Geschichte: Festschrift für Ernst Benz* (Leiden, 1967), 337.

7 Miller to Franklin, June 16, 1761, in *Franklin Papers*, 19:324.

8 *Chronicon*, 59, 60.

9 On the name "Ephrata," see Alderfer, *Ephrata Commune*, 60.

10 "Visit by the Provost Magister, Israel Acrelius to the Ephrata Cloister, August 20, 1753," *Memoirs of the Historical Society of Pennsylvania* 11 (1874): 373–401.

11 Bach, *Voices*, 99–107; Erben, *Harmony of the Spirits*, 48–49, 197, 200, 221.

12 Bach, *Voices*, 25, 38; chap. 7 ("Heavenly Magic").

13 Dennis McCort, "Johann Conrad Beissel, Colonial Mystic Poet," *German-American Studies* 8 (1974): 12, 14.

14 Martin, "Ephrata Cloister," 166–67.

15 Aaron Spencer Fogelman, *Jesus Is Female* (Philadelphia, 2007), chap. 3 ("The Challenge to Gender Order").

16 Bach, *Voices*, 28, 33, 109–12.

17 Martin, "Ephrata Cloister," 88.

18 William Fahnestock, 1835, quoted in Bach, *Voices*, 141.

19 Martin, "Ephrata Cloister," 173, 176.

20 Martin, "Ephrata Cloister," 131.

21 Miller to Franklin, October 10, 1786, *Papers of Benjamin Franklin* [unpublished, available online at Franklinpapers.org, years 1786–87]; *Chronicon*, 161.

22 Charles Brewer to Bernard Bailyn, June 17, 2018. I am most grateful to Professor Brewer, an authority on medieval and baroque music, for sharing with me his views on Ephrata's music in an extensive note that he modestly dismissed as his mere *"zwei groschen"* on the subject. It is in fact full of insights and perceptions that improved my understanding, but obviously he has no responsibility whatever for anything I have written in this chapter.

V: THE HUTCHINSONS' NETWORK AND BEYOND

1 Lucien Febvre, "Un livre qui grandit . . . ," *Revue historique* (April–June, 1950): 216, 224.

2 Frederick B. Tolles, *Quakers and the Atlantic Culture* (New York, 1960), 3, x.

3 Lara Putnam, "To Study the Fragments/Whole: Microhistory and the Atlantic World," *Journal of Social History* 39 (Spring 2006): 617.

4 Horst Pietschmann, ed., *Atlantic History: History of the Atlantic System 1580–1830* (Göttingen, 2002), 43–45; Renate Pieper and Peer Schmidt, eds., *Latin America and the Atlantic World* (Cologne, 2005).

5 Jose R. Torre, "The Scottish Atlantic," *William and Mary Quarterly*, 3d ser., 65 (2008): 801; Dana Schaffer, "Atlantic Worlds and the US History Survey," *Perspectives on History* (March 2014), 20; Atlantic World Research Network, www .uncg.edu/eng/awrn.

6 Nicholas Canny and Philip Morgan, eds., *The Oxford Handbook of the Atlantic World, 1450–1850* (Oxford, 2011); Vincent Brown et al., eds., *The Princeton Companion to Atlantic History* (Princeton, N.J., 2015).

7 Wolfgang Splitter, "The Fact and Fiction of Cotton Mather's Correspondence with German Pietist August Hermann Francke," *New England Quarterly* 83 (March 2010): 102–22.

8 The main participants were Aaron Fogleman, Northern Illinois University; A. Gregg Roeber, Pennsylvania State University; Renate Wilson, Johns Hopkins University; and Marianne Wokeck, Indiana University.

9 Neil Safier, ed., "Itineraries of Atlantic Science: New Questions, New Approaches, New Directions," *Atlantic Studies: Literary, Cultural, and Historical Perspectives* 7, no. 4 (2010). Papers from another seminar were also collected and published together: Malick Ghachem, ed., "Slavery and Citizenship in the Age of the Atlantic Revolutions," *Historical Reflections / Réflexions historiques* 29, no. 1 (2003).

10 The full texts of the responses to the questionnaires will be on file in the Seminar's archive in the Harvard College Library. In inviting comments, I noted that what the respondents wrote would in no way be identified with an individual by name.

EPILOGUE

1 Recorded in full in Bailyn, *On the Teaching and Writing of History* (Hanover, N.H., 1994).

2 Paul F. Lazarsfeld, "An Episode in the History of Social Research: A Memoir," in Donald Fleming and Bernard Bailyn, eds., *The Intellectual Migration: Europe and America, 1930–1960* (Cambridge, Mass., 1969), 270–337.

3 Harold Nicolson, *Diaries and Letters, 1930–1962,* ed. Nigel Nicolson, 3 vols. (New York, 1960–68).

4 Mann's reading of "The Prodigy" is available on YouTube. On Mann as ironist, see Erich Heller, *The Ironic German: A Study of Thomas Mann* (Boston, 1958); Mann, "Humor and Irony" [1953] in Henry Hatfield, ed., *Thomas Mann: A Collection of Critical Essays* (Englewood Cliffs, N.J., 1964).

Illustration Credits

German Sectarians of Pennsylvania, 1708–1742, vol. II, Julius Friedrich Sachse, 1900

p. 141: From *The German Sectarians of Pennsylvania, 1708–1742*, vol. II, Julius Friedrich Sachse, 1900

p. 149: From *The German Sectarians of Pennsylvania, 1708–1742*, vol. I, Julius Friedrich Sachse, 1899

p. 152: From *The German Sectarians of Pennsylvania, 1708–1742*, vol. II, Julius Friedrich Sachse, 1900

p. 155: Library of Congress

p. 156: Courtesy, The Winterthur Library: Joseph Downs Collection of Manuscripts and Printed Ephemera

p. 157: From *The German Sectarians of Pennsylvania, 1708–1742*, vol. II, Julius Friedrich Sachse, 1900

p. 220: Te Naval Historical Center

p. 233: Louis Fabian Bachrach ©

Text Credits

The following works were the original sources for the relevant sections of the book. They are reprinted here in revised form with the permissions of the authorities indicated.

"The *Apologia* of Robert Keayne," *The William and Mary Quarterly*, 3rd. Ser., vol. VII, no. 4 (October 1950). Reprinted by permission of The Omohundro Institute.

"The Index and Commentaries of Harbottle Dorr," *Proceedings of the Massachusetts Historical Society*, vol. 85 (1973). Reprinted by permission of the Massachusetts Historical Society.

"Stephen Johnson" from *Perspectives in American History*, IV (1970). Reprinted by permission of the Charles Warren Center for Studies in American History, Harvard University.

"Context in History," the Charles Joseph La Trobe Memorial Lecture in North American History, 1995. Reprinted by permission of La Trobe University, Melbourne.

Memorial Minutes for Samuel Eliot Morison and Oscar Handlin. Reprinted by permission of the Faculty of Arts and Sciences, Harvard University.

Index